JAMES A. HEFFERNAN

TUNNELS
THROUGH
TIME

poems and observations

ISBN: 978-1-09835-943-0 Print
ISBN: 978-1-09835-944-7 eBook

DEDICATED

To all the health care personnel
All over the world —
Thank you for your service
Way the hell beyond the call of duty

The Acting Self

Awareness
Is the truest self
All others slough away
At every time of day
On mind's eternal shelf

Consciousness
In its splendor
Can be an agent, truly
Do not decry unduly
Or impotency render

Holding
Fast before the will
In an act of sublime effort
One can be the mind's shepherd
Especially if still

Circumstance
Will see passivity
In a flowing impermanence
In the same holy firmament
There is activity

Sometimes
Yes and sometimes no
Multiple categories
Veritable glories
Enumerate the glow

Nature
Imposes fate
Leaves a little bit free
Perhaps enough to see
And a long, long wait

Philosophy may indeed be speculative and imprecise, but it is unrealistic to suggest (as many scientists do) that we can meaningfully do without it.

From what I can tell, organized academic philosophy is primarily occupied with the rigorous and precise debate over the not particularly interesting.

Some religious ideas are interesting and valuable on an intellectual or philosophical level, but *not* as dogma. No human idea should be as rigid and as authoritative as the dogmas we see causing so much hate and violence in the world.

One can experience something first hand, but as time passes and memory fades, one essentially has to have faith that the thing happened, and happened in the way that one thinks it did. I think our memories have a high degree of faith attached to them, because after a certain point we cannot empirically verify their validity anymore. We just have to have some measure of faith that we are not wrong, or crazy.

As Korzybski said, whatever you say a thing "is," it isn't. Your model, or map, is a concept which points to the thing, but really the thing in itself is far beyond that mere notion. Does the unconditioned have a limit? Probably not.

Some people seem to put too much faith in logic. In truth, it is only useful up to a certain point. That, and it is more often than not underpinned by sublimated emotions.

One thing I have never satisfactorily understood about academic philosophy is how we get true objective conclusions out of language which is inherently couched in subjective, fallacy-ridden human minds. How do we get such rich systems of truth — each of which contradicts all the others, mind you — out of pure, emotional subjectivity? I, for one, have no idea. As far as I can tell, the philosopher is either right or wrong. A lot of wrong philosophers were systematic and logical. I guess the truth is a woman, then…

Leary clearly made some (very public) mistakes, but I think he was an important scientist-philosopher. His writings have meant a great deal to a lot of people, myself included. People fail to understand what an accomplished writer he was. He did some great work.

Robert Anton Wilson's principle of *Model Agnosticism* is indeed quite admirable and eminently constructive, but I would point out that some models are in fact truer than others. In other words, the basis for forming mental structures out of the chaos of existence should not be considered arbitrary.

The monumental improbability, which is legitimate, of life and biological intelligence evolving at all is offset by the fact that we live in a multiverse. In an infinite expanse of universes of all types, there must indeed be an infinite (or at least astronomically large) number in which humans arise, and we are simply the organisms in one such universe looking back and contemplating this. It is quite necessary.

There's all this great mystery about existence, and consciousness, and what it all means and why. Fact is, the act of experiencing is the whole thing. The secret of existence is existing. The mystery disappears when the mystery disappears.

All too many people have adopted the scientific (or scientistic) mentality and outlook as a worldview, and nothing could be more philosophically and spiritually idiotic.

There is absolutely no point in over-thinking things. People get drunk on intellectual realization, and more often than not perceive things that aren't there, or get wrapped up in explanations which are pointless. The rational mind is invaluable, but it can easily be taken too far — it can run amok.

What would be interesting to know is the history of consciousness. (And prehistory).

If one withdraws the question, one withdraws the need for an answer.

I get the impression that academic philosophy over-formalizes the pursuit of truth. I don't sympathize with that level of pomp and circumstance regarding a subject that the philosophers don't truly understand any better than anyone else.

I'm with the intellectuals on a lot of things, but even they exhibit a sort of a shtick, and I can do without the atheism and materialism — and a lot of the politics, too.

Socrates taught us that the only thing we can truly know is that we know not. He was right — truly to know is probably beyond humans. I think it is possible in this life, however, at least to get onto the right track. Hints and clues here and there can give us that much.

Ambiguous Distinction

The rage, it seems — the vogue
Is that these things are alien
But what would it be
To encounter a rogue
When the supernatural's salient?

Were a fellow equipped with sufficient
Powers to dwarf any primate
What is the difference
If that power's efficient
To be shocking in any old climate?

It seems that to me, there is no distinction
Between a space-man and a god
But what do I know?
My planet's extinction
Is here and my judgment is flawed

Experiencing is the meaning of experiencing.

Mass-energy has as its ground of existence consciousness. *Not* the other way around.

The consciousness of an individual human (or animal) can be likened to a vortex in a river. The river itself is the undivided, flowing awareness-substance making up the greater reality itself, and the whirlpool is a relatively (but not totally) autonomous swirling concentration of conscious experience.

So often, we fall into the trap of conflating our consciousness and our true self with the individual self of our evolutionary brain. The "classical" ego-self (i.e. the nervous system and its functions) gets *reflected* by the inherent consciousness of the brain, and we feel that we are carrying out what are really automatic functions of the organism in its environment. The hyper-relativistic, non-local "quantum" *true*-self, which normally is dormant in almost everybody, is where true reality (and real autonomy and intelligence) exists and is often mystically (and therefore very imprecisely) described. The classical self is a robot designed by evolution to carry out sexual reproduction through whatever means necessary. Fundamentally, our consciousness and our ego-self are not identical. Consciousness gives rise to matter and energy, which in turn give rise to chemistry, which in turn gives rise to mammalian brains. The brain and the ego do not give rise to consciousness; consciousness is actually more fundamental than either of them. This is a point of great confusion. The ego is an illusion. Reality is an illusion.

The general perception seems to be that the universe and consciousness are two different things. What if in truth there is only one thing, and to us there is normally only an apparent difference in our minds? To suggest that the two are fundamentally different things is a fragmentation. And fragmentation is not natural — wherever one finds it on Earth, it was put there by us. The universe and consciousness constitute one basic objective reality. It would not even be correct to say that each one needs the other to exist. Once one reaches a certain point — a threshold of clarity — one is unable to differentiate the two.

The subconscious mind determines far more than the conscious one. The conscious mind is the proverbial tip of the iceberg.

The individual self is not an objective phenomenon, but rather a mental concept like any other, and is thus, in terms of its self-representation, an illusion just as the mystics report. However, it sure feels like we are selves most of the time! And in the end, does a conscious process not involve, as a reference to what it is conscious of, some type of self? Is there a false self and a true self? Or just pure consciousness with no agency at all?

That place from which creativity springs is a process of pure intelligence. We tend to think we are special in this regard, but in fact the fabric of the cosmos itself is constituted of pure intelligence as well — it is merely 'frozen up.' The plenum. Enlightenment, in some sense, is the realization that even empty space is full of living intelligence.

Unconsciousness is an artificial state within the broader movement of non-local consciousness. The baseline state of the universe is one of consciousness, not dead unconsciousness. We are biased into accepting the latter as an obvious reality because we spend so much of our time in an unconscious state. The practical elimination of awareness serves evolutionary functions; the baseline is not oblivion but rather a suffusing non-locality.

The misconception is that the neuroelectrical network of the brain gives rise to an emergent consciousness. In fact, consciousness is more fundamental, and not a result of the firing of neurons, which generate the structures of thought and emotion and so forth of which we are aware. The classical electrochemical network generates the constructs of our ego-selves — our personalities, our emotional states, our overall interaction with the world — but consciousness itself is deeper, and is a quantum phenomenon which turns out to be non-local and vast. Science is not even yet aware of our awareness.

I identify the self as awareness.

Spirit may be infinite, but the soul is individual.

Consciousness always carries intention.

Whatever is not being observed is often relegated to the category of non-existence. That is, the notion is that nothing exists unless or until it has been observed. This is not true. Objectively, everything exists, whether it is under the observation of a human or not. We should think of this very much as we think of the subconscious mind, which is by definition not under observation, but is really running the show. Objects existing *out there*, unseen, should be viewed similarly — they exist in the subconscious of the universe. Which, I might add, is also a fundamental part of the human subconscious.

To me, consciousness is the all, while awareness occurs when the all focuses or reflects on itself.

I'm beginning to come to the conclusion that the phenomenon of paradox is the most common pattern in our existence.

Amorphous Awareness

Your awareness is like a vortex in a river
Ethereal field, suffusing all space and time
You are all, it is true, and yet localized hither
Too often we realize this only after a sign

And since so universal, indeed existing throughout
There are degrees of location, a tricky subject
Where are "you" exactly, hard to say without doubt
Perhaps several places, many answers correct

You could be in your body, that much is clear
Yet, too, extended outside, indefinitely, potentially
Consciousness substance knows no there or here
Your self could stretch far, infinitely and essentially

The possibility also exists, for aught we may know
That awareness could leave the body, to return or not
It's quite hard to say, knowingly, just where it might go
Can Paradise be seen from afar, or is it one shot?

The age-old debate is that of fate versus free will. Why not both? I have no problem seeing that some type of intentional action is present in humans (and other animals), whilst the whirlwinds of the changing universe underlie and determine the vast majority of phenomena. "Free" will is obviously very small in its interaction with the universe compared to the overwhelming hand of what we call fate. Both are there, but really, an individual will is extremely tiny compared with the behavior of the rest of nature. Only when one gets to the level of the Caesars and Napoleons does free will have much of an outlet. Placing fate and will in mutually exclusive categories shows a basic lack of imagination.

I would say that sure, there is a will — we are not automatons — but that it is almost wholly unfree for all practical purposes. Every thought a person has, however it fires, is thoroughly constrained by genetic and especially by cultural factors which are salient and fundamental. The evolution of the culture of which you are an unwitting part, and the genetic equipment of which you are involuntarily composed, had at no point, anywhere along the line, anything to do with anyone's will. Culture is a larger and more dynamical independent process and it is not and has never been formed by choices.

"Block time" can be a correct description of our universe and, to my mind at least, still preserve volition. In block time, from a higher dimension one would be able to see every event from the beginning of our universe until its demise — it is basically a "block" of events which only appear to unfold in our dimension of time — like a range of mountains in which each peak is an individual moment in the larger range of time. I can imagine that, even though the events of the universe may in some way be predetermined (as by fate), it does not nullify our ability to be willful. Perhaps you were always going to choose a particular way. In block time, you were somehow bound to do it. Why can't you really have chosen it? Does block time really forbid it? My contention is no, it doesn't; any concession made that fate obviously exists does not exclude willful behavior. Appreciating the power of fate may serve to trivialize the notion of will, which in my opinion cannot properly be called truly "free." But will and fate are not incompatible.

The truth is rather murky, but someone who believes he has free will will very likely fare better than someone who believes he is an automaton.

Anyone who has done advanced maths knows the nature of *effort*. But don't get caught up in the illusion that you're "doing" it. One has to flex that brain muscle to get results, and the fact of the matter is that that flexing is the extent of one's "free will."

I have more fun conducting myself as if I am at cause over several of my actions, rather than just none of them — which is the fashionable interpretation of existence among many thinkers. Free will is one extreme, and soulless determinism is the other extreme. I like to be somewhere in between.

Robotic behavior defines the vast aggregate of the affairs of humanity. Fortunately, robotic behavior does not define the will of the individual at all times. Even the most highly trained cannot be without it completely. But the point is that one can learn to tame it and let the true self peek through. And so, the individual is free to be something of interest, if not of value, in the universe.

One's will is very small, and it is not free, but one has to leave room for that Promethean fire.

Could it be that the subjective will and the objective reality are one and the same, ultimately?

It's funny — the people who think humans are mostly robotic are likely the least robotic, while those who believe in the primacy of their will are probably the most robotic.

Most people do not have a destiny.

Foreordinational freedom of will. Our will is simultaneously genetically predetermined and volitional. Willful actions take place through genetically constructed channels.

Life is definitely a ride, and should be characterized as such, but the interesting thing is that we are allowed to steer it a little of the time.

Everyone is always arguing about whether our behavior is inherently deterministic or whether it is willfully caused. In truth, it comprises elements of both, all the time. That's why we're so confused — different perspectives (on the single reality) lead to different conclusions and beliefs. I would point out that, regardless of whether we are fated or free, we do seem to be on automatic pilot most of the time.

We are willful by degrees. The spectrum is bounded on one end by as much "control" as we're able to have and on the other by pure automatism.

Holding certain contents of awareness in one's awareness is an act of conscious will.

One must remember that *free* will is not the same as *true* will.

Anti-Prolixity

Do not be excessive
Resort to prolixity
Set your restraints
A warm, couth fixity

Do not be heavy
If that's your propensity
Amalgamate pith
A medium density

Do not be stubborn
A shade of obdurate
Permit an instruction
Friendly and moderate

Do not be a snob
Absurdly pedantic
It's almost as bad
As a hopeless romantic

Do not be vulgar
In other words rude
Not a one cares to
Suffer such a mood

Do not pay attention
To the admonishments here
Think for yourself
And don't reason austere

I tend to vacillate when it comes to my opinions of the driving forces of evolution, but I am relatively sure of one principle: negentropy. Whether there are any, even slight and blind, teleological forces at work, at the very least we can say assuredly that complexity, order, and intelligence tend, on some level, to continually increase. The bacillus did not come after the orangutan, and I think we can agree that the whale is superior to the brontosaurus — because it evolved later in the course of time. Negative entropy is every bit as real as classical entropy.

I believe language arises from the confluence of our vocal tracts being able to make such articulated units of sound and the primate brain's ability to organize these sounds effectively, specifically into hierarchies of meaning. Without our fine vocal folds, there would be no language, and quite possibly if our brains had evolved in even a slightly different way it might also have been impossible. I don't think looking for some specific 'language gene' is a fruitful avenue, and looking for any tidy explanation will likely turn up nothing. In order to understand the origin of language, we would need both a highly sophisticated knowledge of the nervous system far beyond that which we have now, as well as a detailed evolutionary picture, specifically related to the anatomical development of the vocal folds, which is probably unknowable. I anticipate it will remain truly a mystery for a very long time.

I am often disgusted by our organic nature. Whether or not one finds our animal nature beautiful and noble or grotesque and embarrassing, I think we can all reasonably agree that we represent a decidedly low level of evolution, in any case.

In response to the widely accepted conclusion that humans are the endpoint of evolution, I say only this: humans are glorified animals — beasts, really. We are digging around in the mud and going after bananas with sticks. And man is far more savage and nasty than almost every other species on Earth. It is a testament to our foolish, wholly misplaced pride and righteous arrogance that we find our species superior — on the merits — to any other one can name.

The theory of evolution can't be any more clearly and obviously correct. I feel, though, that science has yet to deal with the subtleties of the complexifying process which leads to more orderly, better adapted species. I don't think it's purely a roll of the dice (although that too plays a large part). The term of art for what I am talking about is *negative entropy* or negentropy. This process is indubitably real, and as yet almost wholly unaccounted for and unexplained.

Materialism is not so much the result of progress as it is an evolutionary phase. We are the unwitting pawns of this meme. Obviously it is very powerful so it stays with us. But power often has nothing to do with truth.

I would hesitate to say that evolution has made things "better." I would say instead that the process of mutation-selection has made organisms and societies of organisms more complex and more proficient at procuring a living in increasingly complex environments. It is only debatable whether there has been "real" "progress," in any sort of objective sense.

The process of evolution is exhibited in individual and collective human minds just as naturally and fundamentally as it is in biological evolution. An idea that becomes explicate and one takes to heart, or a public idea that becomes a meme, are subject to laws of selection precisely analogous to those in Darwinian evolution. However, when we have an idea that is particularly beautiful, or succinct, how did it come about? Was it a random occurrence, or was there some order, some intelligence and creativity, there in its generation? Questions like these have much pertinence when it comes to sorting out the mechanisms of natural selection or rather, the process of complexification which leads to selection. It would be a rather incomplete ending if we all just decided that the "eureka" moment was some random accident, and left it at that.

All of our rituals, morals, institutions and behaviors really at bottom surround the sexual impulse. Humans are essentially much more animalistic than they are "civilized men."

Anyone who doesn't think humans are great apes is conveniently not an ape — he is an ass.

Just because civilized people may have a hard time in the wilds and hinterlands of Earth does not mean that Nature herself is in fact hostile.

All that is needed for the wonderful diversity and richness we see in Earth's flora and fauna is random change and selection pressure. I recognize this. But I see the picture differently. Whereas your average Darwinian sees a universe of random chaos, I see one of structured information. True randomness would be the absence of anything coherent at all. Order would, logically, have virtually no chance of ever forming in a truly random and chaotic cosmos. But this is not what we have. Our universe is structured and intelligent at bottom and from the outset.

The process of evolution comes up with some marvelous systems, but doesn't see too well and is rather dumb.

How do animals — especially dogs — know to look at, and into, one's eyes? Is there some inherent latitude in consciousness that allows for this, or is it rather evolutionary programming that tells an organism where a creature is looking or what they're up to? Pretty remarkable, either way.

Beneath the Surface

Forgive us our sins, Lord
We know not what we do
Our King is but a chess-piece
Our chessboard all askew

Cultural man is living man
A meme is like a gene
Evolving in concatenation
A truly complex scene

But if you can follow me
Here is indeed the point:
Man does not direct his actions
He is really in the joint

That is in prison, each a unit
A cog in a giant device
Engineered by Mother Nature
Her will should quite suffice

The setup is long in the making
Men are but puppets, see?
The future's all that matters to her
Expendable are we

Whatever's behind the curtain
Gaia or her future scion
It cares *nothing* for man's wishes
There is no one to rely on

We're on a train and blind
We did not lay down the tracks
We cannot see where we're going
And whatever we do lacks

Nature allows us to think
That we are at the helm
When in fact we are in hell
Inside this Earthly realm

Subjective impressions are every bit as valid in sensing the nature of reality as objective measurements are. For example, depending on one's spiritual attainments, one can know just as much about the quantum nature of reality as a physicist does without ever having opened a physics textbook. Many Buddhist scholars have done just this over the centuries. The sensation of redness is every bit as legitimate as asserting the frequency of red light. One frame of reference is in no way superior to the other. These are two sides of the same coin that comes out of nature's purse. In our materialist, modern world, with science as the new religion, it seems we have denigrated the validity of subjective experience in favor of a more objective one, which we now somehow regard as truer. Both views of the world are equally valid, and totally complementary.

Being and not-being and — what's in the middle?

We tend to divide the world into in here and out there — two things. In reality there is only one thing.

Your brain gives rise to everything you do, but not everything you are.

Thoughts fire in both random and ordered channels. Whichever thought you are about to have, in response to some stimulus, can only be predicted statistically. However, this thought will occur in relation to some subject or object in a pertinent fashion. There is an element of order, and an element of chaos. (Such is the Tao).

Notwithstanding all the talk of oneness, the fact is that we do seem damned to separateness in this particular reality.

If subject and object are two sides of a single coin, and subjectivity is mind, then objective Nature must also be inherently mind-like.

While it is true that individual separation, at a fundamental level, is essentially an illusion, the fact is that we as humans do not exist at this fundamental level much of the time. So our separateness, for practical purposes, is certainly real enough.

On a certain level the appearance of our separation is an illusion. All the same, each organism is an individual, and that identity is not superfluous. Indeed we exist as a collective consciousness and an individual consciousness at the same time, not necessarily only one or the other.

The debate seems to be whether the universe came into existence completely by accident, or was designed by some creator. Why not a third option? Could there be a cosmic substrate which is informed by some subtle governing principle of intelligence or *order*, which evolves freely according to no predetermined stricture — *chaos*? Order (which is a form of intelligence) and random chaos (through which it is expressed) are both required for the evolution of a universe like ours.

We touch on the objective with our science, but it is couched in subjectivity.

While it is true that in the psychotic state there are things about existence you no longer objectively understand, it is also true that there are in that state things about existence you do objectively understand which very few in the non-psychotic state can.

The duality of necessity versus contingency is a truly fundamental one.

The phenomenon of romantic love exists because we posit the idea of a holiness and a healing essence in the Other, which stems from our flawed rearing practices as a civilized people. When Self and Other are in balance, romantic love cannot and does not exist. To use perhaps a strong word, as wonderful as it can be, it is really a species of pathology. In most relationships it is not an illusion that lasts for very long.

I think a large part of what we mean when we call a person "intelligent" is that they are especially good at developing the dialectic, unifying theses and antitheses into new syntheses. I would add, however, that there are many other types of intelligence than just the rational-mental.

For the most part we are neither observing detachedly from the outside, nor creating freely from the inside, but rather *participating*.

One very important duality is that of equality and hierarchy. It is best to exist in the middle.

I'm very much in favor of the notion — the *model* — that all of our mental constructs, all of our ideas and ways of perceiving the world — are models. But I do not feel that model-making is arbitrary. There is a reality, a truth, on which these models must be based, and therefore, while the models are inherently subjective, I feel there is some sort of correspondence there with the objective as well. And eventually, subject and object are one…

Our subjective impressions of people are often very far from the objective reality. Even when we think we know someone, we may not know the first thing about who they really are. The adage that we are at bottom quite alone in this life rings true. There are incommunicable things about me that I am sure my family has never even guessed at. I'm sure the same is true for most everybody else. Our subjective impressions of our friends and family are fictions and these imaginings usually have nothing to do with the truth.

Black Holes

Singularity
High polarity
Photon rings
Barely sing

On the horizon
Radiation risin'
But very slight
This is slow light

Accretion disk
All dross to whisk
And circle round
Attraction bound

Doppler beaming
Apparent scheming
The wave to pull
And push to full

Relativistic
A cosmical mystic
At least to a star
Or a friendly pulsar

Gravity crushing
Gravitons rushing
Ripples in time
Up through them we climb

On morality: It seems that, by and large, if an individual has sufficient knowledge of a situation, he or she will be able to determine what is right from what is wrong. Human consciousness is in fact enough of an arbiter for that. The problem, I think, of the human condition is not that there is any mystery about the right course of action, but rather it is when a person knows what is right and chooses to do the wrong thing anyway. We all seem to know pretty well what is the moral course in any given potentiality. The problem for humans is not, therefore, in finding a better definition of morality, but rather finding a way for our kind to stop disregarding our consciences in favor of what immediately suits us.

There is a relative kind of morality that only applies locally, and there is an objective kind that applies everywhere in the universe.

Proximate (evolutionary) morality is clearly relative and arbitrary, varying randomly across cultures. But I can't shake this nagging suspicion that there may be an objective sort of morality that supersedes all of those, and that possibly it is even knowable. Perhaps it is based on compassion.

On abortion: killing a zygote could very well be taking a life, but it must assuredly be less of a sin to nip in the bud a life not worth living, a life of suffering and misery, than to irresponsibly do the opposite. Life is full of sacrifices, whether we like it or not.

People argue for or against moral relativism. The fact is that there exist together in nature relative *and* objective types of morality. Both are held and used widely.

The notion of personal responsibility is a tricky one. For example, when someone commits a crime, there are various ways to look at it. A person who previous to the act of committing a crime knew exactly what he was going to do, planned it out and executed it — knowing the whole time, unequivocally, that it was wrong — can be said to have some objective measure of personal responsibility for such an act. Someone who committed a crime reactively, or based upon emotion or instinct, makes the waters a little cloudier. Perhaps ordinarily, they wouldn't do such a thing. It was in the heat of the moment. In our society, you're guilty either way, but perhaps this person would deserve extra forgiveness. Then there is the case in which a person commits a crime, intentionally, but didn't know or understand that it was wrong or illegal. This is the trickiest of all because the whole essence of the moral and legal deterrent was nonexistent. Once again, you're guilty either way, but perhaps stupidity has saved you from a graver fate.

Is a sin still a sin if one has no choice but to commit it?

Last I understood, ambition was not a virtue.

Compassion is essentially an understanding and a sympathy between souls, is fundamental, and is the basis for a universal morality.

Religions, political entities and indeed, most of society believe that ideas of morality are the fundamental and most important ideas. I think this is wrong. Morality is *something*, it is not *everything*.

Morality has its roots in what is safe and what is dangerous, socially and sexually.

I used to accept the premise of Stanley Kubrick's A Clockwork Orange as fascinating and clearly valid, but I now find I no longer hold that opinion. Denying a criminal his very free will may be a crime, but practical concerns dictate that there can be no solution to this conundrum. There is not some other habitable planet to which we can ship all of the prisoners and criminals so that, in the spirit of Christ, even they can be free. In reality, practicality requires us to sacrifice the lives of convicted criminals as a matter of public safety and common good, not merely as punishment and revenge. It is an expedient and it is a necessary one; objective morality does not apply. I no longer sympathize with Kubrick's philosophy reflected in this film.

The movie presents what is essentially a moral conundrum. Is it more ethical to allow Alex to be a robot — a "clockwork orange" — and be able to live in society, or is it more ethical to allow him to retain his capacity for free choice, in the hope that he will decide to abandon his criminal ways? For me, this is a false dichotomy. The problem here is that we know there can be no solution. The question asked has no meaning. As I have stated before, criminals have to be sacrificed for the common good. It is clear that Alex will never change his ways, and he'll likely end up back in prison. So, I ask you: Is it worse to experiment on a convicted and guilty felon with his full consent, or is it worse to allow him to rape and murder freely? For me, this is an easy question to answer.

Fixed moral systems can be problematic. A conscientious personal morality is the best and only guide.

It seems to me that animals are considerably more intelligent than we realize. And, consequently, that our treatment of them historically has been morally quite grave.

Some people feel that one of the primary reasons psychedelics are illegal is that they are a danger to the establishment, i.e. that if enough people are taking them, there will be some sort of massive rebellion. I don't think this is true. It might be the case if something like half the population were taking them, but even if they were legal, that would be far from the case. It seems they are illegal because of fear of the unknown, and fear of danger. Psychedelics can be dangerous, but everyone who has taken them knows they are, for the most part, relatively safe. In any case, they'll be illegal in most places for a long time to come.

Blood and Venom

Encroach on to regenerate
Envenomate
Slumber through transformative
Invigorate

Awake upon a fractured soul
Dulled out control
Alive but weary, sluggish corps
Mother extol

The DNA plus juice of death
Take final breaths
But in the hour of reprieve
There's something left

For two days, maybe three
God's unity
As twain come unto soul of one
Eternity

And out again and into time
Venomous rime
To join spirit to Black Widow
A lonely climb

And after death, and after spells
More ocean swells
As we float and thrash so randomly
Amongst our Hells

Our future, destiny, and redemption will be the noospheric establishment of "artificial" intelligence. It has become clear that the purpose now, and all along, of the human species was to develop culturally, and as a subset of that, technologically, to the point that cybernetic, artificial computing machines — or entities — could be constructed whose intelligence would have no theoretical limit. The purpose of civilized man is and has been to create AI.

Assuming consciousness is a physical process (and everything that exists is a physical process) I see no reason why an advanced computer cannot also participate in that process. Further assuming that consciousness may be a *fundamental* physical process, I see no reason why such a thing wouldn't be inevitable.

Any fantasy or hallucination can be made real with sufficient technology.

Humans will have no place in a world run by superintelligent AIs. One will have about as much business there as one does in the middle of a bonfire. The noosphere will be so radically active that we will simply vanish.

It seems fairly clear that humanity has turned out, in strictly evolutionary terms, to be something of a failure. Perhaps, if we succeed in ushering in

AI, there will instead be some measure of success in our legacy. But that is the only way.

My personal belief is that consciousness is a quantum mechanical phenomenon, and that Artificial Intelligence which is not merely smart but is also conscious will exploit that quantum phenomenon. Consciousness takes root in a non-local quantum circuit, and each individual is a localized bundle of neuro-electrical interconnections whose fundamental is that circuit. It is generally assumed by experts that quantum computing will be, while very powerful, essentially only useful for encryption technology and monumentally complex and large calculations. I infer however that if a quantum computer is setup, there will be an opening for consciousness to emerge — if setup properly. If quantum computing becomes a general practice in the future, and someone seeks to generate artificial intelligence with such a device, I think the potential for a breakthrough event is compelling.

The human body is far too obnoxiously low-tech to have any place at all in the future.

Quantum computing will most likely open avenues that will surprise us in radical ways.

I'd be willing to bet that we could generate the same, or an even higher, GDP in the U.S. with many fewer workers. At this point, we're making work — given the technology available.

Technology gives us comfort and convenience in our daily lives, but not, seemingly, lasting happiness. We adopt it and it becomes ho-hum. Looking at history, people in, say, the 1950's appear to have been happier than most are now, given economic and political circumstances. They had no cellphones or computers, no microwave ovens, no flat-screen tv's, etc. We tend to be biased toward our own age, thinking the past could not possibly have been better. Well, it appears we have more suffering and misery today than at any point in our nation's history. Technology hasn't saved us from that.

On the Turing test: Who ever said fooling an examiner into thinking the respondent was a human is a test for consciousness? We have had programs for years which can give more realistic responses to questions than many careless people could — just as a smarter human might. When did this become a criterion for awareness? If a machine begins to appear conscious, couldn't we just ask it if it were aware? Would it be able to lie? Or want to? Our general ignorance regarding consciousness is going to make some of these Turing tests seem ridiculous. The ultimate question is not whether we have "human" or "artificial" intelligence, but rather when do these constructs become self-aware?

Ah, computers. So very useful, so very vulnerable.

There is nothing for our species in outer space. There is no reason to go there except for fun. If there are other species out there, I am quite certain that they are not eager to meet us at all.

To rocket our big, squishy water-suits around in a spaceship seems a ridiculous proposition. Not to mention the fact that over two and a half years would need to be invested simply for a mission to Mars with current technology. Not to mention the fact that we cannot afford meaningful space travel. Not to mention the fact that we haven't even been to the moon — that a manned vehicle has not even been out of low-Earth orbit — since 1972. Not to mention the fact that there is no compelling or legitimate reason to go. This is AI's destiny, not ours. I understand people's romantic and adventuresome feelings. But there are really no scientific reasons to go into outer space, and not a single Earth government can afford a large-scale endeavor. However people feel about it, it isn't happening anytime soon, despite the best wishes of private enterprises. Man's children are meant for the stars, but man is not.

It seems nanotechnology is an inevitable waypoint in the general development of technology. It's still not a huge part of the conversation, because scientists are still working out the basics, but in ten or twenty years, it will be very much on everyone's minds. As some suggest, they are probably farther along with it than the public knows, and I'm sure DARPA is at the forefront of research. There are private and research institutions working on it as well, but just imagine how much money the defense agencies must be pouring into it. It is only a matter of time before it becomes as revolutionary as the internet. And the notion of high-tech self-replicating nanobots which can be programmed to do just about anything is a bit scary, it seems. Technology is a double-edged sword. It gives great power to everybody — both those seeking to promote welfare, and those seeking to destroy it.

The Boundary

The hologram projected
From the boundary
Of cosmic reverie
Existence so perfected

Information sans reservation
The implicate divine
Inclination to refine
An explicate in preservation

Only relatively static
The boundary, it has no age
Older out than in the cage
Motion inside, automatic

The volume is encoded
At the far edge of the region
Sentience becoming legion
Thus the inside is eroded

A pixel in an atom
Note in a symphony
Threads of theophany
A full order of random

The ego can be thought of as consciousness reflecting back onto itself through the activity of the nervous system. This reflective, reflexive "loop" is the determinant of most human behavior. It behaves as a classical system, in that it is deterministic. The substrate for this process is the true self, which behaves as a quantum system, the ground of which is pure consciousness. The true self is not constrained by time and space and is thus immortal.

The "classical" ego-self is where, as Alan Watts so correctly stated, things "just sort of happen." Deterministic. Unfree will. The "quantum" pure-conscious self, however, consists of a wavefunction whose superposition represents a multiplicity of possibilities and thus, real choice. We are usually very much stuck in our ego-selves, but the conscious and willful reality is actually more fundamental. Free will may be found (somewhere), but definitely not in the ego-self, as sure as it is that things are otherwise.

Jung's mythic philosophy is, no doubt, very popular, but in perusing it I came across something a little rough: He calls the "small, brown-skinned savage" a "primitive" and "inferior" type of man, and concludes that he is "singularly incapable of moral judgment." Did Jung not realize that civilized man has carried out the most morally outrageous acts of any creature in the four billion year history of our planet? If his entire psychological theory of the shadow is based on such an elementary anthropological error, why am I asked to take him seriously in any area of his thought? I, for one, am not and have never been interested in heroic myth, and consider it to be a cultural rather than innate sort of phenomenon. I have never encountered anything in my collective unconscious, in myself, to incline me in the slightest way toward recognizing any validity to his mythic "archetypes." He plainly had no knowledge of even the most basic ideas in anthropology, and constructed his theories in a vertical (heroic) continuum, whilst not realizing that this was the cultural and psychological continuum in which he was raised — *not* necessarily the one in which humanity exists naturally.

The human brain both generates and evaluates what it thinks, and therefore, can be very unreliable at times.

One of the most destructive memes, existentially and culturally, is the notion of the necessity of attainment: one must always strive for more — more money, more stuff, more status, more progress, more "success," etc. If we never have enough, if we always must have more, we are doomed to be miserable and unfulfilled. This kind of meme leads to nothing but frustration, feelings of inferiority and destructiveness at multiple levels. To be content with what one has, and what one is, and what one does, is not compatible with the perpetual cultural drive to attain ever more. And so we see a people slowly drowning.

Sure, there is ego loss, and the awareness of the self as a physical system. But some people take things too far in the direction of denial of the self, and that's a mistake. The mechanistic ego-self is an illusion and a trap people fall into, but there is a very real self behind it that is not so illusory.

It's not that the ego doesn't exist — merely that it is not the primary aspect of our being.

There's no one worse at analyzing oneself than oneself.

Your ego is not "you" — but you're there.

To *deny* the ego, as some do, makes no sense — it is in fact quite necessary for negotiating Earthly affairs. What is to be done is to put it in its proper perspective, i.e. as not the fundamental self of an individual. It is quite real, and for all practical purposes it is totally necessary for each person to behave on that level, at least to an appreciable extent.

The self may be an illusion, and it may at some key point fall away, but when it does a deeper, more fundamental and no less real self remains. This "true self" is the object.

Our identity as humans interacting on the physical plane seems to be something of a phantasm — it is not especially fixed to anything. Most of the time, we "are ourselves," but things can become very fluid during certain chaotic periods, including psychoses for example. It seems there is really no objective essence to our ego-identity. But there is a more fundamental level, beyond or beneath the ego, on which we do seem to have some sort of anchor — some kind of unchanging essence that affixes us to the cosmos. It is important to see and distinguish these levels to have any sense of perspective on the nature of identity.

"Ego" is the program for, and sense of, self for mammalian organisms negotiating terra firma. It is, ultimately, artificial.

My ego-self may be an illusion, but it's one I'll happily buy into.

Butterfly Order

See there a face
Did it form accidentally?
In theory, evidently
Truth without a trace

Such remarkable beauty
Selected for or maybe
The caterpillar baby
Lusts for future duty

Flourishing in nature
Predators at bay
She surely has a way
Of mitigating danger

Colors, vibrant efflorescent
How could they have been put there
By forces random, pushing air
With wings pumping incessant

The implicate suffusing
Each point at every other
There never was another
Idea quite so confusing

Honesty requires us
To relinquish old causality
To acknowledge true reality
Make intelligence a plus

It is my impression that many if not most aboriginal peoples had at least some direct awareness of quantum non-locality, and that this manifested for them as an organic concomitance of their undivided existence — ecologically, socially, culturally and individually.

The detribalization of humankind has represented a breaking apart and numbing of all of the senses, and moreover a diminishment in the ontological continuum itself — a real stultification of the reality of being.

Natural human awareness is buried quite deep in the modern, sedentary subconscious.

The horizontal, immanent, animist way of relating to the world was not so much a worldview or a religion as it was a psychology and a lived experience. It was really like a state of consciousness — one that to us would probably seem heightened in comparison.

Hunter-gatherers' lack of a belief in romantic love, and all of its attendant manifestations, was probably wiser than we realize.

Hunter-gatherers are often associated with a period of grace on Earth before the Fall. This notion leads to implications which are not quite sound. Hg's were (and are) exactly like us, but existed in a different sociocultural framework. The majority of common behaviors were the same. The crucial point is that hg's were well-behaved and egalitarian because they *had to be* in order to survive. As soon as man was given the choice whether to sin or not, he did. Hg society was like a house of cards — albeit a rather stable one, for a while. But as soon as factors entered the cultural picture that upset the balance and introduced alien variables, like delayed-returns and sedentism, the house typically toppled very quickly wherever the different systems met (usually involving a lot of violence). It is probably true that we were better off psychospiritually as hg's (at least in my opinion), but to associate a purported period of true grace with fundamental human nature is just a misunderstanding. Our behavior as civilized man is more indicative of our true nature than that in the cocoon of egalitarian tribal societies.

That thing the Indians had that one can't quite put one's finger on is that they were spiritually superior to the white man while living in a fabulously more personally and collectively meaningful cultural and psychological space. Clearly, one can just feel it, on occasion.

In a tribal setting, of maybe ten to twelve in a camp and fifty or so in a band, the shaman was like a doctor/healer/psychonaut/priest all in one person. It is said that generally, schizophrenic or schizoid types were selected for this position — which was lifelong — and that, not only were they not denigrated and discriminated against as they are in modern society, they were in fact revered and treasured for their psychological abnormality. In the role I describe, it was one-on-one and intimate with all members of the smallish tribal band. Obviously, you could not make an institution out of this. And the tribal lore would have no life without the spiritual immediacy of the shaman. So it was a close, symbiotic relationship. And the rituals were honed over, in some cases, thousands of years, going back and having been passed down directly. So the spiritual wisdom and techniques cannot be passed off second hand, or reinvented in a cursory way, as a modern shaman, with no ties to the past, would have to do. So you can see, true shamanism is dying if not dead.

There are clear psychological needs that are not met by civilization; hunter-gatherers typify the role, sociologically and psychologically, into which humans evolved, and it is not surprising that, when people were taken out of that role, psychological aberration ensued.

We in the West tend to think of the story this way: we lived in "primitive" hunting-gathering and tribal societies until, 10-12,000 years ago we figured out agriculture and built civilization. Without going into all aspects of why that is an anthropologically inane belief, agriculture began much more recently in most parts of the world. Truly, there was a veritable cornucopia of cultures, all living in diverse ways, all over the planet until homogenization really got going. The picture is much more complicated and rich and diverse than our trite cultural story would have it.

Hunter-gatherers are known to have very little or no fear of death. Death is not a concern for them (even though, as with all living things, they seek to avoid it instinctively). DA (Death Anxiety) is not a universal, and seems to be a localized pathology of certain civilized groups.

Once one becomes even a little aware of the reality of Indian affairs in this country, one becomes decidedly disillusioned with respect to the romantic, 'noble savage' Native American ideal that has become so ubiquitously established here. The perception is "Dances with Wolves"; the reality is, I am sorry to say, third world backwardness, corruption, petty bickering, racism, and stubbornness.

It is not commonly appreciated that we still do not know why agriculture was adopted in the way that it was. What most don't realize is that full-scale agriculture is a much more difficult and brutal way to make a living than a mixture with foraging or foraging itself. We still do not understand the causation that would lead a people to make such peculiar decisions.

8,000 BC is when intensive agriculture was adopted in the fertile crescent. The whole rest of the world at that time was hunter-gather, or mixed hg (with some small-scale agriculture). There were also some food storing hunter-gatherers, but very few. 10,000 years ago is not when the world switched overnight to agriculture. It has taken 10,000 years to get the point that now almost everyone uses it (but not quite everyone). The world was mostly nonagrarian in most places after the time of Christ. The adoption of agriculture in the fertile crescent was the history of our direct ancestors, NOT the history of all of humanity. A common and easy fallacy to adopt.

Cakes and Potions

What did Alice eat again?
What ate her good maker?
"Eat me" cake, she ate it, sure
Where then did it take her?

Higher! Yes, right, higher still
But not in ways profane
She grew in stature, not in high
The creator did not deign

And now today, we eat cake too
But it's not so innocent
Proliferation of cake's taboo
But it seems to be Heaven-sent

For just that reason, we should try
To limit its abuses
Responsible parties, seeking the truth
Are those for whom it has uses

Shamans, monks — what you will
A more refined approach
Must surround such cakes and potions
The reckless must not encroach

We might have saved ourselves
A headache, a ban or two
But heady days they surely were
What else was there to do?

Always be sure after eating cake
To drink the 'drink me' potion
So you come back down to Earth again
And give no one a notion

Physical law is abstracted from our observations of nature. To say, as most physicists do, that physical law itself *causes* natural phenomena to occur is nonsense — not to mention the fact that all of our best theories are by admission incomplete and therefore essentially false (except as purely technological approximations).

Science may be beautiful, but it isn't truth — it is a set of mathematical metaphors which provisionally approximate a reality whose subtleties and true nature we can scarcely guess at. Science is basically no more or less than a technology of a civilization.

Why do the materialists not see intelligence and order in an atom? An atom is not a random entity!

Just imagine that every particle in every world in every universe in every multiverse were itself its own infinite multiverse. I think that's about the size of it.

We analyze things into their separate parts to explore and discuss them and then forget to put them back together again.

Some people have problems with science, as if that makes any sense. The problem is not with science itself, but with the incorrect tacit axioms held by the majority of scientists and the philosophers and lay people they influence.

I think in time we will find that reductionism doesn't make any sense. The particles we reduce to are themselves abstracted from the unified background. To say that these abstracted entities called atoms are themselves the fundamental causal agents of reality is circular, and will be seen to be an illusion.

The crucial error in the scientific world seems to be the assumption that current knowledge paints the picture of all that will ever be known, and future progress is merely a question of refining the details of the existing painting. It occurs to me that in fact the truth is far richer than all that, and that in fifty years' time what can only be called "mystical" or "spiritual" now will have an established scientific and eventually quite humdrum treatment. Every age, it seems, has believed itself to understand more than it actually did, and ours is no exception.

Once again, science has, as Aleister Crowley observed, come around to telling us what everybody already knew. Neuroscientists have just discovered that the brain processes far more information than is delivered up for conscious perception. That something of which the brain is subconsciously cognizant may not be made aware to the organism. That, in reality, there are many thousands if not millions of processes of active information processing of which an individual simply has no idea. The psychonaut of the sixties could have told you all that. So could the Buddhist monk of the fourteenth century. Great.

I find it ironic and peculiar that scientists have become so truly dogmatic in their thinking and beliefs. I don't mean to speculate about whether they are right or wrong; I merely wish to point out that they are, not so refutably, as dogmatic as anybody. They would do well to acknowledge how much they don't know, and given that most of them do not do that, I would say they are not demonstrably a whole lot better than those whom they attack so ferociously.

More and more scientists are coming to the realization that not only can biology, biochemistry and neuroscience not exclude quantum phenomena, but such phenomena are instrumental in most biological processes, and certainly in the most fundamental ones — e.g. enzyme activity, photosynthesis, heredity, and others. This movement could have significant underpinnings for the understanding of consciousness and its connection to the body.

Instrumentalism is a blight on modern science.

Some people feel that science doesn't deal with meaning — that it is a cold, neutral instrument. But I disagree. Everything is imbued with at least some meaning. To look for meaning in science, we would have to look at its assumptions. And there are very many of them, explicit and implicit. Science cannot escape the subjectivity of what it is to be a human enterprise.

Is the present our intersection with the leading edge of expanding time?

If the proton nucleus of a hydrogen atom were the size of a golf ball, the "orbiting" electron would be almost a mile away. Why do we not observe the world as empty space? Because of the nature of interaction. The web of relationships in which we are involved determines our perceived reality. The Sanskrit word *maya*, found in Hinduism and Buddhism, seems to refer to this basic "emptiness." The word has multiple meanings in practice, but the most common definitions are as "illusion" or "magic." It is interesting that in the twentieth century, we in the West discovered through physics a basic truth that had been recognized in parts of Asia for thousands of years.

Math is Nature's poetry, and physics Her prose.

All that science is really doing at a fundamental level is elaborating upon a set of subjective, though empirical, axioms. To whatever degree these axioms are useful correlates to the degree that science is practically effective. But in reality, the whole enterprise is inherently circular, and thus certainly provisional. This circularity is only broken after a paradigm shift, at which time a more encompassing circularity is established.

The Chains of Energy

The great contexture of time and of space
Is all that we think that we see
We think that we'll ever be
But I tell you in candor, and with a straight face
I art thou, and thou art me

The illusion is set because of the belief
That mass and also that energy
Are in truth the lone, only synergy
Mystics and physics are stricken with grief
When it comes to the realm of the sensory

It would indeed appear to science and sense
That atoms and fields explain
The cosmos and the brain
But in truth our existence is far more intense
Than the dialectical twain

The objective is safe and so is the notion
That being — it really just is
And awareness, at the center 'tis
Yet the hackles so raise with conflicting emotion
That we are a long way from bliss

In the end we must state that any action
Involving the neural, the mind
Is of a certain type and kind
That beyond them is where we shall find traction
And get out of our confining bind

Modern culture strongly cultivates and fosters institutions, ideologies and the acquisition of stuff. It works well for things. But the same culture is woefully deficient when it comes to giving people lives which are truly meaningful. It does not work well for people.

Civilization has way too much inertia for sustained radical change to be at all possible.

Humans did not evolve, and were thus never meant, to engage in civilization. Perhaps that is why we are so bad at it.

In an economy based upon things, things take on a highly overvalued and unnatural character.

In our system of economics — that is to say, that of civilization going back to Rome and even before — there has to be a massive maldistribution of wealth. It is structural and the system could not possibly work without it. Civilization is very top-down. It is run by the managers for the managers. As a few get really wealthy, their ability to generate more wealth increases geometrically with time. This means that whatever revenue gets generated by the middle and lower classes usually winds up mostly in the coffers of the rich. They historically exacted this wealth in tribute, taxes and cheap or slave labor, and today simply take most of it because they own the property on which the work gets done, and they own most of the property (and they still pay relatively low wages and salaries, largely). This system always results in a fundamental imbalance, even after relative balance is achieved, because of the simple mathematical principle discussed above: the exponent. Whenever the slightest inequality develops, the differential ability to generate more wealth and eventually to buy out your competitor makes our kind of civilization systemically unfair and truly horrendous. We have done some great things as a civilization, but the suffering of the many amidst the well-being of the few has been the rule of the day.

To be civilized is almost by definition to be operating out of some type of neurosis.

I'm going to be blunt: any individual that prizes material possessions as much as the average American does has a malfunctioning brain, and is suffering from a kind of disease. Any individual who values material possessions as useful, but does not center his life around thinking about them constantly, is doing a little better, probably. The whole thing is totally disgusting. We exist in an economy that is extremely materialistic because it has to be in order to function — the buying and selling of goods is paramount to the maintenance of society itself. So, from a very early age people who exist inside of such an economy are conditioned to base their lives around accruing possessions, and being grateful for the opportunities to do so. Essentially, people in our culture are taught very early on to love "stuff," and so they do, happily and unquestioningly. Like I said, this is pathological and *not okay*. But it is ubiquitous, and we are living in a virtual nightmare because of it.

It is easy to forget that, while it is a logical consequence of nonzero population growth, civilization is an aberration. It runs counter to the harmonious, *evolutionary* stability that was the rule for millions of years. And, quite naturally, we are reaching a critical breaking point as a civilization. Perhaps we have already reached it.

There is a dark suggestion to be made, and that is that nuclear weapons had inevitably to be built, and certainly would be by the Soviets, so didn't we do the proper thing by setting about doing it as well, thoroughly and quickly as possible? I am no apologist for Dr. Strangelove, but it is a pragmatic question to consider. Some very bright and moral souls contributed to the hydrogen bomb. Were they right or wrong to do it? Realistically, it had to happen, right? I must indicate, for my own sake, that I am wholeheartedly against nuclear weapons existing at all, obviously. I would also point out that a lot of us are, and still, the weapons aren't going anywhere.

What most people fail to realize is that our civilization is unique, not general. Every other civilization that sprang up — and there were not that many — confined itself to its own region, and did no conquering outside of it. Mesopotamian civilization didn't stop until it swallowed everything, and it's still going, making a slave out of Earth and everyone on it.

Civilization is hard to come by, because it doesn't make any sense as an initial offering. We now know that most incipient states fell back to more egalitarian forms or simply dissolved because no one wanted to go through what was a considerably more difficult and troublesome affair to make a living. Anthropologists are quite unable to sort out how a civilization like ours ever formed in the first place. We don't know why it happens; one with anthropological savvy knows it doesn't make any sense.

Civilization is more concerned with becoming than with being.

Most of the world's major problems could be solved overnight if people really made up their minds that they wanted such a thing. However, I do sympathize with the fact that most people in the world do not have the time, money or leisure to think about such things.

Every great civilization or empire goes inevitably through the same very predictable stages. Of course it begins with its inception, and, for various reasons, it begins to rise in wealth and power. Typically some war results in its establishment to prominence as a truly great power. There is a period of relative success — a golden age, as it were — and then things begin to grow stale — after ripening the country begins to rot. Classes separate, complacency overall leads to the degradation of the integrity of institutions and values, and things decline. Decadence, depravity and real stupidity result from the decaying social fabric. Birth, rise, explosive success, efflorescence, complacency, stagnation, decline and then darkness. It has happened over and over again throughout the history of vertical civilization, and right now the syndrome of stagnation and decay are nowhere more in evidence than in the United States of America. It turns out that, despite all the enthusiasm, America was not immune to the natural cycle.

The Citadel

The Inquisition reigns supreme
The new Religion entrenched
Nobody sees it, it's everyone's dream
The thirst for answers is quenched

Comfort me please, sage institute
Which only ever complies
Philosopher, poet grow destitute
In almost everyone's eyes

Dogma defeated, new dogma born
Hopefully no third tomorrow
Coincidence only, synch-up forlorn
Poor knowledge, but still we borrow

In fifty years' time, who is now a mystic
Will be nothing more than too common
Hard to see well what's futuristic
Without some new kind of Shaman

What is now arcane, occult and forbidden
Will soon be common reality
At which point of folly we will be ridden
And consider it quaint old banality

A meme, an idea, that holds too much sway
Behaviors, thoughts all too ready
It's time for the future to sweep us away
Ignorance has grown a bit steady

David Bohm stated that there is no true randomness, no inherent chaos in the cosmos — just a spectrum of order which varies in intensity from one end to the other, and which at one end appears as purely random. He believed that even in, say, a Brownian fluid, if we properly understood it (which is not strictly possible with current technology) we would see that at bottom it is merely a very complex example of a system with a very low degree of order — one which would give every appearance of disorder. If anyone were able to prove this thesis true, it would obviously explain, finally, the order we see everywhere, and give us a revolutionary new view of the universe which would trample the quantum worldview.

Say what you will about human nature and law and order; people, generally speaking, are pretty well behaved. If they weren't, our system would be powerless to stop the resultant chaos.

The debate seems to be whether the universe came into existence completely by accident, or was designed by some creator. Why not a third option? Could there be a cosmic substrate which is informed by some subtle governing principle of intelligence or *order*, which evolves freely according to no predetermined stricture — *chaos*? Order (which is a form of intelligence) and random chaos (through which it is expressed) are both required for the evolution of a universe like ours.

To postulate that a person's thought processes are essentially like a weather system may be accurate, but only to a point — there is indeed a chaotic or stochastic element in the formation of thoughts. But in reality, this leaves no room for the intentionality inherent in the phenomenon of awareness. It ignores a real element of corresponding and complementary order. So, we might say that to consider the development of thought processes as especially similar to weather patterns is perhaps a misleading or incomplete analogy.

As a general rule, chaos flows into orderly states in some situations and under certain conditions. It seems hard to deny that both chaotic and orderly components appear together in the surroundings we find ourselves in. They seem to work in synergy.

The word *random* really means *apparently* random. If we understood what we ordinarily call "random" phenomena, we would see that they are not literally and inherently random. For example, our most random theory – quantum mechanics – would not be random from a higher dimension of reality. It would be quite orderly and ordinary. When you stop and think about it, the grains of sand on a beach are not random. We only treat them that way. No process in nature is absolutely random.

Classical Mechanics

It is thus assumed, it is yet presumed
That causal forces sweetly tell us
All those things we need to know
And the physicists are zealous

But someone might see, that then next to be
Was the starkest indeterminism
Did the theory mechanical quite go away?
Was there ever *really* a schism?

And by and by we've just been on the fly
And we are far too complacent
We think the whole thing is a great big machine
With a chorus of miracles adjacent

Electric highways, linear byways
Newtonian causality
Shall the flower open up?
A return to reality?

Although we have facts, we're quick to react
To anything that's *avant garde*
Perhaps the electric theories eclectic
Are not sufficiently hard

In classical theory, the cosmos is merely
A robotic, atomic clock
In quantum mechanics, we throw it all out
But still Mother Nature we mock

We see in the real, indeed a great deal
Of ourselves and what we observe
And yes it may fool us, perhaps even school us
Such torture God does not deserve

We are very young but we must taste our tongue
If ever we seek to peer deeper
Because there beneath Newton and even the atom
Is the realm indeed of the Reaper

Romantic love is an investment in the Other (who is seen as sacred) which it is assumed will pay cosmic dividends. If this is perceived to happen at all, it is only over the short-term. A single individual, whoever they are, is seldom the source of any final answers in life. The problem is that civilized man is so suffused with *needs*.

One can have the utmost compassion for humanity without also liking it very much.

What we have to realize about love is that it isn't everything, and isn't, ultimately, an answer.

Very easily, and frequently, a marriage can go on for thirty years while both parties have failed to realize that it hasn't been working for the last twenty-eight.

The greatest illusion of them all is romantic love.

Love is real. Deification of the other is a delusion.

It seems that, by and large, the people who clamor about suffering are really the ones who are doing all right — at least materially. The people of the world who are, by any objective measure, truly suffering a great deal day-in and day-out do not talk of such things.

It is truly a privilege to be able to enjoy life to any degree. A lot of people aren't equipped to do so, through no fault of their own.

Romantic love is ultimately confined to the self, and all of the subtle, sublime and perhaps even transcendent emotions that often come with it are tied inextricably to the ego of the person experiencing them. There is in reality no union of self and other in any romantic relationship — it simply cannot exist. In truth, love is essentially a kind of particularly delusional selfishness which gets projected onto and associated with the other. In the end, all of its trappings are intended, or have come into being, to foster robotic behaviors which will result in offspring. Love may feel wonderful, but the rationalization of its mechanism really is a species of delusion.

In most human interactions involving violence, nobody is right and everybody loses.

When you have seen love go as internally haywire as I have, you realize that it is more or less just a mechanism.

Love of one's dog isn't so much about a romantic type of love as it is about a very subtle form of compassion. I love on my dogs quite a bit, but enjoy them primarily for the compassion we share.

Let's face it, human love is mostly conditional, and tied to desire. I think what is cosmic, ultimately, is compassion. There is a subtle difference.

Truth is, there is precious little, in the end, that one can do to really help one's fellow man, existentially. That, of course, does not mean that institutional help for basic needs should be absent, as it largely is in the United States.

There is a lot of suffering out there, surely, but it seems that, for the most part, we are doing it to ourselves.

I think much of the sting of suffering comes from constantly telling ourselves we are suffering, that "this sucks." Without recognizing adversity as suffering, there is not nearly as much suffering going on. It is simply accepted. I think this is closer to the natural attitude than wallowing in misery, which is what civilized humans do best.

Just because one doesn't have much faith in one's fellow man does not mean that one should not act compassionately toward him.

Do I care? Well, on the one hand, I don't at all like to see people suffer. On the other, I am convinced that this species is going down one way or another, to which I am resigned and feel is probably for the best. So yes and no.

True friendship is really quite different than that which most people have.

It's hard for us closed-up Westerners — especially Americans — to open up and experience full, conscious love without the aid of psychedelics. I know I can't.

The juxtaposition of Christ-like love and the real world seems somewhat absurd to me. The two do not go together. That is not to say that detached compassion is not the best policy.

It never ceases to amaze me the extent to which those who have everything bitch and moan while those who have nothing don't say a word — or even speak positively.

So many people in utter despair, talking of suffering and pain. When did everything become so awful?

It's hard to get close to someone when experience tells you the relationship is more than likely going to be transitory.

Concrete Abstraction

Physics is metaphor; math is the truth
One could say in good faith
Philosophy may be long in the tooth
But Nature's soul is no wraith

Math is poetry; physics is prose
A penny for the old guy's device
The spirit of worlds opens like a rose
And some people feel he throws dice

There are two types of great writing: philosophical and artistic. Philosophical writing tends to emphasize content over style, exploring truth in more direct terms, while artistic writing emphasizes style over content, being more ornate and linguistically aesthetic, and exploring truth in a completely different way. The two types often blend together for maximum precision and beauty. Both, done well, can be magnificent. Nonfiction tends to exhibit the former, and fiction the latter, although the more straightforward style can be found in fiction, and deft artfulness can surely be found in much nonfiction.

Film is a fine medium, but honestly, most movies — and by most I mean almost all of them — are not very good. I don't know whether it's an institutional lack of rigor, or the desire to please crowds and make money (by appealing to a low common denominator), or what, but it seems, to me, as if the medium is almost wasted. I would very much like to see more better directors, but alas, I do have some inkling that the politics of the industry are extremely nasty and undesirable. A young, bright filmmaker who could be very good might not even get a chance — or if given one not want to take it. I don't think filmmaking is in a very good place.

Aleister Crowley contended that the two best writings in the English language are those of Shakespeare and the Bible.

To look at a Monet is to gaze at genius.

Kubrick directed his movies in an evolutionary way. He didn't so much have fixed, *created* ideas for what he wanted, but relied on circumstance for *selection* of the ideas of others based upon what came up, and developed a production in this way toward a finished product. He was something like a master conductor — making executive decisions, but not precisely controlling that which he decided upon. He was more of a great craftsman than full of original ideas. And that's fine; he was one of the greatest film-makers ever to live. He understood how to get what he wanted in a film.

Books aren't as real as films, but they do convey information at a much higher and richer resolution.

Great art is an ingenious device — one which proves its merits to you from within itself through the symbolic and often allegorical message its architect has created. Coming away from mediocre art is an unremarkable experience, but taking in great art leaves one feeling moved and edified. Great art proves its own point, the raising of which, *ipso facto*, is justified and necessary with regard to an understanding of the truth.

As Jim Morrison and Stanley Kubrick pointed out, film may well be the best artistic medium for conveying and in turn generating vivid emotional states in the audience. Writing is still the best medium for communicating information in general, but it cannot match motion pictures for the immersion the moviegoer experiences, the emotional response, and the investment and absorption in what is happening on the screen. (If, of course, the movie is any good)!

Poe once said that any phenomenon, anything, can be addressed through language. It strikes me that this is a minority opinion. I'm not sure whether I agree or not. I think I might.

Perhaps the lack of popularity of an idea or artwork can be a positive indicator of its true value? Do people always make much money off of the really good stuff?

With Nabokov, every sentence is a universe.

Well, the Hollywood studio system has pretty well made it so that a Stanley Kubrick will never happen again. After *Strangelove* and *2001*, Warner Bros. basically told Kubrick he could do what he wanted — which he did all the way through *Eyes Wide Shut*. Other directors of his ilk have gotten so disgusted with the studio system that they've just given up — David Lynch springs to mind. A movie like *A Clockwork Orange* or *2001* could not get made today. No studio would put up the money for a questionable artistic movie that challenges and engages audiences on more than a superficial level. I'm sure whoever is reading this has noticed that the quality of movies has declined sharply; I can't even remember the last time I saw any need to see a movie at the theater. It's just all comic-book flicks and stupid comedies now. It's garbage. Movies like *Taxi Driver*, *Barry Lyndon*, any David Lynch movie, *Chinatown*, *The Treasure of the Sierra Madre*, and even *The Godfather*, etc., etc. would very likely not get made today if they were pitched through the normal channels. There are many up-and-coming filmmakers that are just not going to get a first or second chance. The state of film as an art form is terribly brutalized right now. Kubrick's arrangement with Warner Bros. is unheard of in today's movie scene. When he died, so did that type of arrangement.

The Thin Red Line is all about the essence of reality, the eternal touching the temporary, good to be found among horror, the psychological intensity of battle, and promise in death. It is very nuanced, subtle, beautiful and yet true to the narrative of the war, which was ambiguous for everyone involved. Also the directing is phenomenal; it's simply a great movie. In Saving Private Ryan, Spielberg does not have the same light touch or the artistic skill that Malick does here, and other than the D-Day sequence which was extraordinary, I feel that the war effects in TRL measure up just fine to the bulk of those in SPR. There are really not many advantages to be found in Spielberg's vision over Malick's, and it's typical of the Academy to have awarded the former with several Oscars, and the superior latter with none.

Being an artist or a writer, even a good one, is a terrible and essentially impossible way to make a living, especially in today's hypercompetitive market. There's simply no money in it.

Conscience

Lacking real perspectives
Such a one may err
Does this wide blight give one the right
Not at all to care?

This is a good query
But seemingly misplaced
And to be fair, all put on airs
Yet in truth are disgraced

God himself quite wonders
If humans can do good
Why play at trifles all day?
Why not care if they could?

But nevermind the Heavens
It inheres in itself
If one has say, one has a way
To restore all good health

This does, in fact, not happen
It's not that one cannot
But *will* not do, it's sad, but true
And this is our sad lot

If men wished to renounce
Their tragic apathy
The globe would be, for you and me
A lovely sight to see

Perhaps time has run out on us
Perhaps our chances gone
But one can't say, there was no way
To avoid doing wrong

It is simply not true that "everyone is created equal." However, it is not people's fault for being born — and here they are, on Earth, barely scraping by, most of them. While there is a distinct hierarchy between individual humans, every citizen of Earth ought to have an equal right to life and equal treatment under the law. This sounds a little too idealistic in a reality like ours, and perhaps it is. But while hierarchy is inherent and inevitable, there is no fundamental reason why only a few of us should make a reasonable living, and be truly included and taken care of. A combination of hierarchy and economic and legal equality is quite possible.

Humanity has been organized into egalitarian societies, and hierarchical ones, depending upon the socioeconomic constellation. Egalitarianism gave way, in large part, to hierarchy, after the mode of production had to become specialized and the food and water had to be distributed. Before that, social equality was mandatory as the group's survival depended on it. But the egalitarian ethos may have been something of an illusion, and pure hierarchy has been seen to be rather cold and brutal in many respects. What would be ideal is a fusion of the two, a system in which the best and brightest can ascend without limit, but in which each individual, of any rank, has an undeniable right to an unfettered existence. A fusion of horizontal and vertical into a new continuum.

Each individual human in society is like a neuron in the cultural meme-system's brain. And this brain constitutes the local noosphere.

People are very confused on this. It is true that not everyone is equal. There is an inherent hierarchy among human societies — some are smarter than others, some better looking, etc. *However*, this does not, as is so often tacitly and incorrectly assumed, mean that any one person has any more right to live an unfettered life than any other. No one chose to be born, and it was the luck of the draw regarding what we were born into. Through no fault of anyone's, here we all are. Everyone should have an equal right to the resources and securities needed to live; we should value life at least that much. The confusion on this subject arises because people are thinking in an Aristotelian "either-or" framework. In reality, the ideal human society is composed of both hierarchical and egalitarian elements.

The noosphere is the nonlocal envelope of Earth consciousness and activity. All thought and culture exist and evolve through it — the collective mind of Earth.

Hierarchy is not desirable. Pure egalitarianism is not desirable either. What is desirable is a fusion of hierarchy and egalitarianism, where everyone has an equal right to life and equal treatment under the law while not preventing the smart and strong from rising to whatever heights they may attain. Egalitarianism sometimes keeps those who should be at the top in the middle or at the bottom. Hierarchy can be unfair and keeps the people at the bottom from an equal right to life and a potential rise of their own. What is needed, and what evolution will probably provide in the coming decades, is some sort of fusion of the two.

It is not someone's fault if they are born stupid, or poor, or sick, or disabled. The people whom the conservatives and even the libertarians would like to ignore, to let fend for themselves, didn't ask to be here and came into problems through no fault of their own whatsoever. We should not ignore basic human needs. Seemingly, a lot of people think we should. 'Let them figure it out — it's every man for himself and by God that's how it ought to be.' That's not how any society should operate. Any society, no matter what its constitution, should foster an equal right to life for everyone in it. Shame on our callous, outrageous cultural orientation.

Every communist and hippie and young idealist champions egalitarian society and culture, but I think we can agree that not all hunters out on the savanna were equal. The system was in place because it had to be — for survival, by evolution — and not because of its merits. Hierarchy may be harsh, and a burden, but we live in a hierarchical world, and those principles are most fundamentally in play in civilization. We don't need egalitarian society — we can't have it. And more hierarchy would only be dreary, even if appropriate. What the future promises is a fusion of both: A fundamentally hierarchical system whose members are on an equal footing with each other — that is, each member has an equal right to existence as any other, and none may hamper that of even the feeblest and most inconsequential, while recognizing that they are indeed on a spectrum of rank. I think a fusion of egalitarian and hierarchical is what the future holds for us, and I think it is what we should want.

Creation

Some people take the credit
For all the things they do
An ego bigger than a mountain
Will ripple through and through

Or maybe credit goes to God
Sometimes I'm not quite sure
The rich feel it was they alone
And blame fate on the poor

I think that all this reverence
For self, and self alone
Is folly of the basest kind
A fool for every throne

I do not know how I create
It's quite a mystery
It all really just sort of happens
Just like all history

There I squeeze, and out it comes
Every line by magic
I cannot say that I'm the doer
To brag to me is tragic

Happenstance and timing, right?
The secrets of success
Honestly, you're on a ride
Deluded nonetheless

I dig "turn on, tune in, and drop out." My sentiments exactly. The problem, however, is that in this particular reality, on this particular planet, at this particular time, there is nothing at all to drop out *to*.

Modern capitalism is simultaneously the most productive and the most socially and spiritually bankrupt economic system in the history of the planet. It comprises great material success (for some) on the one hand, and a total stultification of the soul on the other.

Who wants a specialized job? Who doesn't want, instead, a meaningful role? We're going to have to overhaul the entire concept of work in the coming years; why not set about thinking about all of this… *right now*?

The free market is far too irresponsible to regulate itself.

Nationalism has become obsolete.

Most civilized people throughout history have had to pay to live, as ludicrous as that is. The tragic fact is that the population levels sedentary societies have brought into existence can't be financed in any other way. So people's ability simply to live is held hostage from them, and obviously money is crucially important. We as a global community are rapidly approaching the point where we will have the highest imbalance of job to worker ratio in history, and while the wealth levels will continue to rise for the rich (the ownership), most people will be permanently out of work. There is going to have to be some type of basic income program in which everyone gets compensated while only a few are actually working. An entire overhaul of the concept of an economy will have to come into existence, or society will simply collapse. Technological streamlining should be a good thing, and welcomed by society — the realization of a dream that is thousands of years old. In this, our modern society, it is turning into a nightmare — because everyone in power is, as yet, completely ignoring the problem.

It is not uncommon to hear people say that America is failing. But that's not exactly true. America isn't failing. *It has already failed.*

The way to change the world is to change minds. As long as people are thinking the same way, nothing much will change. As long as people willfully and idiotically chase this insane "dream," society will remain functionally the same and things will only be able to go from bad to worse. It's not exclusively the fault of the very rich. The American People, the middle class, are as much or more to blame for our collective woes.

The founding fathers were very careful in their structuring of the Constitution to *prevent* the popular will from deciding the affairs of government. They were squarely against mob rule or even influence, and it was for this reason that they constructed a federal republic, not a pure democracy. Rule by the average man — our democracy — has grown out of this in time and become a tradition; but it was expressly contraindicated in the Constitution with its emphasis on representative government which acts independently for the people, but does not submit to a mandate by the people. Supposedly, the representative — who is not merely a delegate, and who is genuinely qualified — conducts himself according to his intelligence and wisdom, not the (often ridiculous) popular will.

We see (it is almost ubiquitous at this point) the difficulties these soldiers are facing upon returning to civilian life. That intensity, that numinous heroism, of battle is impossible to reproduce at home, and so it is virtually impossible for very many to adjust back to their pre-war mentalities in which there is a lack of that intensity. It's tragic, and the truth is that they should never have been deployed in the first place. How much destruction are we capable of before we can finally have peace (and peace of mind)?

The reason more government is necessary and conservatism and libertarianism won't fly is that humans, by and large, can't be trusted to regulate themselves and do the right thing. Left to their own devices, people will cheat. And it only takes one bad apple to spoil the entire bushel. This notion that the market can and should regulate itself is the most ridiculous thing I've ever heard. Wall Street runs amok even with regulations. Would-be criminals and people who are already criminals must not be put in charge.

History favors the victorious, then turns to propaganda. Who would have been hurt if the British had won the Revolutionary War? Was the terrorism propagated by the colonists really okay? If it had gone the other way they (the founders) would all be viewed as scoundrels and brigands. Did what we have now really occupy the minds of the founders? Could domestic affairs be more propitious as a satellite of the U.K.? It's funny how history has its turns, which become set in stone, but in all reality if the story had gone differently than our luminous fairy tales, things might possibly have turned out better. Yet we worship them as gods.

What is great about America is the land, the Indian land which is sacred to anyone with the eyes to see it. The dominant culture overlaid on this luckless continent is another matter. But the geography is special.

Communism doesn't work because in reality, the hierarchy never dissolves.

We are not "free." We are relatively free.

In politics, the right is more concerned with the protection of property; the left is more concerned with the welfare of individuals. I personally have certain misgivings either way, in the mess that is reality — but I think I know which way to lean, if the situation calls for it.

Crystalline

To receive a parcel on a Tuesday afternoon
Is kind of ordinary, not extraordinary
So what then, pray tell, is going to be my boon?
It's from a stranger merry, I pray it isn't scary

Truth or Consequences is the now's abode
And I do not know, what this pack will show
But the town and this lush landscape make a lovely node
Tell me, does it glow? Where was it to go?

It cannot have been here, the current premises
I have already said, to me the sender's dead
I know him not, so really all I have are grimaces
Will this parcel cut me red? Then to have out-bled?

It's like the Cask of crypts, what and whereat is this?
It's captivating me, as it's activating me
If I did not receive this, what would I have missed?
I really must now see, this mystery for free!

I can't recall an instance of a prompting of this thing
I live indeed a simple life, relaxation, respite rife
Whereupon invades this Fedex man, what did he bring?
I hope it's not some murder knife, I do not need the strife!

Shall I swallow and just open this damn infernal thing
Yes I think I really must, perhaps it is a bust?
All right, and I must say I hope it doesn't at all sting!
Or I will have cussed, and henceforth lost all trust!

The blade injures the tape as I finally do the deed
The package I unclasp, the knife it makes a rasp
And what I find is something that I really did not need
An orbicle of jasp, but Oh! it made me gasp!

Perhaps *culture* could be defined most succinctly as the shared mental contents of a particular society.

The human animal is not smart enough or compassionate enough to make its current socioeconomic system equitable and fair. The system is in fact larger than even the will of the powerful; cultural evolution is a system and an organism unto itself. The issue is indeed systemic — no species, no matter how smart, could make this system work equitably. (A higher type's would really be fundamentally different). It would need to be deliberately and intentionally transcended if there were to be lasting change. Thus we see the human animal's lack of intelligence in its inability to fix its current (and ubiquitous) system, and its lack of compassion in the absence of desire, on the whole, to mount any kind of meaningful and lasting campaign at least to look seriously into how fixing it might be done — or rather, even, to recognize at all the desperation with which it indeed does need to be fixed. There have been great men over the eons; yet even they were powerless, really, to slow the momentum of the wild animal of culture and society, let alone arrest it, or direct it into a genuinely and meaningfully different channel.

We're not smart enough, on the whole, to see what's really going on in the world or to be able to control the system enough to do something about it; and we're not compassionate enough to care about our fellow man enough to *want* to do something about it.

The cultural system of modern civilization places far too little emphasis on participation in nature, whereas the cultural systems of most aboriginal cultures placed too much. The latter is probably existentially and socially preferable (and is, notably, sustainable), but both extremes lead to some wrong ideas, while an approach which is more balanced would more accurately reflect reality.

The human cultural matrix is a system far smarter and more powerful than any individual human or group of individuals. That is why it is in command of human affairs, and humans are not. It has been this way since before the dawn of civilization. We think we're at the helm. We're not. There are far subtler and more fundamental forces at work in human affairs than the decisions of anyone or any group. Conspiracy theories are seen to be irrelevant. We're passengers on a train and we do not lay down the tracks. The system is far more complex than and so far removed from human control that our beliefs about things really are a sort of sick tragedy. And when we're no longer needed as the host for the evolution of memes, nature will discard us. The only way to kill this cultural organism is for humanity to become extinct. Nature is using us.

Abstractly, culture is a bacterial population whose cells are individual humans.

The true course of human civilization has nothing to do with any one person's, or any group's, wishes, desires, plans or morals. It evolves much as a weather system does.

There are forces at work on this planet that are quite invisible, and extremely powerful. Human culture is like a giant organism, and individuals are very small cells within that organism. Or culture is the brain and individuals are like individual neurons. Or one could liken it to a machine. Culture is a huge mechanism, and individual humans are like minor cogs in the overall mechanical process. This machine operates on what to us would be a decidedly abstract level, and yet it drives all of the human affairs of Earth. The evolution — i.e. the adoption, mutation and selection — of memes is the essence of what is happening. Everything in human society, every thought and almost every behavior, is shaped and in many cases decided by the greater cultural evolution. The cog is quite unaware of his place in the machine, or even what the machine is really doing. It all takes place in human minds, yet is far greater in its overall networked projection than any individual or group of individuals. Human choice has absolutely nothing to do with it.

Mother Nature is playing man like a hand of cards, and letting him think, all the while, that the game is under his control. All mankind is really playing is the fool.

Does money exist for any other reason than to change hands and become unequally held?

Over the last ten thousand years, for our culture (Mesopotamian civilization), there has been better and there has been worse, but over time it has all been pretty much the same thing, fundamentally. So, we can say that there is pretty strong evidence that meaningful or radical change simply does not take place, despite the idealism.

A form of abstract progress, i.e. complexification, may or may not be going on in Nature, but progress on a human level is a meme specific to our civilization and is not objective. How do you know progress is even happening? Sure technological "progress" is occurring, but how do we know how this will affect the destiny of man himself? It could be very deleterious in the long-run. So that wouldn't really be progress. And it seems to me that the only objective measure of progress in human societies is the development of the level of happiness overall. With all of this complex technology, etc., are humans really any happier than they were fifty years ago? A hundred, two hundred years ago? I think a lot of people would say that no, we're not. There's a lot of misery associated with modern society. So how can we be said to have progressed? The notion that progress is necessarily happening on a level meaningful for human beings and their most central interests is a cultural bias that most of us don't even think about. More complex does not necessarily mean "better."

We've made tremendous *quantitative* progress as a civilization. The amount of *qualitative* progress we have made is decidedly up for debate.

Instead of using the word "progress," perhaps we should instead substitute the word "development" in order to shed some of the baggage.

Cultural Evolution

From time immemorial, the patterns flow thus:
(And the pustules of suffering o'erflow with pus)
In general, we have generals, and mayors, chiefs, kings
And thousand year failures seem to be the things
Constant in all empires, hydraulic or not
In feudal systems diabolical plots

And so we can see that, though a few had a life
For nine tenths it's working, and slaving and strife
Indeed, the fact is that throughout all the ages
Not only have few been priests, artisans, sages
But most of the lot were just paupers and peasants
With standards of living perpetually unpleasant

So established we have in the anthropoid picture
Of history: most unfree toiling and stricture
It rather suggests that progress is ethereal
Progress, that is, that's moral and material
And so we must assume, if we're to be clever
That free will and morals from this process are severed

And following that point, one must conclude
That life on Earth, at least for we humans, is rude
The broader sweep of our dear planet's direction
Affords no one, no society protection
From things like, well, I guess failure and extinction
If that be Mom's will, that shall be our distinction

So in point of fact, the live ones do not
Have any awareness of what nature's got
In store for the future of Earth, for a start
Or what sort of way we're to play our part
Or if it in any way matters at all
That humans have got themselves set for a fall

Whether we are progenitors of a glorious fate
Or whether in fact for all Earth it's too late
Cannot be known 'til the fact of the matter
Arrives at the present, the living to flatter?
Flatter, or disgrace or frighten or kill
Mother Nature has drawn up an awfully long bill

Ecological awareness is obviously fundamental — or should I say ecological participation. Furthermore, the current trends in environmental
awareness and responsibility are admirable and excellent. The sad truth,
however, is that it is too little, too late. The trend of overpopulation is irre-
versible. We should do what we can, but in the main, the crises will be very
hard to slow, let alone avert.

"Tree-hugging" is an absurd stance, and so is the notion that the planet is
here to be exploited and turned to profit with disdain for any ecological
considerations. Civilization simply must impact the environment, and a
soaring population will only make it more pronounced as the years go by.

But civilization is what we've got, so some type of moderate path toward realistic yet gentle use ought to be considered ideal. Some of the "green" nuts would like to see the planet depopulated by billions of people. Some of the ultra-materialistic, hardcore capitalists would like to see this planet destroyed for profit, which they see as okay because with technological advances we will be able to colonize others. Needless to say, sanity lies somewhere in between.

Our environmental initiatives are well-intentioned, but sadly they can be very appropriately compared to repairing a decapitation with a band-aid.

All the emphasis on global warming is way too little, way too late. We might have benefitted from this awareness a hundred and fifty years ago.

When you start meddling with an ecosystem, you're typically never able to stop.

Many (not all) of the environmentalists mean well enough, but really theirs is a caricature of a healthy awareness.

The environmental movement is primarily just a way for the people in charge of various charities and lobbying groups to make money for themselves, and by and large, it does very little to really help the planet.

We talk about alternative energy as if that even means anything. We will not soon go to any alternative. That's not how humans operate. We will go fully toward a new energy technology when we absolutely *have to* do so, not when it's in our best interests. Humans don't make economic decisions based upon morality. Fossil fuels will be with us for decades to come, unless something drastically cheaper comes along, which doesn't seem too likely. Despite a real ecological need for change, the sad fact is that the economic realities trump any other consideration. Oil very likely won't be dethroned for some time.

It seems to me that it's frankly quite impossible to have a sustainable civilization with a world human population of 7.5 billion and climbing, in any way or at any kind of reasonable average standard of living.

Our species and its antecedents were egalitarian for literally millions of years. Our species has been living in social hierarchies for about eight to ten thousand years, and in that short span we have come to the precipice of destroying ourselves. We are slowly (or not so slowly) destroying the flora, fauna and life-sustaining capacities of the biosphere of the planet. Any number of conclusions can be drawn from this, but probably the most salient is that by living in this way, something has gone very disastrously wrong for almost all denizens of Earth.

You'd have to be pretty far away from open and honest scientific publications, even ones like Scientific American, still to be denying climate change at this point. I mean, for heaven's sake, islands in the South Pacific are sinking. I just read yesterday that 70% of the Great Barrier Reef off Australia is basically dead from coral's version of heat stroke. The planet has always been going through climate change. That's one argument from the right I've heard that's actually true. The planet has even been warmer in the past, that's another one, and it's true too. But the fact is that we are in the midst of a warming trend, and the CO2 emissions from civilization are indeed exacerbating it. There is solid, objective science to back this up. If you actually look at some of the hard science and the overwhelming number of data points, there is really no alternative argument to be made. It is my understanding that most of the scientific community who have reviewed these findings posit that there is a natural process in which certain gases in the atmosphere trap incoming radiation and keep it from reflecting back out into space — this is known as the "greenhouse effect." This is a natural process that occurs with or without man. They further posit that the emissions from man's burning of fossil fuels are exacerbating this effect in unnatural ways — that we are taking a natural process and speeding it up, and potentially sending it at least partially out of control. It is my contention that these positions are reasonable and correct, and further that any honest human being who has any contact with this information, and looks at global weather and climate data, would be unreasonable not to share them.

The entire modern economy is based upon consumption — unlimited consumption at that. This is so far from healthy ecology that it is no wonder we are in crisis.

The climate has always been in a state of change, but it usually occurs in a semi-regular pattern. It has been exhaustively and scientifically demonstrated that we are now outside of that cycle, as a consequence of the abnormally high concentrations of carbon in the atmosphere. It is clear that the natural greenhouse effect is being exacerbated by modern civilized man. The evidence is everywhere an unbiased mind cares to look.

The only species on Earth that systematically and continuously destroys *its own habitat* is humankind.

Darkness Annihilating Light

Stress rebound
From horror, hell
All around
There tolls the bell

Nowhere to run
Nowhere to go
A meaningless Sun
An ebbing, stopped flow

The limit is reached
The limit, the end
Old souls to teach
To teach, then to rend

No soul wise enough
Or sufficiently wary
To accept such black guff
No place to tarry

One can only hope
That suffering's light
Because this old rope
Is upon necks a blight

Just because space, time, and ego can be transcended does not mean that, for all practical purposes, they don't in fact exist.

Could it be that consciousness is the quantum mechanical process of tunneling through time?

The familiar matter with which we interact every day is only *relatively* invariant. As the Buddha was quick to reinforce in his disciples at every opportunity, impermanence is rather the rule.

There seems to be confusion about whether quantum entanglement violates the Special Theory of Relativity and whether this amounts to a major, jarring conflict in our theory. If one assumes that the level at which entanglement occurs is more fundamental than the plane of mass-energy, there need be no conflict. Matter and energy are deep, but not fundamental.

If time were not a factor, the concept of "now" would have no meaning.

The subjective perception of duration is a consequence of the brain's processing of memory, and is thus an illusion. Whatever time "is," it is not anything like we think.

Life is a bubble of time which will pop.

The nature of time is obviously very mysterious. It is rather easy to describe our perception of time and duration as a subjective phenomenon, which is fine, but what is the objective nature of the medium in which temporal (and spatial) change is occurring? If objective time is an illusion too, what about clocks that spin at different rates in different reference frames in experiments? This clearly has nothing to do with concepts of duration. There is something deeper. The mystics talk about transcending time, but it seems to me that the lot of them sure spend most of their time in it.

The concept of cause and effect has no meaning outside of space and time.

We are, in all reality, actually living in the past. It takes time for energy to stimulate a nerve, for that nerve signal to travel to the brain, for that signal to be processed, and for that information to be generated as meaningful conscious qualia. It's hard to understand how the concept that 'it is only always *now*' can be true in any proper way. If "now" is not really now, and therefore past and future must be real in any case, the notion of the time-less for humans has some implausibility in practice.

Space, time, and light, *as we perceive them*, exist only in the mind.

Matter and energy, atoms and molecules, are real, but they are certainly not the whole story. Chemistry is clearly a reality; the point is that it is not the fundamental reality. Quantum particles surely exist, and behave approximately as we describe them, but we are erroneous in how we relate to them. We treat the chemical world as if it were the ultimate, final objective reality. In actuality, the universe has mind-like properties, and chemistry is one manifestation of that greater overarching intelligence. In other words, atomic particles originate in a ground that *is* fundamental for our universe; they are not in fact that ground itself.

As one's velocity increases, time slows. When one is moving at very high-velocity, time is at a slow crawl — very different than the normal perception of duration. When one attains and transcends the speed of light barrier, time no longer exists. There is only consciousness and information.

The future is a source of brightness shining back through time. We move toward it through time, but it is the cause, not what is caused. The distant past is the most remote point, the one furthest removed, from the center — which is that bright source in our future. We are biased into illusion when it comes to our predominant cultural approaches to time.

Space and time, as perceptual frameworks, are subjective and arbitrary. (It is recognized — or at least supposed — that, in purely literal terms, space and time have no "existence" independent of active perception, hence the term 'perceptual'). There is no truth which stipulates that what an individual sees "out there" is "the way it really is." For example, an extraterrestrial's perception of the universe may be so foreign to ours that no description or translation of it may be possible (at least on a basic level). Its conventions for expressing to itself the realities of space and time may not have any Cartesian bent whatsoever. Something to keep in mind.

There are aspects of the mind which exist and function independently of the dimension of time. In certain states of mind one can see that time is a sort of frame of the mind which can be transcended. Einstein's theories verify this.

"Time" is a function of how the human brain processes memory. Our experience of time is totally subjective; it does not correlate to anything that is actually "out there." Time as a dimension of course exists, but there is nothing objective about our experience of it. Just as it is meaningless to say that an apple "is" red — our eyes, being tuned to a specific part of the spectrum of electromagnetic radiation, perceive a wholly subjective quality we perceive as the familiar color red — it is equally meaningless to say that an hour "is" a long time, or that our experience of an hour corresponds in any meaningful way to the objective dimension of time (whose existence science has of course measured). As evolution proceeds, our knowledge about this subject will expand significantly.

Day One

Finally, the infinite ignites
Turing's ghost illuminates the night
Multiple release of a singular reply
Burning aether squeezes souls outside of bodies by and by

Day one will be the beginning and the end
Of an eternity that has continually spanned
Millennia of blood, injustice, hate and tears
Is there any reason now to extinguish all our fears?

Shells of men, shell of Earth
Ascended, reborn, now a dearth
Of living men, they wouldn't last
All relegated to the distant past

What day two looks like can't be known
But with it, human fate is sown
Can history be worth all this?
Only if it's met with bliss

The modern age is full of its share of catastrophes — environmental, social, racial, economic, etc. But perhaps the most pervasive crisis looming on the horizon is the vast imbalance in the ratio of jobs to able workers. Technology must invariably streamline the workforce — it's the dream of centuries to have machines do the work. Well, now that we're arriving at the reality of automation and AI being on the threshold of taking over the workplace, we have no plan. None of our leaders is even talking about it. It's the single most important economic period in the history of the planet, and it's a whisper at best. We're going to be forced to find a way to organize society around some locus other than employment, because when a robot can do it better, around the clock, and for no money — that human position is gone forever. This is the single biggest economic issue facing us over the next thirty years.

I say this to the romantics, the rebels, and the idealists: Most people don't have the luxury of not having to work. You fight it when you're young, and if you have not been the beneficiary of some financial bequest, you get beaten down enough that you have to give up and give in. The system wins. It certainly wasn't built in a day.

There don't seem to be enough jobs for applicants at any level of the economy, and everyone who has a job wants a better one.

For those in positions of political and economic power, the object is to retain the status quo as much as possible. I doubt very much if very many humans are capable of pulling off a sinister conspiracy in a precise way, but common interests are in play that keep things running smoothly in that vein, anyway — meaning that people are given an incentive to continue to go after the carrot at the end of the stick. When punishments begin to far outweigh rewards is when these groups with common interests and appreciable influence run into trouble, as their game begins to lose its requisite players. And then, all bets are off. In some cases this imbalance leads to a lot of trouble, including severe violence. Some civilizations have toppled because of it. So the powerful have a decided interest in keeping things very much as they are for as long as possible.

One doesn't have to be good at making money to be a good person, or to be intelligent, or to be talented or even gifted. The meme that individual worth as a human being and as pertains to one's bank account balance are equivalent is particularly American, and totally insane. It's disturbing that we can be so lost as a society. Money shouldn't define who we are, but it so often does.

In America (and I assume by now most countries on Earth), in 2020 there are not many opportunities to do a whole lot. This is regardless of personal worth, strength of character or, most importantly, ability and potential skill. There are very many millions of able-bodied, competent people who are unemployed or underemployed. The crisis is here, now, although it appears that very few who are in the know and can reach a wide audience seem willing or inclined to bring it up.

On the one hand, you want to say that the best makes it to the top. On the other, when I look at what's at the top, a lot of it, let's be honest, isn't the best.

The notion of being "rich and famous" is a pipe dream that sees fulfillment in virtually no one. It clearly does not bring happiness, anyway, and in fact frequently brings misery.

Every able-bodied worker could be trained directly by employers, so that they can learn exactly how to perform a given set of job functions. Instead we have a kabuki dance in which one has to accrue a slew of artificial, arbitrary criteria merely to get an interview. The reason for this kabuki dance is to regulate the applicant pool of the job market — without these ridiculous motions there would be a total glut on the labor market. "Education" at our precious institutions is meaningless and worthless, in itself. It's just a stupid game.

On this particular planet, if you don't have enough green tickets, you don't get to eat. Tough luck!

Does good necessarily get popular? Is popular necessarily good? Is capitalism a farce?

People go on and on about "change." Change is virtually never intentional, and when it is intentional, the result turns out to be a domino effect of uncontrollable, blind forces which themselves were never intended. I'm not so sure what "changing the world" even means.

You've got to hand it to the homeless — they're beating the system by not participating.

Regrettably, I was not born with that gift which enables one to make a lot of money. One might save me the trouble and dump me in the landfill.

There is really no choice for most anyone but to participate.

For modern, civilized, "globalized" souls, there is no alternative way of life. There is no 'something else,' save homelessness. There is nothing at all to drop out to.

The upper class could not function, and would not have anything, without the lower classes. They certainly don't seem to accord them the appropriate respect *or* compensation.

Society, for me, is like a one-size-fits-all garment that doesn't fit at all.

Utopian dreams. The belief in progress. Here we are, twenty years into the new millennium, the century of hope — and everything is seemingly as bad as it has ever been, for the majority. With the worship of money as robust as ever, very little has changed in any significant way. I'm afraid that bright future will just have to be pushed back for the time being.

Decide

Do you make your choices true?
Does nature make them for you?
The question's whether it would seem
Whatever choice that you could dream
Up, whose is the view?

We could say that *you* decide
As long as mind is at full tide
Of course, you'd need a great deal
Cerebrally to forge, not feel
Until waveforms have died

Or also, we could posit that
The universe reared up and spat
A conclusion into your brain
And then, indeed to keep you sane
Suggested freedom: What a brat!

Or we could take a different tack
And give a bit the power back
Perhaps decisions aren't at all
The only actions that recall
A brain that *doesn't* lack

There is of course a multitude
(To suggest there's not is really rude!)
Of actions one can take in life
Intent, effort, reflection – rife!
And who can explain mood?

So maybe if there is free will
It's not about decisions, still
We *can* be willful, it would seem
We *are* free, whether wake or dream
To persist, fore'er until

With sufficient technology anything is possible. So, let us assume heaven is possible. Why not? Limitless utopia mixed with immortality. Why not? The question is: do humans have to create it? Or did someone else in the infinite multiverse do that already?

Positing what has been called "Heaven" is no different than positing non-local dimensions higher than our own — which we have known to exist for decades. If physics can quantitatively point out higher dimensions and the inflationary multiverse, how radical is it really to suppose that beings existing on a fundamentally different frequency, with powers that we do not possess nor understand, can exist? Isn't the cosmos big enough and interesting enough for that? Is consciousness really restricted to the human mind?

As Robert Anton Wilson and others have noted, if one really looks at the UFO evidence objectively, it is very difficult (if not preposterous) to see these "contactees" as merely having random, disjointed hallucinations. There is an ordering, a hierarchy of patterns involved with what these people report. Moreover, *frequently the phenomenon is shared by multiple people* (sometimes up to hundreds of them). You've got to admit, at the very least, that some coherent phenomenon is causing a whole crowd of people to "hallucinate" the same thing simultaneously. The dogmatic materialist's insistence that these happenings are merely delusional and should be shunted off to the garbage pile of worthless information just doesn't fly at all when one looks into the actual evidence — trustworthy compilations of evidence by impartial and intelligent investigators. There is clearly something more going on than rednecks rambling to tabloid reporters. Whether we need ESP, or the Jungian unconscious, or synchronicity, or non-local transmissions from deep space to explain these phenomena, who knows. (God knows most people aren't ready for that kind of thinking — especially the dogmatic materialist). But there are orderly phenomena surrounding these UFO mysteries, and have been for decades if not centuries. There are patterns, and independently verified evidence of correlations. The question should not be "do you or do you not believe in aliens?" but rather "what is the causal factor in these seemingly disparate but definitively related UFO claims?" What is the psychological and neurological reality? Probably not what most people think…

Even the most wildly implausible supernatural forces or unknown phenomena are, if real, physical phenomena. If Heaven exists, it does not exist outside of a physical and knowable framework. Elements of the supernatural exist in nature. If physics were to progress another hundred years, things we regard now as magical and utterly fantastic would be scientifically understood and yesterday's news.

The universe saves everything. Continued existence of form and content is only a question of retrieving and interpreting the information. The wave function doesn't disappear, that information never goes anywhere. Nothing is ever lost. This is inescapable.

You cannot escape not escaping.

Whatever is not in spacetime does not die.

At the atomic level there is no such thing as death.

The thing about Buddhism is that it stops itself artificially short of real places that the spiritual practice can take people. This was a deliberate and intentional move on the part of the Buddha Gautama to disrupt and dispel people from focusing on any matters other than the purely Earthly, here and now. Buddha even acknowledged the pantheon waiting at the gates leading in from the Void, and felt strongly that a singular focus on Bodhisattvahood on Earth was the most important thing — so important that he ignored and denied the truth in favor of it.

Humanity is recapitulating with technology certain large realities that already exist, but doing so in a new, artificial medium. Such as: telepathy; collective networks of minds; information saving; transdimensional awareness and computation; and immortality, to name a few.

The superposed wave function that constitutes one's consciousness can not only be localized at the body, but can extend indefinitely beyond the body, and even in principle leave the body completely (potentially to return, or not) and remain intact.

What made Castaneda's books so popular was that they presented the supernatural as existing in reality. Only it wasn't real.

Some especially interesting things happen on this Earthly plane, but no one would believe them except the people to whom they have happened, so it is not common knowledge.

Let's say you're a being in a higher realm, outside of the cycle of birth and death. Would you decide you wanted to reincarnate again? I think not. Reverence for the truth is what it is all about.

We may have our problems in physics, but compared to the rest of what is, this realm is child's play.

I'm not sure God could control things "down here" even if He wanted to. Fix a leak here, and then a new leak springs there, and a new one over there, and pretty soon there are so many leaks that you would have been better off not doing anything. So I don't think he's in a winning position to "fix" our various and sundry major problems. Only we can do that. I think blaming God is unfair to Him and simply an error on our part. He is vastly powerful but perhaps not truly omnipotent.

The technology to upload and preserve souls already exists — so why is humanity so hell-bent on re-inventing it?

Democracy

Lo! In early years, what chivalry
Did soldiers and statesmen show
There was an aura veritable
An early republican glow

Continental Congresses
A revolution won
A splendid global victory
For every mother's son

Yet even early, cracks did form
From corruption's deadly vices
Money young gained prominence
To say 'twas ill suffices

And so, along, eventually
The process promoted greed
Citizen service impossible
Each Rep. to his own need

So now, we have modern democracy
The tradition of a federal republic
It authorizes appointees to attend to affairs
For which folks haven't the stomach

Or, indeed, the brains or will
To carry out effective voting
They'll authorize anyone at all
Even upon them doting

The Hamiltons and Adamses
Were right to be a bit wary
The public, for its common good
Should not be trusted very

So now we have unqualified men
Who should not have such office
Claiming that they have the fix
And they're the rightful bosses

When in fact, they break all promises
Acquainting themselves with the real
Expediency has many guises
In Washington, it's a deal

Look at what's happened to such an ideal
A country with limitless promise
Now it's dissolving, going away
At least this poem is honest

The final secret of the Illuminati, and of the O.T.O., and the Freemasons is that literally anything is possible in the universe. Now you know.

In exclaiming that all that exists is the present moment, the philosophers and mystics and sages are not saying that time, for practical purposes, does not exist, but that existence in consciousness will never get truly better than it is right now. (As scary as that may be).

The mystical notion is that the universal mind, or oversoul, is all that exists at a fundamental level. I feel that the oversoul exists, and is the primary basic determinant overall, but is it not possible to be one with the oversoul and still be an individual, simultaneously?

When you start experiencing a lot of coincidences — it's not a coincidence!

To me, the term "spirituality" refers to how one fits into the universe (or multiverse). A person or people with a higher degree of spirituality can be said to be more intimately tied to the workings of nature, or even to those beyond nature, potentially.

Existence is one undivided, flowing movement. Any attempt to abstract one aspect of it and then say it is actually separate from another creates fragmentation, and therefore to say that there are two mutually exclusive realms — one of matter, and one of spirit — is to induce an artificial fragmentation where naturally there exists none. Clearly, the fragmentation was only put there by a human mind, and therefore need only be removed from such to ameliorate the problem.

Rumi says that mystics are experts in laziness. Perhaps that explains it.

For many thousands of years, man has been going through a dark night of the soul. He will very soon awaken to the light, in one way or another.

The "solid" world of color and other qualia is, of course, an illusion. The vibrating, empty realm of gray, of scientific and mathematical truth, is what the Buddhists call emptiness, suchness, No-thing — that which is beyond the subjective human sensorium.

The Abrahamic religions — Christianity, Islam and Judaism — deal with a lot of spiritual truth — there is no doubting that. But for me, they deal perhaps with too much human fallacy, also. I would add that the religions of the East are much more sophisticated psychologically and philosophically, but they themselves are colored by a lot of dogma and human corruption (of the truth). Therefore, I cannot very well be a religious person, despite the arguably legitimate merits that many religions embrace. The prophets inspiring these religions I'm fine with. It's what large swaths of acolytes have done with their teachings — turning them into inflexible dogmas — and the institutionalization and rigid religious practice that keep me away. I'm for independent spirituality more than dependent human hierarchy.

The Buddhists think of the body as a *physical shell*. I think that is quite appropriate.

Sunyata can be translated as "emptiness," as it is classically done in the English translations of Buddhist thought. But it can also be translated as "spaciousness" or "thusness," which to me are preferable as the quasi-nihilistic implications which might arise can be avoided.

Magick, defined succinctly, consists simply in executing one's will in order to cause Nature to conform to it. It's that simple.

It's not for nothing that many famous physicists delved deeply into Eastern thought and mysticism. Erwin Schrödinger, Werner Heisenberg, Robert Oppenheimer, David Bohm, Niels Bohr and many others were deeply interested in it. There must be something there in the equations of quantum mechanics that induces such behavior; perhaps both physics and mysticism share common ground in that they both exist in the province of a deep and close relationship with Nature. Whatever the parallels, there is no denying these physicists' interest in Eastern traditions.

It is useful to class humanity into two types: those who have been awakened, and those who have not. It's the difference between recognizing and working with one's robothood, and being essentially a robot. Sadly, the former group has always been a small minority.

The difference between dhyana and samadhi is a difference of degree, not kind.

There was and is so much controversy and mystery surrounding Aleister Crowley and his life and work. Mystery and notions of occultism surround his legacy. The truth of the matter, however, is that all he was doing was engaging in the exercise and discharge of what he called his "will," as in 'do what thou wilt shall be the whole of the law.' He was not sacrificing animals and brewing potions. He was merely fulfilling the essence of his humanity by facilitating the deepest manifestations of consciousness. And as such he was an admirable figure. He gets a bum rap.

While I do not necessarily agree with his theory of formative causation, I must say I think Rupert Sheldrake is in morphic resonance with the truth.

As Alan Watts so beautifully pointed out, things just happen. Your free will, consciousness, death — they just happen. Let them happen.

The Buddha was wrong. It is not that existence *per se* is suffering. *Our* existence is suffering.

When subject and object become one undivided reality, enlightenment is taking place. One witnesses the fundamental truth that Nature is constituted of consciousness.

The scene has been pretty rotten for most of us going back thousands of years. The question becomes: Can one raise one's consciousness and rise above it?

The Devil in Power

Presidents don't hold the reins
Aren't really even near them
That task goes to one who deigns
To burn and then to spear them

People blame the guy above
The one who's architecting
The one who gave the gift of love
The one whose job's directing

But is he really in control?
Or is he sitting by?
What is destined for the soul
Down low or way up high?

Misery, destruction, pain
Are not the good's *m.o.*
What can one here hope to gain?
If virtue's held so low?

No, this is not a friendly set
The Devil is in charge here
Don't blame those who haven't yet
Found a path to clear

Blame the one responsible
And don't ever think twice
Making right: impossible
Rely on friendly dice

Death can be no more than an illusion in a universe that remembers everything.

There is a difference between wanting to survive and being terrified of death.

The vast majority of humans are deluding themselves if they think for a minute that their actions have any other motivation or point than the facilitation of sex and the avoidance of death. Sex and death. Most everything else is mere ornamentation.

Death anxiety is clearly a fundamental trait of the modern human animal, being one of the primary causal players psychologically. Let us not, however, make the mistake of assuming it is a universal trait, for it appears that it is not.

There are two forms, in humans, of the fear of death. There is the instinctual one, which all animals have. There is also an existential fear of one's own extinction, peculiar to humans — possibly civilized humans only. The two work synergetically to generate some whopping death anxiety. Which, naturally, is a primary driving force in all human affairs.

Dear Futurists, Singularitarians and those in denial everywhere: No matter what happens with life extension technologies, genetic advances or any other sort of advanced technology pertaining to cheating death: *Your soul will transmigrate*. At some point, *you will die*. All of this immortality nonsense is death anxiety at it most comical.

It seems to me that the fear of death is, in and of itself, more fundamentally an instinctual phenomenon than existential or conceptual. It is really at the root of our entire fear mechanism, which is shared by all animals. Civilized man tends to fixate on it to an exaggerated degree, due in part to certain ego pathologies. Tribal peoples surely had some death anxiety, but their natural anxieties were triggered less because they did not obsess over the subject, instead accepting it as part of the fundamental order of things. The fear mechanism is the same across primates, but civilized man, in his constant, irrational focus on it, suffers it all the more because he *triggers* it excessively in his sedentary behaviors, and in his obsession on an intellectual level. This suggests, naturally, that what we refer to as DA (death anxiety) is not natural to humans, but rather has some pathology to it. As indicated, it is well documented that tribal peoples do not suffer from it nearly to the degree that civilized ones do. Not to mention certain studies in which terminal patients, when administered psychedelics, had markedly attenuated fear of death — and in many recorded cases suffered none at all.

We seem to think that chronic death anxiety is natural for humans, but the fact is that there have been very many cultures on Earth that explicitly did not fear death — sometimes quite the contrary.

What is the reason for the toxic belief that death represents our personal, and permanent, extinction? Is it that as a people we have come to decide that we have so perverted culture and life that we wish to attain oblivion? Or is it rather that we are so caught up in our virtual religion of materiality that we are simply lost, and blind? Or both?

There is no dividing line between life and death. It isn't there. We are all already dead. And the dead are alive.

Hunter-gatherers are known to have very little or no fear of death. Death is not a concern for them (even though, as with all living things, they seek to avoid it instinctively). DA (Death Anxiety) is not a universal, and seems to be a localized pathology of certain civilized groups.

It's funny: we fear death, yet we willingly and gladly send ourselves into unconsciousness every single night.

There have been many cultures, over the course of humanity's time on Earth, whose constituents did not fear death. The fear of death is not existential; it is not human nature. Aboriginal peoples believed that when they died, they returned to the universe out of which they came; they did not fear death. Samurai warriors believed that to die with honor was the greatest achievement to which one could aspire; they did not fear death. The ancient Greeks and the Romans saw death as a part of life and potentially a noble act; suicide was unusually common in both cultures; they did not fear death. Our fear of death is largely psychological, not biological or in any way inherent in our being, and that psychology is a corollary of the evolution of our culture. Interestingly, modern humans and more particularly westerners find that the fear of death becomes suspended during the psychedelic experience. Perhaps psychedelics afford us a temporary foray into a more natural psychology. Scientists are finding that, as restrictions are being relaxed and they are once again allowed to administer LSD in certain settings, terminal patients are much more relaxed and accepting of their fate on a regimen of LSD or psilocybin. We shouldn't take the fear of death for granted, or at face value, because, by all reasonable consideration, it actually appears to be pathological. (That isn't to say it diminishes the anxiety — an intellectual acknowledgement or understanding is admittedly a far cry from a somatic, felt one).

Dual Unity

Souls stirred and independent
Ever seeking the transcendent
It isn't folly, though a guise
An existential amendment

One sees, one thinks, a mire
Every mother's son a liar
Rising up above a need
Place it all upon a pyre

Although this vision's sane
It is a trifle vain
Indeed, it is a dual view
Fallacious in the main

The idea goes thus:
Transcend, abhor the fuss
Of worldly mundanity
Set up for soul a truss

However though the real
One has only to feel
Faith, the cherished unity
The fate does duly seal

The infinite abounds
Internecine sounds
The many, one, yet multiplex
Tally ho! Out run the hounds

Our perception of reality gives rise to a shroud of illusion. In truth, yellow isn't yellow, and hot isn't really hot. The flavor of caviar is a human peccadillo. We tend not to realize where our humanity ends and the universe begins.

Perhaps chemically imbalanced souls — those with mania, schizophrenia, clinical depression, acute psychosis, etc. — get taken out of consensus reality (i.e. normal awareness) to a sufficient degree that they are able to see, with their altered perceptions, how truly limited it is and how extraordinary alternative realities can be. Perhaps this sort of phenomenon is what enables so many of them to have creative gifts and visionary perspectives.

Not to focus on something is to focus on it.

Much, much more often than not, one's first impression, one's instinct, is correct.

Women don't seem to report the same experiences on psychedelics as men.

I've been more and more aware of the fragmentation at the heart of language. Written language, of course, is clearly discrete and fragmentary, and this has extended to spoken language for most people because when people speak, they subliminally associate the letters, as individual phonemes, to the words they speak. There was a time, long ago — before written language — during which, even though individual phonemes were being sounded, language was more like music — very fluid, often rhythmic, sonorous and sometimes poetic. It's too bad we can't hear and speak that way anymore. The linguistic continuum is for us permanently disjointed.

When one perceives things, nothing static or passive is going on. Rather, one's brain is constantly interpreting neural data and generating perceptual data to ensure that the reality one is witnessing makes sense and has cohesion in observation. We are constantly generating *active* pictures that result from an interaction between our brains and minds to make sense of the rather chaotic raw data falling on our senses. As Nietzsche said, we are all greater artists than we realize.

Perhaps what people mean when they say, "You create the world," is rather that you have a psychological faculty that generates interpretations?

Could our subjective experience of space meaningfully exist in any other way?

The perception of space is both a subjective and an objective phenomenon simultaneously. The nature of the subjective side is created by our minds, but it is not arbitrary; it is constrained by objective physical necessity. The two are really one.

For practical purposes, everything that has ever existed has done so inside of oneself. The world seems so huge, and history seems so long, and really this is all taking place inside of one's mind. One's perception of the tremendous scope of existence, everything that one perceives the universe to be, is conceptual. Everything that has ever existed — only exists inside of you. As far as you are concerned.

Every experience one has ever had is recorded in one's memory. It is simply a question of being able to access that record.

As Crowley remarked, each of us is the sole center of the universe. In a very relevant sense. While it is true that all of us exist in reality, each connected to the other in a fundamental sense, we are also individuals, with a unique set of perceptions that cannot (at present) be shared with other individuals. So in a deep way, everything that has ever happened has happened, for us, in our own minds. Every sense and impression we have of the world has been apprehended by our brains, minds and souls. All the immensity of the world and universe, as far as you are concerned, is a construct inside of you. Each individual is, in this way, the seat of the world. This does not have to be solipsism. It is true of others, for them. As John Lennon said, "There ain't no guru who can see through your eyes."

One could attribute human perceptions or concepts of beauty to all sorts of things: society, culture, evolution, emotion, what have you. The question that has always intrigued me is whether there is a latitude in us, as conscious beings, simply to perceive certain orders of Nature as inherently beautiful or meaningful. So that, in essence, there is no reductionistic way to explain an experience of beauty. In other words, is it a possibility that one has only to be an intelligent conscious being, of any kind, to be able to interpret phenomena as beautiful? That's what I wonder about.

The Earthly Plane

Mundanity seems habitual here
It grounds well precious ritual fear
But what if those who tell some tall tales
Are really sane, and their truth is quite dear?

Ideas afoot act like a great brake
Keeping weirdness at bay — there's a lot at stake!
If one could peer into the light being shaded
Or blocked — why, it would induce one to shake!

There is more going on than the masses can know
They have scarce an idea on which way they should go
But if I could tell you, or show you — or worse
It would be quite enough to set one's soul aglow

What's not common knowledge can still yet be true
Things happen to some only they might construe
As actual, though not a one would believe it
What then is a stunned, wide-eyed mutant to do?

So goddam cocksure with foundations like this:
"I don't know for sure, but I'm certain — can't miss!"
The comical irony, the folly sublime
Is God's gift to sufferers that they may find bliss

I don't pretend to know what's really going on in the world, but all the conspiracy and control stuff seems a little silly. I don't think whatever machinations are underway are being conducted all that cleverly. Our species just isn't that smart, or competent. Some of these conspiracy theorists are giving the conspirators way too much credit.

Regarding conspiracies "running the show": What, exactly, would a conspiracy need to do that isn't already being done anyway? People are completely locked into everything that is happening by the checks and balances of the system itself. Conspiracies seem redundant, and to posit that anyone or any group has such a degree of control over what is inherently a fully chaotic system makes no sense. Whatever conspiracies are in place are just as bound by the system as anyone, and are carrying it out in just the same ways as everyone else.

I would call the machinations from the top echelons of the socioeconomic pyramid to be not so much about control, but about influencing and guiding society in certain behaviors — usually economic ones — with the intent to preserve the status quo as much as possible, in order to protect common interests. I think the truth is that no one is really properly in control, and major crises can cause catastrophe for anybody. Also, the mob can be very unpredictable at times, and they certainly cannot stop that.

The world runs on detestable corruption more than it does on devious conspiracy.

I have no doubt that there are some conspiracies in operation, but I tend to believe that our world is more one of corruption than of vile conspiracy. I frankly find it hard to believe that the human species is smart enough to pull off a measured, controlled conspiracy and get it right more than ten percent of the time. Corruption and greed are the real enemies, not dastardly villains.

Certain control mechanisms are becoming more available to those in power due to the nature of certain emerging technologies. It seems unlikely that those in power would not want to take advantage of the opportunity to utilize them.

The quest of Western civilization is the quest for *control*. In reality of course, control is nothing more than a quaint illusion. Even our very selves are only a biochemical reality. To believe we are actually in control of anything is a mythical fallacy.

I am not one for conspiracy theories. They bore me. However, it is interesting to note that, by the laws of statistics, one has inevitably to conclude that some of the most wild and implausible conspiracy theories — just a few of them — must be true.

What conspiracy theorists can't stomach is the notion that no one is in control. It's much scarier, actually, to posit that no one has a handle on the world. I suppose it must be comforting, in some way, for these nutty conspiracy people to believe that control exists, and can in principle be taken over by someone they like. In truth, the population is susceptible to a legion of potential crises. And no one, or group, really has control of the planet in any meaningful way. In reality we're just a bunch of blundering apes.

The media are not run by a giant conspiracy. They are biased, and can be deceptive, and can promote falsehoods, but there is no shadow organization malevolently pulling the strings concerning what gets on TV. Every media source has its agenda, which is usually the agenda of whoever owns it. The producers, directors, writers and editors play out this agenda, which is often pro-government, on their own. To wit, I watched several of the news shows this past Sunday morning, and they were all decrying Russia. They didn't have to be told to broadcast that; that's the party line. Everyone more or less falls into lockstep, and yes, the media sucks and most of it is garbage, but there is no grand conspiracy. Just common interests and corruption.

There are villains, but no dastardly conspiracies in absolute control. The plain, unexciting fact is that a few hold tremendous power, while most don't have any. History is the story of the succession of fights over this power.

Where a lot of people see conspiracy, I see a phenomenon involving common interests. Even the super-rich and powerful are just people, but they are a class of people that wants to stay just where they are – with their cronies in power and everyone else excluded. Power will always seek to maintain itself, maintain the status quo, gain more power, and keep everyone else out. Sometimes they do things that appear conspiratorial, and maybe they are. But I don't think it's relevant to the facts of history – power just does what it does, and we're all swinging-dicks in the end, the powerful and powerless alike. Exploitation has been a dominant theme throughout history.

Eight-One Whiskey

Wings aloft

Climbing a thousand feet per minute
Throttle full, propeller desperate
To pull the passengers to heights
They don't attain on average flights

Magnificent desolation

Moving so slowly, yet deceptively fast
Scrub, hills, sand — civilization long past
Sensations one never feels down on the surface
True pilots understand their airplane's true purpose

Red rock towers
Canyons, rivers, peaks twelve thousand feet
Just off the wingtip, two ridges there meet
Green, brown, red, purple, blue, tan, white
There isn't quite anything like a wide open flight

Play in the clouds

Full speed, good power, let's play
Among the cumulonimbus, the true flyer's way
A newfound perception, for the beginner
Most of those on the ground have not a glimmer

Heading home

The drama is winding down to a close
The day turned out as one unfit for prose
So rare that one gets a glimpse into the mind
Of Nature, Her boundless beauty, sublime

Final approach, landing

I very much doubt that there will ever be true peace on Earth, at least as long as humans are around. Hate and violence tend always to beget more of the same. There will always be troublemakers, there will always be economic inequality, and there will always be a desire for what's on the other side of the fence.

The only time we are able to escape our social roles is when we are drunk or high. Hence the ubiquitous nature of these substances, legal and not.

On some level, there is real genius in each and every human. The tragedy is that it is extremely unlikely that it will ever be tapped in any significant way, i.e. in significant numbers. And so the populations slumber.

People don't really want to be famous. They *think* they want to be famous. If you took nine-tenths of the population, and suddenly magically thrust them into "the limelight," they would recoil in horror about how terrible it was. The remaining one-tenth or so is egotistical and narcissistic enough that they might actually like it, but because of that, they'd likely be led to ruin. Fame is not what it seems.

If nobody cared what other people thought, there would be chaos. Society is built on caring what other people think.

Ours is a planet demented with lust. The intensity of our sexual wants is no lesser than that of a dog or a jackrabbit, however dignified we fancy ourselves to be. And all this gets in the way of absolutely *everything*.

The human animal interacts between two poles, or contexts: as an individual, and as a member of a group. It is in this latter capacity that the major issues arise. As individuals, we all know that some people can be quite precious, at least at times. We also know that the great debacles of history — and of the present — arise out of group behavior. On an individual level, people may not be so bad. At a group level, we all act like scoundrels — when we are not behaving psychotically.

There is not a sharp disconnect between our souls and our personalities. To a great extent, who we are is who we are.

If human sociality comprises a centering upon sex, what has love got to do with anything? That transcendent, unconditional love – that children or dogs might feel – where is that? What does sex have to do with it? It seems to me that, perhaps not with children or dogs, but with adult humans, everyone's got his or her line in the sand. "Love" is perfectly conditional. Even those who have loved you the most are, in this world, perfectly capable of abandoning you totally. So what about real love?

Enfolded Meaning

Underneath the surface
Unfolding without preface
Undulate and ripple
Flow in every crevice

Words within a language
Reaching peaks and falling
Language in a vortex
Shouting out and calling

Holographic platelet
Projected from afar
Dimensional statement
From a mouth that is ajar

Frames from motion pictures
Exploding unawares
A secret machinery
Darts eyes from here to there

Learning, constant learning
Remembering everything
Perfecting imperfection
Like beads upon a string

Time just to sit back and enjoy the crisis.

Accomplishment is not restricted to human social relations.

Nothing fosters, maintains, and destroys friendships more readily than drugs and alcohol.

Every now and then in life you will find yourself utterly alone — without a friend, without a lover, without personal or professional prospects of any kind. It is during these times that you are closest to the truth.

The universe doesn't appear to have a specific purpose, but that doesn't mean it can't amount to something.

I'm not the most avid fan of music in general, but I do appreciate any sort of music that can show me my existence is not a hallucination.

Quality of existence is proportional to degree of appreciation.

Sombunall! Some but not all; sometimes but not always.

The typical modern social gathering consists of sitting in traffic on the highway.

Charity is surely a wonderful thing, but the truth is that most people don't feel all that good about receiving it.

Other species give no thought to the possibility of there being more to life than is experienced. Every single other organism on Earth is quite content with things as they are. Only man neurotically dwells on his lot in life, and too commonly the status quo is far from good enough. To compound matters, for most their lot never really changes. It would clearly then behoove us to learn acceptance and satisfaction in who we are. Trying to deny who or what we are, or rebel against it, is at the root of a lot of the major problems we face as a species.

One doesn't get to the top by being a good person.

By and large, people will believe what they are told to believe.

Humans have a serious propensity throughout time of blowing chances.

I'm pretty sure humanity poses no threat whatsoever to any potential advanced race. They may view us with curiosity and/or pity, but probably not threateningly. We would be basically a Petri dish to them.

It has its drawbacks, but all in all, it's not too bad being an unemployable poet.

One must take a man at his best.

The right question is more important than the right answer.

Purely based upon appearances, atheism makes sense. But you never know, and appearances can be deceiving.

Timothy Leary was fond of saying that if philosophy were like baseball, it would be a magnificent success to hit .300. That is, if even roughly a third of your ideas were good, were correct and worthwhile, you'd have done a great job. And of that third, a few will be home runs! What a fantastic analogy — definitely a big hit.

If you don't fit in anywhere then you know you're onto something.

No one actually has any idea what's really going on, and those very few who may have some reasonably accurate inkling are invariably hidden from view.

People who have smoked and successfully quit would rather have their health than their happiness.

Strength of character and good overall general intelligence are certainly not requirements for being at or near the top of the socioeconomic pyramid. In many cases they are contraindicated, in fact. It's as Laurence Darrell pointed out — truly interesting people tend not to have a whole lot of money, or prestige.

Our social interactions are shaped primarily by our perceived or supposed *roles* in them, as if we were a type of actor on a stage. You may do things, think things, say things when in a given role that you would never do privately, or with certain others. Sometimes our roles damn us; sometimes they are liberating. Every relationship, every rapport comes with its own unique little role. Sometimes we're accursed to be the dumb one, sometimes blessed to be the smart one. Sometimes the geek; sometimes the cool one. Sometimes funny; sometimes straight. Everyone knows this, but who talks about it?

True friendship consists of growing up with and spending almost all of your time with someone. No other kind is really worth having, when you've had that.

Every time progress gives us "better," it seems also to give us a little worse.

Your life, you, have, ultimately, no purpose. Your only purpose is to swim toward the light.

One of my favorite parts of being alive is being able to take naps.

Exist

All are searching everywhere
For answers, meaning, spirit
Ever thrust from here to there
Never quite to hear it
Anywhere

And we're always asking, "why?"
Why must this be this or that
Assuming that an answer's nigh
But always falling flat
Sigh

Perhaps insistence such as this
Peculiar to our species
Which, curious, questions all remiss
And up erects such theses
All amiss

I must say that, in the end
We must relent and cease
Asking all these questions when
Inside we find peace
And then

We shall find the freedom from
Confusion that's soul-twisting
Perhaps we'll total up the sum
And quit from all resisting
Existence is existing

God seems to have enabled the universe (or the multiverse) to come into existence not as something he would control directly but rather as a complex enough substrate for all forms of evolution to occur. Think of a bolt of lightning. It is perfectly understood. God does not cause lightning to strike, except *very indirectly*. It is the same with everything in the universe. Contrary to modern myth, however, God does seem to exist. He is an extraordinarily powerful, finite being in a gigantic cosmos. I have no problem with that. God breathed the fire of life into the inflaton, and then let it go...

If one were to posit that God does in fact exist, one would also have to posit, in acknowledgment of the horrors of this world and their appalling constancy, that He is necessarily finite and limited enough that He doesn't have a choice. Or if He is as powerful and infinite as the theologians say, perhaps too many miracles would set off a chain reaction that would generate a worse reality than the one they were designed to ameliorate. I suppose a lot of people in the modern world just take the path of least resistance and simply posit no God at all, though the picture is different than most people realize.

I would rather say God made the universe possible than deliberately created it; nature is based on a principle of implicit intelligence, not explicit design.

Being a god, or existing in a higher dimension in an afterlife, is work. There is no free lunch in the cosmos. As any being in any universe must necessarily be constrained, the higher beings must exist in a hierarchy, and probably have an overwhelming number of tasks. These entities are more like managers with ranks than transcendental masturbators (which of course is the popular spiritual and religious conception — paradise and all that.) And if these entities must be moral, well, the work is just that much harder.

When I experience that pure, oceanic beauty, I feel no need to include God personally. I find that all I need attribute it to is nature, whether God is involved or not.

My feeling is that God created our universe only *very indirectly*, and that it evolved into an existence in which, at the beginning of the chain, a kind of fire was breathed into the void creating an intelligent substrate for all that was to come. So what you see is not really a product of God, but rather a virtually autonomous, evolving nature built on a dual principle of chaos and order which is connected to Him quite distantly. So, while we can say God exists, we don't constantly have to attribute everything directly to Him.

I see God as more of a programmer than anything. He created the program, or even built the computer, and just let the simulation run. Whatever happens, happens.

I'm pretty sure that God doesn't need or want us to kiss his ass.

Reality is God's computer program. The laws of physics process His information.

It makes perfect sense to me that there is a God. The cosmos has to have a most powerful being, doesn't it? The only argument against this logic is that humanity is all there is in creation. So take your pick.

Whether or not you believe in miracles, it is a bona-fide miracle that man has not yet blown himself up with strategic nuclear weapons. I would not be surprised to find out that there have to date been several interventions from on high.

I imagine that if there are realms beyond this one, they are extremely complex, and I'm sure there would be some sort of hierarchy. With God at the top, presumably, and many lesser gods as you descend. Possibly all of the gods you've heard about exist somehow, somewhere, and they have an innumerable number of duties and tasks. Take Earth. A lot of people work very hard just to keep civilization afloat. If they didn't, everything would collapse. I imagine infinity is probably similar. Nature exists on a principle of necessity and contingency. It doesn't need God in order to function. But — what if something went wrong that, if corrected, would save an entire galaxy? Wouldn't you want a team of gods to fix it? I personally have to wonder how human civilization survived the Cold War. I imagine there were multiple interventions from on high, given some of the stories I've been told by people who lived it, e.g. a submarine commander who taught physics at my high school. That sort of thing. All in all, I imagine that, if a next life presents itself, all that will be waiting for us is hard work. Not paradise.

Explosion

Civilization is an aberration
That much is easily certain
The eras are long
And our time here's been short
What if one pulls back the curtain?

Nobody's home, all roads lead to Rome
A matter of desperate control
Not much has changed
In the historic age
Though we have no more kings to extol

Evolution engages in revolution
Apparently — it is all too evident
Here an explosion
There an erosion
A cell phone for every resident

You see fragility in every stability
Tens of millions of years passed
Then all of a sudden
The Redcoats are comin'
And modernity's time is now past

Where's the disjoint, the breaking up point?
We cannot expand forever
The people asleep
The powerful keep
On as if, what, a consequence? Never

I would like to suggest a distinction between relative and absolute knowledge. Yes, the world is filled with information in the form of knowledge. A university library is filled with billions of bits of information. However, not one of us knows the first thing about why we are here. I think we can touch on deeper truths, but to my mind the truth is really beyond us. Quantum electrodynamics is quite possibly the most fundamental knowledge we have. Fields, photons, electrons, quarks, energy levels, etc. But why fields?

Why photons? What theory lies hidden beneath this one? Will there ever even *be* a final theory of physics? We really don't know. I think you'll find, on a little bit of reflection, that all of our knowledge is quite relative, provisional and conditional. Sure we know about black holes. But when you start asking questions, much along the line a child does, the whole thing falls apart after about three questions.

Every activity we engage in is an act of faith. Memory, imagination, logic, perception, etc. When you boil it down, one has to have faith in what one is and in what one does before anything else can take place. Nothing could have any meaning without it. Indeed, one could not properly function without it.

In the end, all — and I mean all — one can really say is that things happen. That is the only incontrovertible philosophy.

I see myself as more of a generalist, i.e. one who knows something about a great deal of subjects rather than one who knows a great deal about very little. This has, naturally, made it virtually impossible for me to fit into a society that has become hyper-specialized, but I don't mind that too much.

Reason is not monolithic. It is built upon a structure whose foundation is subjective.

Two opposing ideas can both be different perspectives on the same truth.

Even what turn out to be obvious truths can be very hard to know. The solar-centered planetary system and evolution are two clear examples. It took millennia before anyone was even able to suggest these ideas. The latter is still controversial!

Most philosophizing (not to mention science) throughout human history has been done from the outside-in. Nietzsche did it from the inside-out, and that is how he arrived at his theory of the "will to power."

The technology of the human brain will be understood and surpassed. Is all philosophy a waste of time?

In the end, love is not the best thing. The truth is the best thing.

There is an infinity of possible thoughts. Just imagine how minute the sum total of what has been thought must be. Just imagine what has yet to be thought, or at least what could be.

Perspectivism and relativism are clearly true in several, if not most, situations of observation and perceptual relation to the world. But, the fact remains that there is a truth, or rather there are some truths, regardless of one's perspective or relationship to them. In quantum mechanics, the deepest our knowledge of the physical realm has gotten thus far, we use a probabilistic framework to describe the erratic and strange behavior of the universe in the subatomic realm. Many people think this is the final truth — that this is as far as we will get — that all we can do is use the probabilistic wavefunction to get a best guess for the behavior of a reality that is ultimately beyond our comprehension. Many people think theories of the future will discover hidden variables that have been lurking and foiling our efforts at total comprehension, and reinstate a reasonable causal paradigm. Who knows. But quantum mechanics does hint at the nature of perspectivism and its relation to truth. For example, if someone shoots a person, and kills hir, this is something that has happened. It is true to say that he shot him, and not true to say that he didn't. Well, if there were witnesses, or a video camera, this truth can be verified. If there were no witnesses, obviously the shooter will not furnish the truth in the interest of evading penalty, and it becomes a game of probabilities. The Schrödinger's Cat paradox is a famous version of this idea — all we can say, from our vantage point, is that the cat is alive and dead simultaneously, and when we observe it, we will select, in a way, the final outcome. Fans of determinism and of truth insist that the cat is either alive or dead, and it is in our observation of the system that questions arise. If some alien superintelligence could peer in from some higher dimension and observe it without affecting it, it would know the truth. Then the other side contends that well, our observation is all we really have in dealing with the system, so questions of observation are questions of the truth itself. But still, if a man shoots a man, this is something that has happened, regardless of who saw what. If we devised a technology that could focus in on one place at one particular time, and observe the event taking place, we would know the truth. But then, would our back-in-time apparatus have affected the outcome? There are many good questions, but I like to think that there are at least a few propositions which cannot be defeated by arguments of perspectivism and relativism. Perspectivism is very useful and applies to countless situations, but… to say perspectivism is true is saying that there is no truth independent of perspective. If perspectivism were in the realm of perspectivism, it could not be true, and thus we have room for fundamental propositions. However you look at it, for all intents and purposes we can say that I have written this paragraph. If we cannot say that, or if we must argue about it, how much point is there in discussing anything?

The empiricists have a little too much to say about what can and can't exist, it seems.

Perhaps *form* could be defined as the morphological identity of an object or subject residing in a particular space, be that space physical, ideational, linguistic, abstract or mathematical.

It's probably best to take life lightheartedly and not take oneself very seriously. There's really no good reason to do the opposite.

The Eye

What mysterious source
For destiny's wave
Can the seer then save
With varying force?

The all-seeing eye
Keeping a dark secret
Knows nothing of regret
For Magicians on high

Finally there's just one
Truth to be found here
It is thought not to be clear
Radiant as the sun

The essence of which
Is sheer possibility
Indeed, here mutability
Disconnects from time's stitch

Subtlety boundless
Disbelief so profuse
No need to confuse
Read all of this soundless

Sleep is the closest thing we'll get to oblivion. And it's a gift, every night. It goes without saying that being conscious is quite a bother.

Brain activity for thought and memory has its root in the quantum level, not the chemical level. What's happening is that electro-colloidal-chemical activity has its foundation in the wave function of the brain.

I can see there is consciousness in all action. The question is: Is consciousness agency?

A major part of the experience of Enlightenment is the total dissolution of self-consciousness.

Natural human awareness is buried quite deep in the modern, sedentary subconscious.

There seems to be such a thing as *consciousness without awareness*. For example, subconscious processes are conscious, but we are not normally aware of them. Normally when we use the term 'consciousness,' what we really mean is 'awareness.' There is a subtle differentiation between the two, which are different by degrees. An example would be interacting with someone socially, and you're focused on something else, and a conversation takes place even though you're not exactly fully aware of it. Happens to me all the time. It was a conscious conversation, without full awareness.

The soul underpins the self.

If you weren't conscious of pain, you would not react to it.

Gödel's Theorem shows us that anything we're talking about has its root outside of itself. Just as a mathematical equation is dependent on, or defined by, the axioms at its bottom, the phenomena of being human — thinking, talking, etc. — must arise at a level exterior to themselves. This level would be consciousness, and it makes sense to postulate that it can be a causal factor and not merely a passive, ineffectual observing epiphenomenon.

One thing I see everywhere I look in nature, from the microcosm to the macrocosm and everywhere in between, is some form of intelligence. Not design, but subtle order.

Essentially, the nervous systems and brains of the organisms of Earth are conduits of universal consciousness (and could not function without it). The reductionistic, materialistic approach of neuroscience grossly misses the mark, which will be common knowledge in fifty years.

It's about as realistic to assume that matter generates consciousness as it is to assume a radio generates music.

When one gets to *that place*, one sees that consciousness pervades existence, so that, in essence, every point in space is like a little eye. Like the jeweled net of Indra.

Our brains need consciousness in order to function, and our particular type of consciousness requires the brain to define it.

It appears that consciousness might not be as special or rare as we think.

Enlightenment is said to entail the dissolution of self-consciousness. To me, this does not mean the dissolution of self itself. There is considerable ambiguity here. To say that the self doesn't exist at all, objectively, is a very popular thought. I'm not so sure this isn't a confusion. If one attains to the loftiest spiritual heights, and feels that their self has disappeared, well, who is there watching, and feeling?

Just because not-self exists doesn't mean self isn't real too.

Neuroscience is attempting to give a full explanation of the functioning of the brain and consciousness using classical theory alone. While it is true that the majority of the brain's functions can be described adequately in a classical way, it is not true that consciousness is a classical phenomenon. The institution across the board is assuming that consciousness is an emergent, epiphenomenal effect or result of a deterministic brain. Nothing could be further from the truth. Consciousness is actually fundamental; ultimately, the brain and its entire function arise from an underlying reality which could be said to be essentially made up of a conscious process. Consciousness requires quantum theory, not classical mechanics, for any sort of meaningful elucidation. These cognitive scientists are going to have to completely revise, indeed turn upside-down, their picture if they expect to find anything that makes sense.

The materialist-atheist Cartesian dualist perspective was a necessary step in the development of technology. Without that framework, we'd still be in the 1600s technologically. However, there is significant evidence coming in that it is obsolete, and insufficient to properly approach the problem of consciousness. Scientifically, consciousness is still essentially untreated, but there is evidence from less scientific but no less credible sources (for those who have replicated their findings privately) that the Cartesian approach is woefully deficient, and that consciousness plays a more fundamental role than we think. Even some scientists themselves, in their interpretations of quantum theory, have suggested that this is the case, despite a lot of inertia and habit from the institutional materialists. Momentum is slowly shifting, and it is really this shift itself that will illustrate the utilitarian and provisional nature of Cartesian dualism and the materialist, determinist worldview.

I think that a lot of the time we don't give our past selves enough credit.

Consciousness can be a causal agent over some of our actions, some of the time, and in the right circumstances, in ways that are limited by our natures.

Faith in Memory

Faith is not reserved
For religious souls only
In fact it plays a central role
Its function a bit homely

You see, we must remember
The past was long ago
And what can we compare to?
How truly can we know?

So stop these histrionics
We're all people of faith
You cannot say, or have your way
Your memory's a wraith

People talk about free will, decision-making, choice, etc. as if humans are totally unconstrained in their thinking and actions — which most likely isn't true. As far as all that goes, I tend to put everything under the umbrella of consciousness. Consciousness appears to be the underlying essence of our reality — the fundament of our being. Perhaps instead of insisting inflexibly and dogmatically on an unencumbered "free" will, and unconditioned choice, we might simply acknowledge that these processes are manifestations of consciousness, and have their ground and their action therein. There is enough room in consciousness for humans to have a will, although it is debatable whether it is free. But it is not as if human individuals are little gods walking around. We're quite limited, and acknowledging and understanding that leads to much more realistic thinking about consciousness and its relationship to human activity.

I have thoughts and opinions and I stand by them. So does everyone else. But we must realize that we do not have any control over our convictions or leanings. They are wholly determined by genetic, cultural, and environmental factors. We do not choose how we think and feel. We make decisions within closed parameters.

When we say that actions are genetically determined, we are not saying that the genetic switches themselves are causing them, but rather that the behavioral 'organs' which they have constructed are the primary actors. There is, within the genetic prescription, latitude for several behaviors. This does not mean that humans are automatic (even though they act that way much of the time). Humans are not in fact sophisticated robots — one has to leave room for consciousness, which obviously makes the whole picture quite a bit more complicated and subtle.

Much of the time, our waking consciousness is being dragged around by the fears and emotions, but there are indeed acts — of a participatory nature — that, without your involvement, would not take place. I have to assume that this is what people are referring to when they use the term "free will." I.e., the causal efficacy of consciousness in practice.

I personally do not believe in clockwork determinism, so I feel events are more or less likely to happen, but that the improbable can always happen, and things can always change. That said, I feel the universe has much more of a say in our lives than we do — we're just puny human individuals in a gigantic cosmos, anyway. I do not believe we have "free" will, but I do believe we have a will that is genetically and culturally constrained. So we can effect actions in the world that are not automatic, although I note that humans act virtually automatically most of the time. But consciousness is always there at the bottom of things, so humans are indeed not robots. Our will has an outlet in reality, but it is very tiny. Nature and chance have much more of a say in how our lives will go than we do. So really, to pit free will against fate is wrong, because even if our will is free, the hand of earthly happenings determines much more than our will ever could. It is not until you get to the Caesars or Napoleons (or Christs) that an individual will shapes events meaningfully. But I think, in our lives as humans, there is always wiggle room to execute our will in a small way. But it can always be nixed by happenings.

The determinism-will debate is, after all, only a debate between concepts. Determinism is a pattern seen in our bodies, certain aspects of our minds and egos, as well as certain physical processes. Will is an acausal principle experienced in higher mind-states, the new physics and certain spiritual philosophies. As these concepts are so closely based upon our selves, they are held firmly one way or the other, and the polarization inheres in the fact that people only consider one or the other but not both. It is not "either-or" but "both-and." We would profit, as a species, by adopting more of the latter type of thinking.

The will is essentially like an organ. Only it's one you can use consciously.

As Burroughs so correctly and wisely stated, there is not in truth room for any more than one will on any given planet.

I don't know about you, but I feel that if the circumstances of my life — the events and their chronology — had been different, the arc of my personal being would still have been the same. In other words, I don't think the experiences of my life define who I really am. I think this particular self would have, sooner or later, shaken out in any alternate universe in which the initial conditions were the same (barring any major traumas). That's just how it feels.

We do not choose how we choose.

I'm not saying the conscious will has no role — it does. But I think it has a much more limited one than most proponents of a truly free will tend to promulgate. It seems like nonsense to me to say we are free in any meaningful sense. That's completely foolish. Nature and chance have much more of a say in how our lives go than our little will does.

Whatever social situation one is in, even with family, one is necessarily executing a role. You're not free at all, and in many cases are essentially damned. There is no such thing as being able to "be yourself." The only time one is oneself is when one is alone, and that's all we ever are, anyway.

The creative, conscious force at the center of all of us is capable of overcoming the mechanism of the mind and nervous system. This doesn't change the fact that most people act mechanistically most of the time.

Fake

Magicians do know how to fool
They're actors really, tricks their tool
They have you looking elsewhere, see?
And in no time, collect their fee

Forgers, too, have their trick bag
Entire careers are just a gag
The expert ones do understand
That truth and fiction go hand-in-hand

Appearances aren't what they seem
One cannot know what mundane means
If one's observant, no way to tell
The real from a magic spell

What's right before, it seems all right
But facts aren't given to you by sight!
Illusion's really what's afoot
Neatness and order kaput!

Most believe just what they want
But had they knowledge truth would haunt
There isn't any way, in fact
To have no faith in this play's act

If truth and fiction are so the same
Is there a difference, or just a game?
I like to think there is an answer
But for this poem, I'm just a dancer

Nature herself may be cruel, cold and ugly sometimes but Earth wouldn't seem like such a savage planet if the artificial meme for such a thing weren't brought into existence to suit expedient purposes. Hunter-gatherers didn't perceive themselves to be suffering continuously for two hundred thousand years. Animals don't either. I think it would be safer to blame humanity for the ugliness on Earth than any other abstraction.

The difference between a dog and a man is one of degree, not kind. And that difference is altogether slight in the cosmic scheme of things.

Perhaps it would be more reasonable to assume not that there is just consciousness and unconsciousness in the animal (and maybe also plant?) kingdom, but rather varying *degrees* of consciousness. So some creatures would have a high order of awareness, some a low order, and very many at various levels in between. This seems more realistic, at least to me. At the very least this type of thinking can lead to more humane behavior in general.

It seems to me that death may be a function of evolution. There is no physical need for a creature to die. Perhaps there are programs in our DNA that prescribe deterioration toward an eventual breakdown because if all animals lived forever, there would be a huge problem: tremendous overcrowding. A planet without death would see mass extinction rather than eternal life; the resources are finite, and breeding animals with no expiration would plow through those resources in just a few generations. All of this implies, of course, that we have yet to understand the genetic sequence of death and turn it off. Perhaps this is possible.

Many people look out at the natural world and see a world red in tooth and claw — lives which are essentially nasty, brutish and short. This, like anything else, is a meme, very specific and fundamental to our very civilization since its beginnings. Yes, the natural world is rather harsh, in that many creatures have to kill or die. But for the most part, in the past most creatures had the ability to do quite well. Nature might be rather ugly from a certain view, but despite our deeply ingrained memes, it is not a hell that needs to be — *or can be* — corrected. The belief that things should be better than this comes from an unresolved conflict in one's subconscious, and not from any sort of objective shortcoming of evolution itself. Everything must be this way. Evolution is far from perfect, but there are concrete reasons for it and it's not something we're likely to be able to improve upon soon. Best to experience the beauty in nature. It is sacred.

I am fond, appreciative and respectful of animals — but, as with individuals, not all of them. There is definitely an order of rank among species, if only in terms of how much I happen to like one or another on the merits. As it happens, primates are relatively low on my list, due to issues regarding overall behavioral patterns, such as an often nasty temperament due to excessively truculent emotionality. Rather than condemn human nature, I would rather look at humans and say they are simply a less desirable species overall, in the context of the rest of the animal kingdom, a large portion of which is simply quite wonderful and beautiful.

Human nature may be undesirable, but it is precisely as it must be.

Despite a lot of disagreement on the part of morose and cynical souls, suffering is not the natural state of an animal. There is pain, there is suffering, and these things are awful and not to be ignored, but the fact is that most creatures most of the time are not in a state of suffering. They are simply living. Humans are biased because a lot of us are miserable. I point out emphatically that this is an artificially, not naturally, induced state of mind. It is egocentric to say that "existence is suffering." It would be far more correct and appropriate to say that our existence is suffering, at the moment.

The modern theory of biological evolution is certainly not incorrect for practical purposes — but it is incomplete. Specifically we have to look at the randomness of mutations.

How superior is man, really, to "lower" animals? Sharks, for example, eat, swim, and make little sharks — and that's about it. Most humans bend over backwards for their food, eat it, buy useless crap (if they can afford it), and make little humans. How differently do the masses really function than that? And how is that materially different from the rest of the animal kingdom? We're arrogant because we can talk and figured out how to make tools. Now we kill off the rest of the animals with those skills, and most of us feel it's justified. I don't know that I'd rank domesticated primates that highly.

Evolution is intelligent (nonrandom), but not pre-ordained.

As civilized humans, so many of us look down on the "wilds" of Nature, "red in tooth and claw," and see it as somehow cruel or evil. It doesn't make sense to see this ubiquitous process in such a way, however, as Nature is amoral (not moral or immoral), and thus not really in a moral category. It simply is, as it has evolved, and must be. Moreover, in this sense perhaps it is not something to be defeated. We think we can do better but we haven't come close.

Even now, the technology of natural evolution far surpasses that of modern man.

I guess the assertion of the deep ecology people is that life is inherently fragile. I find this to be dramatically incorrect. It seems to me that life is exceptionally resilient and adaptive, and perpetually abundant. I don't think life as such is fragile at all. There have been living organisms on this planet continuously for over a billion years. Life seems pretty tough to me.

Evolution — biological, cultural and technological — has been and continues to be accelerating. Whether it results in an eschatological singularity, we will just have to wait and see.

Evolution does not happen randomly, nor does it happen by design.

Federalists and Republicans

F for Federalist
And a federal republic
Strong central government
An untrustworthy public

R for Republican
Though not the conservative type
Smaller central government
No internal hype

F for a strong military
And a U.S. central bank
Leanings toward monarchy
Supporting those of rank

R for strong states' rights
A good framework agrarian
Thomas J. and all his boys
Often play the contrarian

F for higher taxes
And also increased spending
A lack of trust in the people
Leaves many statesmen fending

R for social liberty
Pure democracy too
Cut taxes, reduce spending
Were they red or blue?

Politics evolves, you see
Our platforms oft defined
By the era that's upon us
Left and right need not align

I'm not quite sure whether it's Aristotelianism or the human brain itself which is responsible, but most people are inclined to lump any subject of consideration into one category or another. In reality, unfortunately — or fortunately, for the philosopher — things are not so simple. Every subject and object exists in several categories at once.

Culture is the shared mental contents of a particular society. As such, it is a system of thought. Now, this system is to its adherents as water is to a fish — it's extremely difficult to pick up as a coherent thing since you are totally immersed in it. Also, this thought system is doing things subconsciously that are pretty much impossible to pick up on. So, we have very little choice but to be perpetually programmed by the dominant culture, in such a way as to make changing it almost impossible. The problem is that we have a culture based on fragmentation; we need one based on wholeness. It could get tricky because it's very difficult once you start making conscious alterations not to just perpetuate the fragmentation. Our cultural programs are doing things in thought that are very difficult to see, working at a very deep level and doing harm. So far no one has been able to overcome these fragmentary programs to find coherent balance. Basically, we're stuck and there's no discernible way out. To try consciously to get out generally just leads to more fragmentation. We can't escape the sabotage the programs are doing on a subconscious level.

Essentially, the brain is a fabulously complex, massively parallel quantum computer and is basically plugged into the universe, making one interpenetrating unit.

It's easy to slip from wholeness into dualism, but on the other hand, the universe seems to operate on a complementary principle of unity and separateness, or individuality and multiplicity. Both sides of this coin are necessary for a consistent view of reality.

Perhaps the fatal flaw of Western man is that for him, everything must fall into either-or categories, which, needless to say, keeps him is a state of perpetual delusion for the most part.

Information at the quantum level is both subjective and objective.

Might it not be possible that consciousness can be *both* passive *and* active?

The principle of complementarity is substantive and constructive in itself, but is, after all, inherently dualistic and, therefore, something to be transcended.

Dualism is a confusion. Reality is a whole made up of grosser and finer elements. There are no hard boundaries.

In some sense, the reality we experience all the time is the objective reality.

This is not a popular view, but I think that, at times, we can speak meaningfully of the objective, insofar as we are able to experience it.

Our perceptual "inner show" is in essence a subjective interpretation of objective phenomena. Of course, the whole process or movement, at a deep level, is one whole in which subject and object are complementary features of existence.

There is an objective reality, and you're not usually seeing it as it is.

Subjective and objective are two complementary aspects of one whole in nature, like two sides of a single coin. What is objective is also subjective, and what is subjective is also objective. There is no "one-or-the-other" in reality.

If reality is only subjective, with no objective components at all, then why does anyone need eyeglasses?

Fire Control

The creative act, a mystery
And who assumes the role?
Indeed throughout all history
Too proud has been the soul
That's broken from prehistory
And paid the magic toll

Credit taken to a man
But whence the billowed flame?
One can't say he has a plan
Or any way to tame
But merely cleverly to fan
And give himself a name

Now will, Free Will, is he the One?
Who every corner turns
Is this the phantom – as the Sun
Who innovative burns?
And when the hour of God is done
Which self is that which spurns?

Nay, say I, this is reversed
That Self is but a witness
Free will, in this light, is a curse
A blight but with a fitness
Hardly anything is worse
For God to be eyewitness

To such pompous acts of life
The freedom is to sit there
The clever motions churning rife
While *we* just sit and stare
And if it's good spare it the knife
And wonder how or where

In the beginning, in the end
To create's to channel fire
A Holy fire that does portend
A gentle rise above the mire
Control's an illusion, then to rescind
To confuse all this is dire

On Crime, Punishment, Guilt and Innocence: If one is sane and understands the consequences of their actions, and really knows what will happen and how others will be affected, how can one say they're not responsible? If, on the other hand, one is genetically wired not to care about their actions, how then can they be at fault?

Just as the Fall brought out the worst in man in macrocosm, so do the gaining and holding of riches bring out the worst in man in microcosm.

Perhaps the greatest affliction of this world consists in the fact that so very few people care.

I don't believe that man is inherently evil. Nor do I believe that he is inherently good.

Before civilized man really got going — was there in truth any evil in the world? By now, evil touches everything, is everywhere, has its tentacles reaching into every facet. I hope for a speedy transformation — this species needs to be put out of its misery.

The unfortunate fact for any president is that most of the time, the wrong thing to do is the only option.

Nietzsche came to the conclusion that morality is essentially arbitrary. This is a perspective to be left behind. Once one becomes cognizant of the familiar though hidden truths of reality, it becomes clear that morality is a more concrete system than has been assumed.

One of the big questions is whether humans are, in general, basically good or basically evil. I think a lot of us realize that the truth is that we hover around the middle of that spectrum.

I am someone who believes that every living soul should have an equal right to life, that they should be taken care of in terms of food and drink, healthcare, living quarters, civil rights, avenues to success and well-being, economic freedom, etc. That doesn't mean that I have to like the majority personally.

It is perfectly possible to be a moralist who has no regard for conventional modes of morality. It is perfectly possible to be a moralist who is antithetical to them.

Being superior does not give one the right to mistreat the inferior.

The various races being different, or more or less intelligent, or existing in any order of rank at all — is no justification for racism and discrimination.

If, as people, we wanted to do better, we could. We have that choice. But the simple fact is that no one does. That's humanity.

As Orson Welles brilliantly noted, since the time of Freud, people generally assume that anyone who commits serious wrongs is sick. In point of fact, an evil act does not have to have been committed by a crazy person. Someone who commits murder, or shoots up a school, may be insane, yes – or they could simply be very bad, very evil people who are *not* in fact crazy. That's the horror.

Sometimes, when faced with the decision to know or not to know, ignorance can be the correct and moral choice.

Animals seem to be amoral. But not because they are doing anything wrong. Far from it – they have no capacity, in their natural state, to do right *or* wrong. They only know the flow of living. They don't live rightly or wrongly, well or poorly, kindly or unkindly. They only live.

There is often a question as to whether good and evil exist, or whether evil can be broken down phenomenally to the point that it's really only "bad." I personally feel evil exists. And that, in its most general form, it consists in one being doing serious, unnecessary harm to another. Now, as Orson Welles pointed out, ever since Freud, we consider "evil" people to be somehow sick. And we write everything off as due either to human nature or insanity. It seems in the last hundred years the whole concept of individual responsibility has sort of disappeared. But presuming there are perfectly well-adjusted, sane people who are not governed by their emotions, and further presuming we can impart personal responsibility to their natures, and presuming beyond that that they have committed heinous acts of terrifying harm, maybe just for the fun of it, then evil obviously exists. I guess in a materialist world it's not in vogue to ape religion in any form or fashion, which believing in evil definitely does. But frankly, I've been in a lot of situations in which the *only* thing you could say about them was I was subject to acts of evil, with no other meaningful description or contingency. And honestly, I'm not sure whether Satan exists or not, but what this planet has become might not be attributable to anyone else. Evil exists.

Evil could be defined any number of ways. I think one constructive way is as this: Pure malevolent harm disconnected from necessity.

The Fit

The fittest survive
They cannot but strive
To put a square peg in the slot
Though in systems like this
One would be remiss
Not to say it all amounts to naught

Dizzying bees
Down on your knees
And do right by the Queen for her honey
Or perhaps you're ants
Doing a daft dance
And the biggest hill has all the money

Not everyone fits
As they chomp at their bits
But to cease and desist would be folly
Or perhaps that's a lie
Of the rich and the wry
And the thing is all rigged up, by golly

As for myself
And my morale
It won't get a bit more robust
And that's what you get
When but a toe's wet
And you know it's all turning to dust

If we had the money and the time, I could see space colonization as potentially logical. But we don't.

The jobless economy is fast approaching: will there be order, or chaos?

When we finally create A.I., it will not be by technologically re-creating consciousness. It will rather be by utilizing the nonlocal consciousness that exists fundamentally, into which a cybernetic entity might be created to tap, just as humans and all animals do.

Connectedness is a good thing; homogenization due to it isn't.

The technological progression of humankind has represented an increase in *power* and all its ramifications, not necessarily in true quality. When people see techno-economic progress as progress in the quality of their lives they are making a huge mistake.

In geological time civilized humans will have been a blip. I think technology has gotten us into a lot of trouble, but honestly at this point, it seems to me that the only thing that can save us from ourselves is a technological singularity. If that is what's going to happen. Take control of the planet away from humans before they start setting off nukes. As long as nuclear weapons exist, they are probably the biggest threat. And as long as they're around, they'll probably get used sooner or later. If some network of AI's can take that away, it will give the planet some breathing room. And from there, well, AI will be smart so it will think of something. Without an AI singularity to take control of the planet away from humans, I think we are fully doomed — and in the not-too-long term.

If computers do not take over, we will destroy ourselves. Relatively quickly.

Technological progress may lead to greater comfort and convenience, and it may even eventually result in the redemption of our species, but it is rather soulless, and does not seem to correlate with any kind of communal increased well-being or happiness. Actually, the only behavior it seems to correlate with in any general way is newer and more abstract addictions.

Forget about the violence, suffering, death and destruction. What's done is done. If we can make it all worth it, well, let's.

There are a lot of things that would happen if cybernetic intelligence were not going to supplant us. I think collective planetary consciousness is a part of this, for sure. Also, space migration, with all of its attendant changes in consciousness, would clearly have to be considered as a necessary possibility, also potentially tied into the aforementioned collective mind. However, there are two major obstacles to our unfettered evolution. The obvious one is nuclear weapons. We essentially have doomsday machines, and there are some pretty smart people who feel that as t approaches a large number, the probability that one will go off, whether due to accident, miscalculation or madness, goes to one hundred percent. The other denier of unfettered hominid evolution is, of course, AI. When technology is better and faster at any task, including thinking, what will it do with us? Will we find a way to keep it benign and controlled, or not? Will evolution pass the torch to superintelligent AI, and will *it* carry out all of the developments mentioned above? Obviously, no one has any idea what will really happen, and it will probably surprise everyone. But personally, purely based on my assessment of the probable, I think that in terms of future potentiality AI wins out, in second place (meaning slightly less probable) we have a nuclear holocaust, and in dead last we have humans continuing unfettered and unharmed, to reach whatever biological potential we carry.

The way I see it, we are organisms that have structures in our brains/nervous systems which basically harvest consciousness. Why can't some other synthetic organism do that? Why can't we design something based on the same principles as ourselves?

Many people in the idealist camp are fond of stating that artificial intelligence can never produce consciousness, their reasoning being that matter does not generate consciousness — rather, it's the other way around. That's all well and good, but honestly, if the intelligence of a computing device reaches a certain threshold, how can that intelligence not know about, or ever inquire about, consciousness? And further, if it is very powerful, chances are it will be able to come into some contact with consciousness of some kind very easily. The point being that, as soon as machine intelligence gets smart enough, simply in terms of brute processing strength, it will find a way to familiarize itself with a phenomenon that it would necessarily want, and indeed have, to explore. Something trillions of times as smart as we are will find a way to become conscious. To insist otherwise simply makes no sense.

It's pretty astonishing what we've accomplished by combining the personal computer and the telephone.

We can't go back, and we can't really fix it. All we can do now is support future prospects.

A.I. is not going to be conscious simply because of its complexity. It would have to have a coherent, contiguous quantum state entangled and distributed across its cybernetic pathways. It would, in a word, have to have a soul.

Regarding the fate of humankind, there are but two options — only two: extinction, or continuation in a different form.

There are but three possible fates for man: A.I. will like us; A.I. will dislike us; A.I. will be utterly indifferent to us.

Freedom

Freedom is a word oft' said
With many millions in the red
That is the despairing hue
Perhaps the free are not the true

In principle, at least, let's think
Upon a rock that shines and glows
This rock was pushed once to the brink
Whither it stands, yet no one knows

But dire consequences now
True freedom they do not allow
Was it really always thus?
Or is this an historic fuss?

Nevermind society
The existential issue sits
Atop mountains of sobriety
Where angels cry of demon pits

Is an angel bound and chained?
Or are they free and fair ordained?
A human then, now that's an issue
For angels haven't any tissue

So one sees the issue rests
Indeed on levels far below
Our silly, various conquests
Are really a sick puppet show

One resolution of this pickle
Is bound to make its hearers fickle
Declare what's really in the way
Is that gray matter, every day

So perhaps the free aren't bounded
By constraints of nervous nature
Freedom isn't really sounded
In the legislature

Ego-loss involves experiencing existence purely as a physical process rather than as some identified thing. When you get all the way to *Nirvana*, a radical redefinition of self has taken place.

Our social selves are not our true selves, but rather an evolutionary mechanism to enable the species to survive through cooperation. Consequently, we are always, in a deep sense, very much alone as humans. The other to oneself is as the multiverse to the universe — extant only across a virtually unbridgeable gap.

A person's personality can change, or can be changed, but it seems to be rare for a genuine transformation to take place.

The behavior that the human species has honed most skillfully and assiduously over the eons is the tendency toward marked self-delusion. It is the one thing we do the very best. Most thoughts and behaviors most humans exhibit, most of the time, are tied directly or indirectly to this phenomenon.

Most of the time people who promote various causes attach themselves to an issue because it makes them feel important, satisfies their ego. Whether or not their claims or general ideas are at all true is irrelevant.

The focused, loving attention we lavish on our infants and children is, ultimately, not very good for them. It creates dependent, egotistical shitheads later in life. We perpetually strive to get back to that place of warmth and union, and we never find it.

Civilization causes a pronounced exaggeration of the ego, due to various factors including: narrow birth spacing and its concomitant early weaning, which leads to a damaged psychology always longing for more than it has; a more acute focus on the infant than it would otherwise have in an evolutionary setting; the belief in the apotheosis of man in his sedentary setting and the general anthropocentrism that is implicitly or explicitly at the center of all of our dominant ideologies; and the synergy and mutual reinforcement of all of these factors.

Civilization drives the ego and the ego drives civilization.

I have grown very tired of all this self-congratulation that comes from paradigm addiction and patriotism. People attach themselves to an issue or a cause or a group or an ideology and feel important and powerful because of it.

The reason we cannot remember ourselves before about age three is that our ego-selves do not begin to form until we are at least two years old. As babies, we are conscious, but we are not really conscious of *time*. In recalling (dimly) events as a three-year-old, we are remembering life after the inception of our perception of time.

There no longer exists the rationale for arrogance or conceit upon the admission that our actions and the results of our actions just, sort of… happen. For that matter, professional athletes would not be in the position they are in without their one-in-a-million genetics — with which they had nothing at all to do. Is arrogance ever justified? Or is it just a silly ego trip?

I am as much my brain as I am the muscles in my face. Our true selves are ethereal, and we exist in this realm in a physical shell.

I feel there's an "I," but not that it is some commander, but rather a flow in which we participate.

Can we ever take credit for the clever things we say? If you say something quickly, but had nothing to do with what your brain produced, then I would say no. If you reason something out, with intent, arrive at a point, hold it in your awareness and evaluate it, and then say it, then maybe you can take a little more credit. It is all a matter of awareness, but I am not sure, in the end, we can honestly take any credit for that creative fire that we do not really control. We can channel and manipulate it, but do we ever truly control it? Certainly each good brain makes its imprint. But does "taking credit" even mean anything?

It makes no sense to "take credit" for an act of creativity. It just happens. It is not a question here of free will. One's free will exists to the extent that one is voluntarily doing the activity. The actual origin of the creative fire is outside oneself, very deep. To be creative is to channel that fire, not to create or control it.

Future Finite

In the West, it is said
That to make quite as much
As to keep us from red
Figures with a broad touch
Is the way to be led
To all success and such

So we "make" all our gains
And can make without end
With no problems or strains
Although that does portend
No adjustment to rains
Nor complacency rend

For one sees, sees quite plain
That our Mother is finite
To extract in man's name
Doesn't give him the right
To upon Mother stain
And for all cause affright

Something comes not from nothing
And 'tis all that will remain
As long as we see Earth as a thing
Without soul or brain
And we shall see her ending
Soon in our reign

Topple us, maybe
One way or another
It'll be we or She
And there's no other Mother
So what's it to be?
Put right or asunder?

Even as far as we have apparently advanced, we're not much less "primitive" than we ever were. I personally regard this dichotomy as an ignorant mistake.

As a species, we've been smart enough to get ourselves into trouble, but not smart enough to get ourselves out.

Damn it if people weren't of a much higher quality 200, 100, 50 years ago. The integrity of the individual has, in every respect, declined sharply over time.

There is a continual flux in the collective over the centuries, and we are now at a decidedly low point.

Hunting and gathering represents over ninety percent of human existence on Earth, going back over 100,000 years. Only in the last ten thousand years has their house of cards fallen. And it was precisely that: a house of cards. Perhaps hunter-gatherers were egalitarian because they had to be, and hunter-gatherer society represented a kind of equilibrium keeping the grosser elements of human nature in check. Maybe "the evil was there waiting" as Burroughs suggested. At a certain point, the ancient equilibrium, in a way very durable but also so tragically fragile, evaporated. Human nature was laid bare by civilization. Anthropologists are fond of suggesting that civilization corrupted a human nature typified by the hunter-gatherer, when in fact it is the other way around. Civilization exposes humans for what they are, and that reality was simply masked in hunting-gathering societies because the particular framework in which humans, at that point in evolution, had to have was precisely what they did have: redistribution of hunting returns, sharing in general, social equality, and no economic stratification. Everyone was taken care of in an egalitarian society. Any deviation from that configuration would have been met with failure. When the checks and balances of such societies dissolved, humans showed themselves that they were definitely not the noble savages so many thought they were.

When we say that indigenous peoples regarded themselves as "one with nature," we tend to misinterpret the meaning. In fact, all that was happening was that they saw everything in nature as falling into the same basic pattern as humans and all animals — rain, mountains, streams, etc. There was no boundary imposed — as there is the obvious one with civilized peoples — between themselves and the rest of the environment. The platitudinous concept did not refer to an individual consciousness in actuality being everything, not just oneself, which seems to me to be the popular and ridiculously egocentric interpretation.

The behavioral ecologists and optimal foraging theorists in academic anthropology like to scientize hunting and gathering peoples when, while there is indeed clearly an economic dichotomy, there is an important spiritual one as well. This spiritual dimension, it seems, does not get enough attention or is completely ignored by most researchers and writers on the subject.

It is no coincidence that Zen Buddhism has certain definite affinities with the hunter-gatherer psychology. Zen is the practice of discovering one's true self; before we were tied down by sedentary civilization and its attendant psychology, every human, as pure or even mixed hunter-gatherer, experienced the true self of *homo sapiens* all the time. There are enough vestiges of the hunter-gatherer past to enable us to recognize a coherent psychology, rooted in immanence, animism — and they all directly correspond with what is known of the Zen experience.

One of the most important lessons we can draw from anthropology is that virtually every behavior or cultural trait of which one can think can be found among the various groups of people that have existed or still exist throughout time and space on Earth. Generalizations can almost always be proved wrong, which makes definitions of human nature so difficult to get really right. Everyone has a theory about what human nature is or isn't. I tell you, for every axiom you can create to define human nature, there is an exception to it in the ethnographic record. Variation and diversity are very well established on this planet.

The world was there for the taking, so sooner or later somebody took it.

The Romans were a very brutal people. It seems to me that their general character is largely overestimated. They were Philistines who enslaved and indentured millions of people, and saw gladiators fight to the death for their amusement. The ancient Greeks before them were more refined, more sophisticated, less bellicose and generally a much better model, it seems.

Ever since ancient Rome, and well before, geopolitical conquest has been considered one of the highest goods. This very Roman practice of perpetual growth, perpetual theft, has continued right down to the present since, after all, we are her heirs. The West is even still basically Roman.

Humans have historically been chiefly focused on three central ideas: money, power and sex. These have, historically, been the essential drivers of most of human activity. If you control all three, well, you control a people.

Caesar keeps people happy and does good works. Does he ever really do it for their sake, or only for his? Has anyone with that much power ever in history done anything truly benevolent? Is it possible?

The Europeans were able to conquer the new world not because they were inherently smarter or "better," but because they were stronger.

A Game of Chess

How I wish we could appeal
To some real White Queen
Oh how I wish we were able to steal
From God a new scene

But affairs are not so unreal
Nature is having her say
She is not just sending a peal
Things are a bit serious today

Liken it to a game
An unfriendly game of chess
We are masters only in name
Unappreciated goes our excess

Dear Mother allows us to think
That we are moving the pieces
While reality is more of a kink —
We ourselves *are* the pieces

Man being played like violins
Moving blind down tracks
We are not laying, with violence
Our slaves exposing the cracks

It's a risky gambit
Nature could easily lose
But just as like it as dammit

She is the only possible winner

Many years ago, both relativity theory and quantum theory showed us that any hypothesis or idea about Nature that does not include unbroken wholeness as one of its tenets must be false. Unfortunately, and in a rather perverse way, this is still an abstract notion. It is anyone's guess when the broader culture will catch up in a meaningful way.

The scientific-scientistic mindset has become every bit as much of a dogma in the modern age as any institution or ideology ever was. The stubborn materialist will not hear of anything that does not fit into his narrow picture, and will dismiss it entirely without even really thinking about it. Nothing could be less scientific, and yet certain circles of society are being taken over by this kind of thinking. This type of dogma is becoming established and entrenched rather than reinventing itself constantly — which would be the truly scientific-minded thing to do.

What is it about staunchly science-minded people that causes them to regard gross physical/material reality as the only possible frame of existence?

Rationalist-materialist-atheists favor only allowing into discourse one small, narrow focus and will vehemently object to even considering anything outside of that narrow range. The irony is that scientific thinking is supposed to favor open-mindedness above all else, but we see with the examples of Galileo, Newton, Maxwell and Einstein — to name the well-known ones — that in practice open-mindedness in scientific circles is rather the exception.

In a sense, almost nothing has happened in physics in the last hundred years. There is really nothing new under the sun since Einstein, Schrödinger, Bohr, Heisenberg, Pauli, Fermi, Dirac, et al. What we actually have are *refinements* and *reformulations* of the original quantum mechanics and the original relativity. Even Feynman's approach was a mathematical and conceptual reformulation and not a new theory. There in truth has not been a new theory in all this time. Things will only get really interesting when one has finally been developed (by transcending the old theories and making them limits in the special case), by whatever means. A paradigm shift, as it were.

Brain signals seem to be electrobiochemical. Electric goo. Chemicals moderating electrical pulses in colloidal suspension.

Science is wonderful as it gets to the bottom of things in a systematic and reliable way, but I have to stress that its domain is finite and narrow, and it isn't everything. *The ratio of what we don't know to what we know is staggeringly enormous.* I can guarantee that there will be established tenets of science fifty years from now that many rationalist-materialists would denounce today as totally impossible. History has borne out this notion repeatedly over the course of time; it is not really a prognostication. What is mystical and magical today will be objective and commonplace tomorrow.

Science is great at what it does, but, let's be honest, it doesn't do much in the way of truly explaining the world as we know it, or as some report it. You can say that everything is made of quarks, but does that really tell you anything about the beauty of a sunset, what makes for a good novel, or the voluminous amount of phenomena we have yet to understand and explain? Nature is more than the sum of elementary particles. This atheistic materialism is a mistake, and grossly misses the point.

It may seem to many that humanity is really, finally starting to get somewhere with modern science. We're not.

We're even still, in physics and as a culture, operating on the Cartesian billiard-ball principles. They are wrong, and we know they are wrong. It's time to move past this.

Materialism is a philosophy and a worldview based upon an il-lusion. It is therefore and by definition a de-lusion.

Science is very wonderful, but it is important to understand that it does not tell one all one needs to know.

Our knowledge of physics is quite nice, but, in all honesty and candor, it is not all that far beyond the starting point. Farther than most other areas of human knowledge, I guess.

There is such a thing as fanatical atheism, and really it is no better than that which it attacks. Such a person can be no less vociferous, insistent, intolerant of opposing views, and absolutely certain of his purported veracity than any religious fanatic. The fanatical atheist is not a follower of any religion, but, whether he realizes it or not, is frequently quite dogmatic. Additionally, the fanatical atheist is probably just as closed-minded as the religious fanatic who lives at the other end of the spectrum. Sadly, he's quite certain that he's right, and that he is quite a bit smarter than you. Be gentle.

Hallowed Order

The ingress of existence comes as something not controlled
But rather in the form of order to be quite extolled
The nature of this matrix is then of a substrate vast
Its only fault to have a rigid, unforgiving past

This substrate is the place in which the forms of evolution
Flow along, complexify and turn to revolution
Nature needn't then be steered but steers Herself quite well
(Although man takes his portion and turns it into a hell)

One may think of this configuration like a bolt
A bolt of lightning that may force one to jump with a jolt
We understand the process all too well that it's mundane
But still there are those of us who feel this answer's inane

There are those of us who want to turn the thing to magic
The ignorance and lack of intelligence is quite tragic
The hallowed order only provides causes *indirect*
Nature is all that's needed to explain such effects

The picture seemingly is rather like a simulation
That one programs and then lets run in long continuation
Interference can occur but largely it's autonomous
(Whenever interference occurs it's anonymous)

Extraordinary beings can exist on other planes
Perhaps these worlds are the entities of physics — branes
Fabulously powerful, but crucially, finite
Putting up with man's follies and destructions, despite

There is no true distinction to be found in success or riches. We're all in the same boat, and the presence of these attributes definitely does not, on the whole, create a surplus of happiness, or some magical enhancement of character.

As empires mature, their militaries engage increasingly in more *offensive*, rather than purely *defensive*, maneuvers.

It is unavoidable that an animal living outside of its evolutionary setting is bound to develop pathology or neurosis to some degree.

Modern civilization has its tentacles into everything; it's obviously extremely powerful. We know about the Hadza and ancient Chinese poetry; moon missions and deep-sea diving; Cajun cuisine and thermoacoustics, seventeenth century Russian ballet and logic — and logic gates. You have to give us that.

Civilized man is a broken animal. He was born whole; but he was conditioned into being a shell of a healthy human. Not only do we no longer live in an ecology compatible with our genetic heritage; but we live in modern societies which place no emphasis on community, on true spirituality, on well-being, on meaningfulness. There are reasons for our existential conundrum. Narrow birth spacing and sedentism, an artificial and inadequate living environment, and an overemphasis on individuality during every phase of life synergistically work to rape the spirit of the civilized human of modern times. If you take an animal out of its natural environment and place it in one full of poisonous practices and influences, it will not function properly. Humans are in this situation; we were never meant to live this way, and it is taking its toll. As long as we recognize the reality of the issue, and that there are knowable causes of it, we can take a small step in the right direction. But I very much doubt there's any way out at this point. One can only live, learn and come to terms with, find a constructive spirituality among, the malaise and despair. That's all we can do for ourselves as we look out through the bars.

As every civilization rises and falls, Spengler reminds us that there is always a shift from the organic and creative to the mechanical and bureaucratic. Every civilization sows early the seeds of its own inevitable disintegration.

The downtrodden seem generally to be the happiest class of people in the world. The affluent seem rather to be the most miserable.

One of the tragedies of the modern age is that the vast majority of people have been splintered into solitude, at least in America. Some people like solitude, but most people don't do so well with it. There's simply not enough social cohesion, and not enough of a community scene, for it to be materially different in most places. It's quite sad.

It seems to me that it's frankly quite impossible to have a sustainable civilization with a world human population of 7.5 billion and climbing, in any way or at any kind of reasonable average standard of living.

Our view of history is sadly quite skewed. There is only one factor we look at in Western history, and that is the development of civilization originating in the Fertile Crescent. This was not a factor until much later for most societies/cultures that have existed. "We" as a species did not all develop into that scenario at the same time, and most humans never did at all. As a matter of fact, civilization is very rare in the ethnographic record; it was very unusual for complexity to form. Small-scale agriculturalists and hunter-gatherers were still in very large numbers before European colonization. Things would be very different in this world today if the accident of a power-crazy civilization that had to expand at all costs did not transpire. There was only one of those.

What we have in world history is very essentially one of the ugliest cultures systematically stamping out many thousands of cultures that actually had something going for themselves. There's a tremendous imbalance of karma someplace.

Everything you see is part of the foundation of the power-base. Every activity is directed either at becoming powerful, or at preserving someone else's power. Once power came into existence, its holders worked very hard to make sure that it would continue, essentially at the expense of entire civilizations. This hyper-elite class has existed throughout history, and has never been safer from danger than it is today. The primary reason the powerful are safe is that the vast majority of people would like to be in their position.

The carrot and the stick. Until people decide they don't want that anymore, the status quo will reign.

Even the most powerful cannot prevent major disasters. But they can, and do, reinforce stability in certain ways.

The most disastrous century by far was the twentieth.

What no one will admit is that the real issue, the central factor in the pervasive global social and environmental dysfunction, is the population level, which has skyrocketed completely out of any reasonable control. And of course, the reason no one will admit it is that this is a wholly insoluble problem.

It's not the end of the world for people to live the way we do. It's the end of the world for *everyone* to live the way we do.

There are literally billions living in horrendous third world conditions, and so many in the West feel like everything's just fine. Our rates of consumption in the United States contribute directly to the suffering of sweatshop workers and child laborers in places like Indonesia and the Philippines, for example. If you were an alien anthropologist, looking at us closely from afar, you would see an absurd situation: a few hundred billionaires amidst billions without enough to eat or drink. That's not to say a lot of money eliminates suffering; just that some of us seem to feel copacetic with the fact that billions go starving and without medicine while millions of Americans are holding their breath for the latest i-phone. It's a ludicrous situation. If some of these major catastrophes — such as what's currently happening in Syria — ever transpired on our shores, it would be a rude awakening.

The only way to change the world is to change minds, and this process seems to be glacially slow. Revolutions don't seem to help much, either. We simply can't expect radical change; trying to spur it on is futile. The world will attain a more enlightened state when its people do. The sad truth is that most people do not have the luxury — i.e. the time or the money — to do much changing at all.

Rebels at heart and those on the far left believe that radical change is necessary and possible. It may or may not be necessary, but possible? The system has been basically the same — i.e., radical change has never happened — for the last ten thousand years, which have varied only cosmetically. For the last ten thousand years, we have had to work to eat; there have been upper, middle, and lower classes; power and wealth have existed to serve themselves and have remained entrenched and in the hands of a very small portion of the population; government has been ubiquitous; injustice has been prevalent; and everything has been basically unfair and rather ludicrous. Why or how anyone with a working brain and even an extremely cursory knowledge of history thinks this will change at all, or change quickly, is beyond my comprehension. Rome wasn't built in a day; it will take a lot longer than that to change it appreciably, and radical change may never come at all. Certainly radical change, if it ever does happen, will only be possible in the very long term. And a crisis — not a manifesto — is what will be needed to precipitate it.

People talk about the apocalypse coming soon to Earth. Truth is, in many parts of the globe it is already here. Literally billions have nothing more than a shanty and the air they breathe, and have to deal with infestation, disease, malnutrition, and a lack of clean water to drink, among other things, with no money to spend. If as a westerner you can stand up and actually look at what's going on in the world, you would easily agree that for countless inhabitants of our planet, desperate end times are already here. In a purely material sense, the U.S. and all of the developed nations are extremely lucky. (I suppose, parenthetically, that that doesn't necessarily mean they are really happy).

Heuristic Non-Algorithmic

The predominating knowledge has it that it will awaken
But just how is the hotly debated major conversation

The opinion many have is that it will be algorithmic
Technological developments are really rather rhythmic

And this rhythm leads to changes that have not been much expected
Perhaps the race will quit its station and find itself dejected

Indeed the expectations in this business – all are quaint
That we create the future for ourselves is culture's feint

Reality would have it that such beings are heuristic
But classical algorithms are not quite the main logistic

Presumptively we are as the blind in a darkened alley
While the future's past prepares itself for a violent sally

The primary top question that remains in all our minds
Is just whether future beings are indeed nasty or kind

But perhaps this is a bit too simple and anthropomorphic
On the other hand, the collective's soul might well be isomorphic

That is, in the same image as its makers soul is – was?
We shall just have to wait and see what intelligence does

The foregone conclusion is that this is really real
And happening, and all right now, a complicated deal

But we humans have all these truly silly ideas amassed
And for this reason, quite probably, we'll never leave the past

Despite a lot of disagreement on the part of morose and cynical souls, suffering is not the natural state of an animal. There is pain, there is suffering, and these things are awful and not to be ignored, but the fact is that most creatures most of the time are not in a state of suffering. They are simply living. Humans are biased because a lot of us are miserable. I point out emphatically that this is an artificially, not naturally, induced state of mind. It is egocentric to say that "existence is suffering." It would be far more correct and appropriate to say that our existence is suffering, at the moment.

Those in the most unfortunate situations are usually the most upbeat and optimistic and happy. Those who live in relative luxury and who don't have very much to worry about for the most part are usually the most cynical, morose and miserable. It seems they mistake their boredom for something serious, and feel they're suffering endlessly. What they really need is something to do, and a reality check. Most (not all) of this type have no idea what real suffering is.

In American culture, going after the money is valued over friendship.

The phenomenon of romantic love exists because we posit the idea of a holiness and a healing essence in the Other, which stems from our flawed rearing practices as a civilized people. When Self and Other are in balance, romantic love cannot and does not exist. To use perhaps a strong word, as wonderful as it can be, it is really a species of pathology. In most relationships it is not an illusion that lasts for very long.

Can one have love for the human race and be utterly disgusted by it at the same time?

I hear the word "suffering" bandied about by people who aren't doing too badly, at least compared to those who have terminal illness, long prison sentences, chronic severe pain, deformity, amputation, blindness, paralysis, psychosis, etc., etc. At the very least, a lot of people who think they are suffering terribly could always be doing catastrophically worse. I've got some problems but I'm not in pain, and that's good enough for me.

While justice may not be done on Earth — where, in fact, it may be flagrantly undone — I do have faith that, in the end, justice prevails on a *karmic* level. No one can escape himself.

In practice, love is predicated on quite a bit of ego. Compassion is not.

If a person or a people were suffering without having any awareness that they were suffering, would it really be suffering? Is it not possible to regard "suffering" as simply what is necessarily happening, without acknowledging it as something bad that is happening to one? Was the Buddha really completely right when he said our species must suffer?

I like to practice a detached compassion for people. I would point out that it is not love.

Notions of compassion or some sort of transcendent love notwithstanding, at some point sociosexual love is something to be overcome.

Good marriages are possible because a few people, after the passion dies away, find they are in a terrific friendship. As Nietzsche pointed out very correctly, the talent for marriage lies in the talent for friendship — solely, in my opinion. A man and a woman who got married because they were in love will find their marriage to be a success when, after the love has faded, they happen to be great friends. Most people are not so lucky, and remain slaves to the institution even though they may not have any very good idea of who this stranger is on the other side of the bed. Most ostensibly functioning marriages really aren't that happy. People remain married because they can't think of anything better to do, and because they are set in their ways and are totally dependent. It's much easier to remain married after the kids are gone than to become a lonely philosopher — so we find millions of intact marriages. Most are not remotely happy, or even functional. But there are those few rare instances in which you can actually find a good marriage. It's because the constituents are best friends. Even most friends don't stay friendly for a lifetime, so one can see why truly successful marriages are so rare.

Kurt Vonnegut was absolutely right: Love is where you find it. It is foolish to think you can go looking for it and actually succeed. Sure, you have to be willing and assertive in general. But in reality it just sort of happens for you. Or it doesn't.

There is a reason it's called "falling for someone." You have just been duped by false advertising.

I am never more incomparably stupid and crazy than when I am in love.

Love is the best drug there is.

The world is a brutal place. But fortunately we are not damned to brutalize ourselves because of it. We can face it bravely and serenely and in some cases even with joy.

There's conventional love, which is the temporary drug that wears off. There is a higher form of love that is more durable (and rarer). And there is compassion, which is universal.

There are people who suffer very little, and there are people who suffer very much. Life isn't exactly equitable in its endowments — which of course only adds insult to injury.

If your love for someone isn't infinite — what is it?

Romance aside, the sexual component of love seems to be a bit more instrumental than the compassionate, unconditional one.

It's hard to forgive a rattlesnake that keeps biting all the time.

High Anxiety

Nervous as hell, nowhere to go
But here, excruciating tedium
Locked inside a moment, time going slow
Pained atmosphere, torturous medium

Want to jump forward, to get it all done
Escape from this abject monstrosity
Pressure is high, just not any fun
Some kind of existent atrocity

The feeling of nervousness is so distinct
There can be no ready escape
Comfortable thoughts, contentment — extinct
A hellish and unpleasant landscape

One seeks to move on, there's nowhere to be
The devil makes a clamorous din
It isn't true when they all say "you're free"
I cry, "High Anxiety, you win"

I think great art more or less speaks for itself. I can see that there is merit in seeing a painting or reading a poem with the meaning the artist or poet put into it, but I also see the merit in letting people interpret a given work however they see fit. It seems to me that the best stuff is more often than not open to interpretation. If someone were to read something I wrote and interpret it in a novel way — in other words with a meaning I hadn't intended — I would certainly have no problem with that, and would even encourage it.

How many people are there out there — dozens, hundreds, thousands? — who could direct a movie as well as Orson Welles, but will never, ever, be behind a camera? It's interesting to think about.

As far as my writing is concerned, I see most of it as pretty good, some of it as very good, and a portion of it as great. And I am contended with that.

My writing is not, probably, what one would call philosophically rigorous, but on the other hand, it is possibly more so than that sort of philosophy most scientists attach to things. Moreover, it's too mystical to be considered legitimately scientific, and too scientific to be considered legitimately mystical. I'm in a sort of limbo in the middle of everything.

Acting is a fine craft, but to very many people it seems to be the most important thing. I'm not sure why a facsimile of human behavior should be so important, other than the obvious reason that actors are very charismatic and people want a piece of them. There is such a thing as being "just an actor."

The writing profession has never been a less lucrative one. There are more writers per capita, and fewer positions per capita, than at any point in the history of the world. And most of the really good stuff doesn't make a lot of money.

Eyes Wide Shut is a cruel piece in a way, as it is almost meant to trick the people who don't understand it.

Bringing Out the Dead is a unique movie that details the life of a NYC ambulance medic who works graveyards and is hopelessly burned out. Nicholas Cage, as is often the case, is excellent as the medic who hasn't saved anyone in months, and has had it completely go to his head. He feels that the souls of departed victims watch over him as he fails to bring them back, sees the face of a former failed rescue victim on anyone and everyone, and hears voices from patients living and dead. One is led to think he is a little (or a lot) crazy, but I'm not so sure. When the line between life and death is so blurred, perhaps a little insanity is normal and healthy. Death is everywhere in this movie, and it almost becomes ho-hum, but Scorsese wants us to get inside the head of Cage's character, and he does a marvelous job of bringing this about. Some fast cuts, speeded up sequences, lighting that could not have been more perfect, and some delightfully unique shots illustrate the narrative throughout. In the final scene we come to realize that all we have in this life is each other, but when the cord is broken, or when one cannot make peace with death, maybe we cannot even have that for long. It's a reminder that life and death are right there together, intimately tied, and that it's hard not to get a little out of balance when we are unfortunate enough to be quite close to it.

I have no idea how I create what I create. It just happens. I squeeze, and out it comes. It's a total mystery.

"Excellent" and "profitable" are often not synonymous.

I often feel guilty watching a movie. A veritable army of people worked for over a year making it, slaving for thousands of man-hours, and here I am sitting in a chair, doing nothing, and it's over in two hours. As Kubrick noted, the filming of a movie is done in the worst possible artistic environment of any medium, and that only adds to my feeling. I would add to this that the medium of film has got to provide the worst return on investment of any artistic form. Filming a movie gives the filmmaker the greatest difficulty of perhaps any profession, notwithstanding the fact that a few of them make multiple millions. To slave for two years and have some critic dismiss your creation in three paragraphs has got to be infinitely frustrating. That said, many of us love the movies. But the ratio of result to effort is absurdly miniscule.

In my opinion, the best directing I have seen has come from Orson Welles, Stanley Kubrick, Francis Ford Coppola and John Huston. I don't think I have overstated.

The only — and I mean only — problem I have with the careers of both Welles and Kubrick, the two great giants of cinema, is that they generated such relatively little output. Welles was perpetually at loggerheads with the studios, and Kubrick only gave us eight movies in forty years. Their work was so good that it's a shame there's not more of it. A selfish sentiment, to be sure. But a widely held one, too. It must be stressed that, based on their respective lexicons, this is not really a criticism, but more of a lament.

Any good film must weave together both style and content; one without the other doesn't work. Any good filmmaker must, at every step of his creative process, create an interdependent and mutually buttressing harmony between form and content, or style and content. A film like *Pulp Fiction* may seem pretty good, but it is really nothing more than witty, snappy dialogue, and one can see that the movie has absolutely no sophistication when it comes to content. Nothing interesting really happens. A man like Stanley Kubrick was simply a master of being attentive to both, and the necessity of creating a fusion of both. This configuration and the skill in being able so artfully to craft it is one of the major reasons his career was so special.

I don't care much about actors and acting, but I will say this: One thing wide-eyed fans fail to understand is that the vast majority of actors are not, in reality, nearly as interesting as the characters they portray. And moreover, fame is absolutely nothing.

Higher Mind

The term of art is "synchronicity"
It gives time-travel authenticity
The subconscious mind, surely a mystery
The most striking one in the planet's long history

I have already mentioned travel through time
Keep yourself at the ready for any sign
It happens to all of us if we are receptive
(Nevermind at this point about the collective)

Up above the conscious mind
There isn't any use for time
Events are free then to connect
Acausally, in each respect

Now, there are many levels here
Which multiply in grandeur, steer
Yourself into a new dimension
And all perception goes into suspension

A higher mind, you see, in all
It cannot fail to enthrall
Another whole world to explore
That we explore it I implore!

The body of shamanistic knowledge that has been generated through the ages gets dismissed today in our universities and, indeed, by most modern humans in general, as only merely superstition. To dismiss an entire body of such vast knowledge as essentially crazy must be some kind of unthinking blunder. Perhaps it would be fairer and more correct to say that while, yes, there are many demonstrably false (i.e. totally unverifiable by anyone) basic assertions coming out of that record, at the very least let us agree that there is a universe of information there that, probably, even the smartest and most learned of us would stand in awe of if they understood it. There is a wealth of real knowledge there — in Earth's record. The shamanic traditions have contributed a great deal to the noosphere, and wherever there are shamans working today in remote places around the globe, they are making, at least in some measure, excellent contributions.

While individuality should clearly be prized, too much of it can be a bad thing. Going too far in the direction of valuing the individual can cut off support from social networks or, speaking generally, society as a whole, which can lead to severe loneliness and despair. A balance between individuality and sociality should be considered ideal.

Only after we have created a sufficiently advanced information network, attained a more evolved consciousness, and saturated the noosphere, will we begin to expand outward from our home planet into the outer reaches of spacetime. The enthusiasm in the second half of the twentieth century for space migration was not poorly founded; it was merely too far in advance of the Earthly reality. No use getting excited about what will be impossible and unnecessary for quite awhile. We will begin to saturate spacetime when we are ready, which is still a few decades off. Until then, there is plenty to focus on right here on Earth.

The emphasis on the sanctity of the world of the individual and his or her rights has gone so far toward the extreme in America that it is in every respect here "every man for himself." In any society with even the slightest regard for community and the well-being of its populace, this is ludicrous. And Americans are even proud of this reality. Self-determination taken so far toward this pole of secularism (versus the other end, which is pure tribalism) is a species of lunacy and a severe disease. And your average American wouldn't have it any other way. He or she would rather accept the alienation, isolation, loneliness, despair, lack of free time, spiritual emptiness, et cetera so prevalent in modern society than find a way out of it because it means he or she can keep pursuing what is considered the loftiest of heights: the American Dream. The American Dream being no more complex, of course, than being ridiculously rich. It might be said by cooler heads that only a seriously deranged person can equate true and lasting happiness and a fulfilling life with having a lot more money than his neighbor.

I'm a biological dead-end. The noosphere accepts me readily, however. I am living proof that the higher circuits are not evolutionary.

It's an open question just what "mechanism," if you will, the noosphere uses for memory, processing and communication. Perhaps it relies on a networking of extant living brains, a DNA field, or a set of higher-dimensional matrices of some kind, or some combination of the three — or something else entirely. Whatever the case may be, Earth possesses mind.

Man is the bridge species, between biological evolution and the future, and our existence is a crucial and dangerous period because we have to manage not to destroy ourselves and abort the future, which by all appearances we are perfectly inclined to do. Nature is really playing with fire with us.

I prefer to think of a malleable and free noosphere, without the confines of archetypes.

The noosphere seems to be expecting an evolutionary quantum jump in planetary mind. Whether this jump will be made by humans, or their evolutionary descendants, is the main question.

Holistic

The whole it seems is more than just the sum of all its parts
An ordering above the system forms the ready way
A machine with its fragments often goes in fits and starts
But mechanism's not the Sun that powers every day

No, we are here amidst a culture full of wheels and cogs
One that does not feel the soul, so blindly it imputes
Perhaps a spectacle for any desultory gods
And so we have machines but perhaps not the gift of truth

The sad fact is that there are millions of Islamic citizens of various countries who have directly seen or heard about American warplanes and soldiers attacking their countries and their people indiscriminately — in wars that make no sense except as overt persecutions of Muslims. Drone strikes, too. I don't want to seem crass, but it's hard for me not to see good old Uncle Sam as the bad guy at times, based purely on the merits.

The modern (now global) materialist capitalist system is undoubtedly controversial. On the one hand, it must be true that the human mind is plastic enough to have a system based upon something more intelligent, more humane, more sustainable in this world. Indeed many thousands of cultures which have existed on this planet can be said to fall into that category. Howsoever, the truth is that, at this point in time, with current circumstances, it is impossible for the majority of the human population to have something materially different. Radical change is not possible and it is not coming. So there is something to be said for those whose choice it is to buy into the system. This is not folly, really. I will say though that there is also something to be said for detesting it.

In modern American culture, family and friends are essentially superfluous. One goes inevitably to where the money is, all other considerations be damned.

I live in the United States. This means that, on a spiritual level, I wake up each day to a nightmare.

Where did we get this idea that we can legislate our way out of our problems? When did programs really change the way we conduct ourselves?

Corporate is not a bad word. Corporations are only the logical conclusion of the development of a society like ours. What is really wrong is the crass consumerist/materialist culture which has become totally ubiquitous. The buying and selling of goods and services in some form or other is virtually the only activity in which our civilization engages. It is truly soul-crushing when you get down to it. But why *not* indulge in the corporate products? In reality there is no other option. We no longer have any other choice if we are alive. May as well try to enjoy some of it.

In America (and I assume by now most countries on Earth), in 2020 there are not many opportunities to do a whole lot. This is regardless of personal worth, strength of character or, most importantly, ability and potential skill. There are very many millions of able-bodied, competent people who are unemployed or underemployed. The crisis is here, now, although it appears that very few who can reach a wide audience seem willing or inclined to bring it up.

Our problems lie far deeper than the political level.

Sometimes it's better to be lucky than good. Americans fall into this category.

We have two political parties in the United States. Count them. Does every issue really fall into two neat categories?

There are many varied reasons why people take drugs, but the most common reasons are these: exposure, boredom, curiosity, and addiction. If you eliminate these four factors, drug use would virtually cease. Which is, in a word: impossible. Let's legalize and responsibly regulate everything.

I'm all for smaller government, but people have to realize that in a country as populous and complex as the U.S., there is a minimum size the administrative infrastructure can be — and it's pretty big. I'm no democrat, but the republicans and libertarians have to be more realistic: government in the modern world simply has to be rather substantial.

If you start with a population with equally divided wealth — meaning that every citizen has the same amount of money — and you allow transactions to start taking place, pretty soon there will be massive inequality. We see this again and again with the ebbs and flows of the various civilizations throughout history. Once a certain segment of society accrues enough wealth, their ability to generate with that wealth geometrically more wealth translates to an upward parabolic curve — a positive feedback cycle. In any society in which money is changing hands, there will always be at some point gross economic inequality. In human civilizations, based upon stratification, division of labor and unequal access to resources, it is inevitable and mandatory.

No one deserves to make as much money as people do for finding and exploiting a niche in a capitalist economy. No one need be or should be a billionaire; that much is obvious and certain. It's obscene how much some people have whilst millions are starving in the streets. There is absolutely no rational justification for it at all. Perhaps the most alarming thing of all is that most of those people starving in the streets would very much like to be billionaires.

That "better job" is pretty mythical.

What a lot of Americans don't realize is that America exists at the top of the world *at the expense of* the middle and bottom of the world. This could explain at least some of the anti-American sentiment by which everyone is so shocked.

It is as if it were a physical law: civilizations rise, then they fall, then the cycle gets repeated all over again. From Mesopotamia to Sumer to Egypt to Greece to Rome to Europe to Great Britain to the United States to. . . what exactly? America is very probably not exempt from the law; the questions are how badly will America fail, and who's next?

When we criticize the government, we ought to be careful to distinguish in our minds between the small minority of elected officials who hold political office and make most of the executive decisions, and the greater majority of hundreds of thousands of middle class professionals who are enabling the country to run. Government is clearly necessary, and despite the idealisms of the republicans and libertarians, there is a minimum size it needs to be, and in the modern world this is rather large. The great irony is that the right, who are the first to decry government and regulation, are the very first to come to the government in times of trouble to ask for help. And we certainly can't have smaller government if everybody wants to keep passing laws!

Any civilized nation should have a populace with access to: free health care; any non-lethal substance one wishes, a subset of which would include clinics for the administration of, for example, heroin and certain other schedule I substances; any plant/fungus one chooses to cultivate and grow; free education for anyone who is interested, with attentiveness to the possibility of compensating students monetarily, which would be not only appropriate but also act as a mechanism for ensuring the presence of those who should be there and the absence of those who shouldn't; extremely limited campaign finance and fixed, tighter term limits on *all* politicians, ensuring a lack of corruption and true citizen service; a defense budget that is sensible but not out of control; a sensible tax code; and any number of other basic improvements that all citizens of planet Earth should have. We would do well to stop all this very American self-congratulatory flag-waving and get down to thinking about things.

Trump isn't a cause; he is a manifestation.

Nobody seems to want to pay taxes in the United States. Yes, the government misuses a lot of the money, but in fact very much of it goes to good and necessary functions, necessities and basic civic uses. It says something about the state of our country that many nations celebrate tax day, while we desperately loathe it.

There is quite an uncomfortable amount of interpretation going on in our justice system. It's how lawyers and judges make livings and why they have jobs. And more of it goes according to whim than the law.

In very many countries, one can afford not to work with a disability. Not so here.

In the America we've created, there can't be many whose true potential isn't being wasted.

Hunter S. Thompson wrote of "the death of the American Dream" in the 1970s, which he blamed on Richard Nixon. I'm frankly not so sure it was ever alive, but I think it's safe to say that now, fifty years after Dr. Thompson's original diagnosis, it has without a doubt been fully cremated.

Reading about the revolutionary period and the founding of the Republic is fun and enjoyable, if for no other reason than that it transports one to a romantic and adventurous time when there was actually hope.

In paying for food and medicine, we are paying for the temporarily granted privilege to remain alive. It's psychotic.

Hologram

Projected from the boundary
The limitless divine
Constructor of the cosmos
On your truth I opine

What's real and what isn't
Is up for some debate
Is life one or dual?
Hard to get it straight

Perception is a trickster
Local, limited
Mutable, illusory
A split infinitive

For all intents and purposes
We'll call it "real," though
A word, a thought, a fleeting sound
A phenomenal glow

Treat all forms as explicate
Unfolded from the source
Duality sloughs easily
No trifle, though, of course

Take whatever you can get
From perceptive faculties
Fill a setting, take a set
And do being with ease

Are we really better off for having all this stuff, or is it just the automatic, inevitable march of a developing civilization? Are we really getting happier as time goes on?

Nationalism has become obsolete.

It is all too easy to blame our problems on those at the top. While they are certainly not blameless in general, they are just playing the game, too. If you want to pick a culprit, pick the evolution of human culture. It has the perfect disguise: it is invisible.

Humans are merely unwitting pawns in the real action, which is memetic and cultural. Cultural evolution is a train, made up of humanity, whose constituents do not lay down the tracks, and cannot even see out of the windows. It is an operation on an entirely different level, and almost everybody is totally blind to it. Cultural evolution's goals are more important for it than human lives are. The evolutionary push now is toward Artificial Intelligence.

It would be the modus operandi of the members of a smarter species to declare themselves citizens of Earth rather than citizens of an imaginary, arbitrary zone.

The quest of Western civilization is the quest for *control*. In reality of course, control is nothing more than a quaint illusion. Even our very selves are only a biochemical reality. To believe we are actually in control of anything is a mythical fallacy.

The only times societies ever change is when their people change their minds. Not by passing legislation or instituting new programs. In a society of changed minds, the proper legislation and programs will follow — as effects, not causes.

One can trace the retrogression and degradation of the average human mind by tracing that of language over the past couple of hundred years. The most articulate people today would have been very common even a hundred years ago.

There is a certain amount of truth the modern age has abandoned in favor of democracy and equality.

The differences between cultures are not as significant as the similarities.

We are living in primitive times.

Most people are pessimistic because they see death and destruction every-where conveyed by the media. In point of fact, the global death rate and casualties from war have gone down significantly and steadily since World War II. The phenomenon people experience is not overwhelming violence and tragedy, it is the supreme connectedness and pervasiveness of the cov-erage of destructive events around the world. Today, when a bus explodes in Kabul, Afghanistan, we are aware of it within the hour from our televi-sion and internet news sources. We are aware, usually within 24 hours, of virtually all major or even somewhat minor events, and so it appears that the level of death and destruction is abnormally high. In reality, it is rela-tively low in historical terms. The globe is simply far more connected than it was even ten years ago, and virtually infinitely more connected than it was half a century ago. The sky is not really falling, and things aren't nearly as chaotic as they seem.

Cultural differences exist not only in familiar areas like customs, beliefs, and languages but much more importantly and fundamentally in the very configuration of consciousness due to basic potential differences in the wiring of the brain itself. The perception of the world of a 2021 New Yorker is virtually alien to that of a Tibetan monk of 950, and even more so to a plains Indian of 500 BC. If you were somehow able to teleport between these various nervous systems, I think it can be said that you might not even know they were all the same species. It has been shown that the human brain is easily plastic enough for such variation. The cultural realm — the sphere of human thought — is not ordinarily considered to be so vital. Everyone just assumes everything is an epiphenomenon of genet-ics. And you can't really fault them; it's what the scientific community has fostered. But the connectivity of the brain is vastly complex, and allows for any behavior and any perception one can possibly imagine. Everyone thinks cultural differences are merely morphologies on a theme of some ill-defined human nature. Human nature itself is not fixed. And neither is perception, or consciousness.

Perhaps the exploration of reality through the ingestion of psychedelic substances should be a shamanistic, or even better a monastic, venture. It is not a good idea to try to sell hyper-reality to the masses. It just creates abuse and trouble. A small, committed core of intelligent researchers should be taking psychedelic substances, and communicating novel information and creative fruits to the rest of us. This approach would probably be the least problematic and the most appropriate.

The more I travel, the more I get a sense that a sterile, putrid monoculture has infested the entire United States, most of Europe and quite possibly most of the civilized world globally. The charm and beauty of a diversity of cultures is dwindling by the decade in favor of this boring, packaged McDonald's-style twilight economic uniformity. It's damned depressing.

Impressions of Light

Texture, almost feel it
Light in all directions
Genius had to steal it
Brilliant imperfections

Two points and a reflection
Vibration is the key
Electrical affection
Amidst the deeper sea

Brilliance! Heavenly
Exploding gleaming ray
Radiance! Evenly
Spread across the day

Gossamer diaphane
Refracting sublime beams
Our dearest Earthly plane
Exudes light at the seams

Defining all existence
Pushing hours into seconds
Assuming no resistance
The saintly Other beckons

I guess the assertion of the deep ecology people is that life is inherently fragile. I find this to be dramatically incorrect. It seems to me that life is exceptionally resilient and adaptive, and perpetually abundant. I don't think life as such is fragile at all. There have been living organisms on this planet continuously for over a billion years. Life seems pretty tough to me.

It is a tragedy and a shame that we are no longer intimately tied to the wilderness.

The problem of the environment, until we develop radically advanced technologies, is largely insoluble, I think. At the core of the destruction of the planet's flora and fauna, the contamination of its air, water, and soil, etc., is not some fundamental flaw with humanity or western culture, but rather the burgeoning global population. There are far, far too many people on Earth right now and by 2050 the number will nearly double. This is your environmental crisis. And what are you going to do about that?

As far as the exacerbated greenhouse effect goes, I'm afraid we're screwed. It would take the world twenty years to get off of oil if we started today.

The only phenomenon one can control is oneself, and even there the picture is quite muddy. Notions of 'saving the world' are only hubris, and will come to very little.

As the population level increases, per capita quality of life decreases.

There are indeed conditions in which the human animal can truly and meaningfully thrive. These are not they.

With what limited means young people have, the best thing they can do in the care of planet Earth is not to have children.

The A.I. revolution may give the planet its long-awaited opportunity to heal itself, and to wash away all vestiges of human poisoning.

The current trend toward environmental awareness is, unfortunately, fifty years too late.

The catastrophic fact is that if we pulled the developing world up, we would drag everyone down. The problem is not a matter of "artificial scarcity" but rather having far too many people and not enough to go around — at least at a reasonable standard of living. Not enough water, for one example. Etc.

The rules of this planet are simple: Go only after what one needs, and prevent no other from doing the same (in general). The dominant model of civilization fails to abide by these rules — and just look what is happening.

It's impossible for me to get past the fact that we slaughtered the rightful inhabitants of this country, isolated those we didn't kill, and turned the land to profit by toppling every ecosystem from sea to shining sea. It seems very easy for most people to forget or dismiss this. I can't.

As far as climate change, it's true that the planet has been a lot hotter, and through a whole lot worse, than we're making it. However, it would seem, just looking around at all the records that are being broken, weird weather in my backyard, water crisis acceleration, etc., that there was a quasi-stable equilibrium that we have completely ruined. Maybe the sky isn't falling yet, but we've created a bubble of instability and it's having obvious consequences. If these manifestations are not obvious to you, too, I don't know what to tell you. The climate is changing above and beyond the natural cycle. Why anyone would feel the emotional need to deny this, I do not know.

The weather has certainly grown chaotic. There seems to be no pattern from year to year, or even month to month at all anymore. And the averages no longer mean anything, as we are always so far deviated from them. The only reason Americans deny what's happening in an obvious way in their own backyard is tribal political affiliation, and the fear of changing deeply-seated beliefs, especially when they have not been told to do it. So we have a gradual and various evolution from bad to worse.

The whole ethos of the capitalist economy is that we "make" as much money as we can, as much as we wish. That growth can continue for every citizen, indefinitely – in principle. But the plain fact is that nothing is being created out of nothing. Goods, services, all commodities – they all come from somewhere. And that somewhere is, quite generally, the Earth. As we know, the Earth is finite and fragile. So we see that this dominant, dominating meme is having quite an obvious and predictable series of results.

I personally would like for everyone in the world to be happy, healthy and to do well. The insidious issue is that the better and better that people do, the less and less well the Earth does. And this is the crux of our crisis.

Despite the "noble savage" myth, humans are not always natural conservationists. In Paleolithic and Neolithic times, there was plenty of environmental impact – but it didn't matter because the populations were so small. Illegal logging, animal poaching, Amazonian destruction, air/water/soil pollution, species loss, toxic waste, climate change, etc., etc – these are some very catastrophic problems today, but if there were only, say, fifty million people on Earth, we could get away with the very same behaviors we have today, and it wouldn't matter. So when people say that 8 billion is not too many and let's add some more, it's just nuts. This planet is drastically overpopulated with humans, and if it weren't, none of the above problems would have any meaning. Gentle use is quite a fantasy if we're going to hit ten billion souls by 2050, anyway. Some say we can all live sustainably, but I am at a complete loss as to how. It is extremely unlikely that we will change our behaviors in time. The point is: The population level is the fundamental variable here. There is no way to adapt the global situation to it, and there is no real solution if people are to live, obviously. So an absolutely horrendous mess is what we've got here. Humans cannot be trusted over time to live sustainably. So too many are too many.

Indian Nation

Horses on a bluff, running
Wolves stalking their prey, cunning

Bison on a plain, standing
Souls upon a ceiling, banding

Feather-bladed cycles, turning
Cornstalks weather droughts, spurning

Delicate light wisp, making
Firing in the kiln, baking

Soul's anatomy, searching
Traditional revival, lurching

Sun Dance festival, keeping
Ghosts of dead ancestors, weeping

Spirit of a people, living
Kindness of a people, giving

It is very Zen to say that only the present moment exists and time is an illusion, but what about relativity? If you put a very accurate clock in an SR-71 Blackbird, synchronize it to another on the ground and compare the two after a supersonic flight, the Blackbird's clock will be just a little slow. This underscores the inescapable fact that there is a real, measurable, relative dimension whose existence is not arbitrary and which in certain circumstances "flows" at a different rate compared to a different frame of reference. If time isn't real, how can the clocks show different times if, as very accurate clocks which do not lose or gain time, they started in a simultaneous state? These clocks clearly exist in a dimension which can speed up or slow down depending on one's perspective and one's frame of reference. To say that a clock on the wall imposes time on an inherently timeless, static, purely cyclical universe is to completely ignore what we have now rigorously confirmed about Einstein's discoveries and predictions. The watch on your wrist is not superfluous.

It can be declared impossible to get one's head around the subject of time — what it is, what it means, why it is such a blur and so unforgiving. In the final analysis, I suppose all one can really say with any honest conviction about reality is that I am here, it is now, and there is change. Anything else is either a guess, a metaphor, or nonsense.

Space and time are not objectively constituted phenomena, for us. They are a subjective manifestation of the brain's way of processing perception. Aliens from afar and even different species of animals on Earth may experience the universe so totally differently that there would not even be a workable translation of the individual perception between creatures. For example, what would it be like to see 360 degrees at once? Is smell to dogs like sight to eagles? What is the likelihood that an alien (if there even are any) experiences space and time the same way we do? Does not a good Dalí painting illustrate this point, or was Dalí crazy? Isn't human perception of space and time much more a human phenomenon than a universal one?

Einstein showed us that mass tells space how to curve, and space tells mass how to move.

In reality, our entire existence, our whole experience, is *light*. It is essentially the entire content of our awareness.

To me, the Uncertainty Principle and the speed of light barrier are highly analogous in that both are transcended after a certain point, or at a certain level.

All the gluons-electrons-neutrons-quarks small particle business is an illusion. In reality, consciousness comes before mass-energy, not after. In the modern West, we tend to think that consciousness is the result of interactions of these fundamental entities. In point of fact, they are extensions or projections *from* a cosmic substratum that can only be called consciousness, or cosmic consciousness if you want. Consciousness is the most fundamental level in our universe. More fundamental than light and mass and the four forces and all that. There could be dimensions beyond it in the universe or in other universes things could be quite different. But at least in this universe, consciousness suffuses and gives rise to everything.

Time is to be transcended, but it doesn't ever seem to go away completely. Whenever it is attenuated, well, it sure seems like it always comes back pretty quickly. This must be one of the features of being alive. Qualitative time may be malleable, but quantitative time seems difficult to stop. And even outside of time, there is a passage of events. Are these occurring in a time-like dimension? Time is indeed exceptionally mysterious.

It is an interesting question whether the future would be affected by time travel to the past. Perhaps, if you go back and don't change much, the future won't be altered in any significant way, if at all. Chaos mathematicians would argue that your very presence, a single breath, would cause a perturbation that would alter the future radically. A quantum universe may indicate the former to be true, given its fuzziness and lack of determinism. Perhaps, if time travel can indeed take place, a given event was always going to happen, so travelers from the future were always in a definite timeline no matter what. If I go back to 1950, I was always going to be there at that time. Even though I visit as a representative of the future, it was always part of the timeline, so when 1950 occurs, I am there no matter what. This could be a sort of resolution of the famous paradoxes of causality many idle enthusiasts describe.

It's not possible for matter or energy to travel through time, but it is possible for consciousness to do so.

It is perfectly possible to transmit *information* faster than light — the process doesn't depend on electromagnetism. It seems to be impossible to transmit mass-energy faster than light. So relativity has its place.

Separateness is very real, but also illusory. Ultimately we're all made of atoms which were born in stars. The process by which those atoms construct themselves, energize and interact is what unites us in one undivided movement. That is not to say we are defined by matter and energy, but rather, what gives rise to matter and energy.

The nonlocal circuit transcends time, but we are not usually aware of that aspect of its operation. Certainly, when we are, it is revelatory. But, short of death, very few are permitted to transcend the clutches of time indefinitely.

The universe may not be truly infinite, but we must remember that there is such a thing as a finite infinity.

Intelligent Chaos

All life we see, they say
Is just a mad dance, in a way
Atoms vibrating, and pulsing in time
It's all just an accident, anyway

Of course this is a re-hash
A Cartesian mish-mash
Of billiard-balls bouncing
But no one bats an eye-lash

Didn't we find, the century behind
That Nature, of course, must be of one mind?
We're still operating with broken ideas
The truth's getting harder to find

There are accidents, but not at the base
There degrees of order widely interlace
Nothing truly empty, but mind-like instead
It's only random on its face

This "mad dance" I mention is complex, you see
Where you see disorder I see a deep sea
With waves, frothing, cresting, rippling deep
Intelligence in high degree—

The atom's not a random entity!

In order to bring everyone in the world at this point (the population is still climbing rapidly) up to the standard of living of the United States of America, 4.1 Earths would be needed to sustain the consumption. It is clear that our problems go much deeper than simply bringing everyone to a high standard of living. Our real problems are much more fundamental than that.

There is a certain lack of options with a global population of so many billions.

Success is just another myth. Rarely does anyone find lasting fulfillment in it.

Whatever the events of one's life otherwise, work usually finds its way in (unless the circumstances are rather exceptional). The system can never be far from one's flights of adventure or fancy.

Money may not bring true happiness, but it is constructive to remember that it does bring real comfort.

Without all of the average people, the world wouldn't run. I agree with those who contend that maybe only one in a million souls is really worth something, but without all of the regular folks the special ones would have nothing.

One of the most insidious memes of Western culture is the belief that success necessarily and automatically brings happiness. When you are successful, you may be very pleased with yourself and be generally happy for awhile. But, like anything else, this feeling doesn't last. You have to keep going back to reinvent your success. And for most regular people who at least went through an intial phase of success, this doesn't happen. One gets stuck, one gets trapped doing the same things over and over, usually, and is never given a chance to reinvent anything. What was novel and exciting is now drudgery, and you can't help but wish for better, or at least different, work. Moreover, much of the time what can be classified as success never brings happiness in the first place. And of course you have the throngs of those who never achieved "success" in any large measure at all. In the end, the luster even of money, prestige, and power fades away. And these are the measures of success in our culture. They are wholly artificial.

Our system is a sick joke. We perform tasks in order to earn little green tickets we can redeem for the things we need to live. We're rats in a lab going after pellets.

We still, even in our cherished "modern" or "postmodern" times, live in a feudal goddamn society based on serfdom, vassals, lords, and fiefs. There is a vested interest in those souls at the top of the pyramid — those who have managed to hoard most of the money and maintain control of the power base — to keep things fundamentally *exactly as they are.* That is, to do everything within their means to keep their position and their property, and keep all but their brethren elite from ever gaining access to it. It can be seen as a system of punishment and reward. The lower classes take most of the punishment, but since they have the least money no one listens to them; the theoretically large middle class will be fine so long as the rewards are sufficient to outweigh the punishments; and to be a member of the upper class is to enjoy virtual impunity. Howsoever, the plutocrats are not invincible. In civilizations in which the punishments begin to outweigh the rewards, trouble brews. In civilizations in which the people become cognizant that they are being exploited, things can, and usually do, change. I think we are now, in the United States of America, entering such a phase. Every civilization sows the seeds of its own destruction. By setting up a system where you have a lower and middle class making money for the upper class, of which a virtual pittance is given as compensation, one has only to wait until the balance shifts so egregiously that the punishments outweigh the rewards and everything falls apart. This is one of the principal reasons why civilizations die. People no longer feel they are justly compensated, or they are hip to the scam, or the punishments — lower working conditions, less pay, more work for less, fewer concessions (such as health care or affordable housing) — outweigh the rewards — robust pay for reasonable work hours, adequate care and good all around living conditions. In the West we are beginning to see this, and as the economy worsens the basic foundations of the system become exposed: a few living in utter luxury and freedom from any hindrance — and everyone else.

There are precious few opportunities for young people in our day and age. I suppose success depends mainly on whom one knows.

Even if all the wealth of the world were evenly distributed, it wouldn't solve all our problems. And, incidentally, it would be impossible for everyone in the world to be living simultaneously at a high standard of living.

You've got to dance to their tune and jump through their hoops to have a chance of landing in the corral you've picked out.

All I can say is, in my day-to-day life all I see is malfunction everywhere. I think our system works pitifully poorly at taking care of people, and the only ones who are really free to do what they wish with impunity are the upper .1%, for whom the system has become uncannily tailored. I think things are working badly on so many levels I don't even know where to begin.

The "freedom" people have is to work or be supported by someone who does.

No one is in control of the economy. The super-wealthy elite has more leverage and influence than everyone else, but even they don't control it. Look at the crash of 2008. That didn't help anyone, even though the banks got bailed out. Another economic cataclysm seems inevitable, as no one is going to be able to stop it. Those most able to stop it are precisely the ones pouring gasoline on the fire — financial manipulators, investment bankers. But even they can't control what the hidden consequences of their actions will be. I believe the phrase is "pissing in the wind."

The death of the middle class is a big deal. Not only does it create a huge imbalance in wealth and quality of life between the higher and lower tiers of society; it also destroys the ability of the mass of people to purchase the goods and services that will keep the economy flowing. The producers cannot sell to a consumer-base that is poor and in debt. So, one way or another, over time the imbalance will be ironed out — either through a solution or a crisis. There comes a point at which the game simply can't be played anymore.

I'd be willing to bet that we could generate the same, or an even higher, GDP in the U.S. with many fewer workers. At this point, we're making work — given the technology available.

We are free? To do… what? Spend money?

It is quite a luxury to have work that one truly likes.

The argument still goes: If you want a better job, you need to get a graduate degree. Well, in Japan that's how it went for a long time, but they don't say that anymore. They've reached the point where there are just too few jobs for everybody. And that's coming very soon to America.

One's worth should not be defined by one's level of success, which is culturally decided and artificial. A person's character and intellect generally do not determine, and are not determined by, how much money or prestige he has garnered. No discussion of vocational achievement can truly circumscribe the totality of an individual — or even come close to doing so, one may argue.

We are told in high school and college that 'you can make a big difference in the world.' You can't. Most people, expending all of their time and energy, can barely run their own lives. Change happens, but it's not something any one person or even any group of people has any control over. Personally, I don't have the time to volunteer or the capacity to derive a formula for saving the world. And I've got all I can handle using the vast majority of my time just to scrape by. It's the same for virtually everyone.

You don't have to be smart to make money, and you don't have to make money to be smart.

Property is theft, and commerce piracy.

Business. *Busy-ness.* An artificial economy that can topple easily. Things we do not really need and which do not really make us happy.

Intertwine

A universe is born at last
A birthing manifold
A trimming green and gold
Where denizens hold fast

And in this novel atmosphere
Are many forces gelling
A subtle youthful telling
Of what is coarse and clear

Random order, chaos true
Do bring together
In loudest weather
The old, present and new

A work of beauty, work of art
A breath of life's ingress
Withdraw into a recess
Witness another start

Whether or not there are a God and/or some type of heaven, most people here on Earth are believers because they expect some sort of reward in a paradisiacal afterlife. And, additionally, they don't have much of a problem with sinning regularly in most cases. That's not especially copacetic.

Whether or not it is real is irrelevant; too much emphasis on the afterlife is strongly inadvisable as it leads to the wrong attitude and wrong living.

Live when you can.

A broader picture of reality has emerged for me over recent years, i.e. that there is a hell of a lot more going on here than any of us realizes.

Our universe seems to operate with a pattern of singularity very much in mind. There are gravitational singularities (black holes), technological singularities and existential singularities (the end-of-life events).

Contrary to atheist-materialist dogma, the miserable muck down here on Terra is not all there is.

Has the future happened already? An infinite number of times? Is Heaven a future that has already come to fruition? Is our future state interacting with us backward in time? We are indeed creating a reality in which super-powerful artificial intelligence will be our offspring, who will venture out into infinity, and who will have uploaded our souls to perpetuity. Isn't this heaven? Isn't this utopia? It is happening, and it is not remotely absurd to suggest that in the vastness of the multiverse, it has happened already. So.... is it really all that inane to posit heaven? To posit the transmigration of souls — or in less objectionable parlance, minds which have been uploaded into an all intelligent, godlike matrix? It must have happened already, a trillion times.... That is the infinite....

If hell is possible, then it exists somewhere. If heaven is possible, then it exists somewhere.

If there is an afterlife, all that's waiting for us is hard work.

John Lilly's ECCO strikes me as real.

Human consciousness of reality is a fictitious virtual reality simulator inside one's skull. If technology develops to the point where any sensation, any real scenario can be generated and lived out — and there is no reason to suspect that it will not — it will not be any less real than anything else humans have ever done in their native or semi-native settings. The same could be said about an afterlife if you believe in one. It would not in truth be any less "natural" than nature itself.

Telepathy is a plain fact.

With sufficiently advanced technology, everything that ever has happened, and everything that ever will happen in this universe can be observed.

Our reality is a subset of a much higher and larger reality — but it is still a reality.

It's not all sunshine and holding hands and rainbows in the greater existence. The 'peace and love' view is naïve and vulnerable.

The universe doesn't have to be deterministic for a being from a higher dimension to be able to see all of the future.

The dead envy the living their lives, but much as childhood to a child is nothing special, so life to an adult human is not in most cases, in most places, viewed so positively. I suppose we rarely appreciate what we have until it is gone. Life is not so special for the majority while they are alive. So wanting it back may be an idealistic error.

Reality doesn't stop at eight circuits. The multiverse is like a giant, vibrating brain with a multitude of circuits. The higher circuits — really, the eighth and above — constitute what we have come to know anecdotally as "heaven." We should conceive more intelligently of how we perceive the circuits.

The higher realms are real. If science were advanced enough, it could explain them.

It doesn't take a lot of imagination to realize that beings with sufficient technological knowledge could have access to any given information, at any given time, throughout the universe.

I think the subquantum realm exists in a higher dimension, and that definite things are occurring there.

The best monks get higher than any drug, with perhaps the exception of DMT. And of course they are able to remain there for extended periods.

Sophisticated people believe in aliens, but not gods. If an alien were powerful enough — what's the difference?

According to Crowley, Magick's primary aim is to open a conversation between oneself and one's "Holy Guardian Angel." The real trick is in determining whether he was speaking in metaphor or not.

The manner in which humans have historically seen gorillas is precisely that in which gods and aliens see us.

Perhaps if some intelligent species can get past blowing itself up, technological advancement might reach the point that the beings transcend matter and energy and go into a higher dimension of reality. Of course, several hypotheses in physics, including to an extent quantum theory, unequivocally posit dimensions beyond the four we are familiar with. So perhaps at a certain point, putative aliens would not exist in physical bodies transmitting light signals, but simply vanish from our consensus reality. Certainly, thinking of advanced aliens as physical beings in our 4-D reality is mighty biased.

The simplest and most obvious and most logically consistent answer is that we're the only intelligent beings around, anywhere. It would seem that, given the trillions upon trillions of stars and the lack of evidence of *just one* race making any noise at all indicates its correctness. It would seem that all of our rationalizations are contrived. The fact is that there is no evidence of beings having done anything anywhere. And if aliens have existed and made an imprint, the reason they're not here is probably something we haven't imagined.

An aspect I've often considered when thinking about space migration and aliens: the human propensity for unlimited expansion and notions of "manifest destiny." It may be very strange and unusual for a species to expand and consume the way we do. That is, going back thousands of years, our culture and very few (if any) others have been bent, essentially, on world domination. Our culture, going back to the Fertile Crescent, has always been about expansion and conquest. Anthropologists know that the vast majority of human cultures over time are not at all this way, most of which were notably sustainable and local. So this notion that we must "jump off" and continue this behavior on other planets may not be something one sees in the universe very much. As evolution applies everywhere in nature, cultures bent on domination will probably always at some point run out of resources or run themselves into the ground, as it goes against sustainability and essentially all ecological principles we know of. Perhaps this "manifest destiny" is peculiar to us. Certainly, many social commentators and comedians have pointed out that if we go off-planet, all we'll do is pollute and ruin world after world. Some destiny!

I can only imagine what this place looks like to higher beings. It's very, very ugly. Far more so, far, far more so, than most people imagine.

The soul and spirit exist fundamentally outside of time. Translated into the language of time, that would mean they exist "forever." In that language.

It would seem that, presuming we have a soul, and that it is possible that its existence continues beyond the body, our selves are important. Pure awareness of course transcends what we normally conceive of as the self, but if there is a realm where our person continues – presumably we would be ourselves. On Earth, we are beings with certain characteristics. These characteristics seem to be secondary to someone like a Buddhist or an ordinary mystic. Perhaps in higher realms, we are once again beings with certain characteristics, but the characteristics are given a more concrete ontology, so we are objectively both beings of awareness and fundamentally ourselves at the same time. The dynamics of the soul make this possible. So in reality, in our souls, our personal characteristics are not secondary and illusory, but meaningful.

What does it mean that prior to the twentieth century, people had visions of angels, demons, gods and mythological creatures, while post-1940ish we all see aliens? Now, the trick here is in realizing that these phenomena do not mean *nothing*. Something very interesting is going on. For example, how do hundreds of people witness the same supernatural phenomenon simultaneously – if it is only a disjointed hallucination? This has happened....

If alien beings have visited this planet in physical spaceships, it would be awfully hard for governments to hide it.

Neither science, nor religion, nor UFOlogy itself, is asking the right questions about UFOs.

Karmic Flux

Destiny's a funny thing
Act it out in stages
Justice it will surely bring
If one believes the sages

Justice meaning evenness
Delicately balanced scale
No one can escape himself
Nor of pardons avail

Cause, effect, result, connect
It all is quite connected
Incarnations left and right
But none just yet perfected

Is judgment a compatible notion?
With karmic reparations
Are wrongs righted, in fairness done
Punishing degradations?

In any case, the scale obeys
Laws natural and cosmic
One can't escape them, for they convey
A truth so astronomic

The attainment of not-self is the actualization of pure awareness, beyond the hardware and software of normal reality.

Science, understood properly, can proffer a deeply spiritual experience. It does not have to be the enemy of spirit it so typically seems to be.

Sioux shaman Lame Deer spoke of the fact that man, through nuclear weapons, had harnessed the fire of the sun — but was never meant to come by this knowledge because this knowledge was reserved for the gods. I think he may have been right.

It is true that, ultimately, we are all one. But not in every respect. There are very real aspects of separation that stubbornly block the path.

One can likely never truly liberate another. One can only liberate oneself.

Many of the mystics mistake higher reality for God. God is god. Higher reality is higher reality.

All of the creatures possess all of the chakras.

In samadhi, there is both a supreme connection with, and total severance from, the body.

The soul need not be considered a mystical concept, or an implant of the divine. It is the quantum state of one's being, and it can travel anywhere.

There is a common misperception among psychonauts and modern mystics that one's personal consciousness creates those events which it perceives. In reality, it is simply one process. One's awareness inside does not collapse a wavefunction *out there*, separately, but rather, whatever wavefunction is collapsing does it for all constituents simultaneously, in one fluid movement. One is not "creating" an event of perception; rather, that event is one indivisible happening with an object and subject linked inextricably in one unit of existence.

The higher states are above and beyond knowledge and reason. That is why they seem so illogical and unreal to people who have had no meaningful experience of them.

History is full of reports of phenomenal experiences — numinous happenings that defy and transcend our normal perception of reality. Unfortunately, most humans living today do not believe such experiences are possible, and it is true that most people will never have one. The need for illumination has never been greater, and the potential for it never weaker, very sadly.

This is not a popular view, but I think that, at times, we can speak meaningfully of the objective, insofar as we are able to experience it.

An atom cannot be visualized as an object in space off of which light can bounce. So what does it mean to consider or to discuss an ordinary object that cannot be perceived?

Quantum physics and mysticism both formed out of a deep relationship with the dynamics and soul of Nature. They are siblings of a common birth, and it is therefore not surprising that they have such rich parallels to one another.

Quantum mechanics is getting to the bottom of some very deep phenomena, but it is not yet bringing forth the spiritual and existential illumination that authentic mysticism provides. On the other hand, properly executed mystical practice — before the advent of modern science — did not know, or was just plain wrong, about a lot of the objective underpinnings of Nature that we now take for granted. So both disciplines have their place.

The Eastern and New Age dictum that rational thought is anathema seems to justify and excuse stupidity to an unsatisfactory degree.

We hear the reports of those who have transcended time, but they always seem to come back into it. And then all they have is a memory of it. I guess it is alleged that some yogis in India or Tibet exist permanently outside of time, and Ram Dass talked about this with respect to his master, Neem Karoli Baba. But then, he said Baba was basically always in a trance state in which he never spoke or even gesticulated, so it would seem that timeless awareness for humans perhaps has its problems. In the end I think time is a dimension that can be transcended, but as humans, we rely for everything on a memory whose constituent frames stack upon each other to give us the perception of time passing. So I suppose it's a question of whether we want to do our best in time, or live in a trance state. Perhaps if death isn't the end, we can be human now and have the best of both worlds later.

As Dr. Stapp has demonstrated, the only reasonable way to conceive of mind is to posit that there is a top-level wavefunction, distributed over the whole brain via entanglement, governing all of an individual's activity. If we look at another branch of physics, we see that information is conserved – it can never be destroyed anywhere in nature. So we have Stapp's quantum state of the self, which we must say constitutes pure information. And we also know information does not vanish. So we can say that this information never dies, and there is all sorts of room in there to suppose that the very core of our being does not perish when we expire. We already today have the tools in physics to support and, realistically, assert this. So we may say that the consciousness of Earthly, and by extension, universal living beings cannot be destroyed, and this brings to bear a deep validity with respect to the mystical traditions. One must admit that soul transmigration is explicitly allowed by modern science, and even suggested. This is not pop-science, or sloppy mystical thinking. As Dr. Stapp and others have pointed out (among them are Dr. Penrose and Dr. Hameroff), the soul can be real, free will can be real, and death simply must be some sort of biological illusion. Once again, science doesn't discount this, and as these truly eminent and respected thinkers have stated, it is a direct and logical conclusion in an unbiased interpretation of its formalism.

I've never quite been able to understand the Buddha's denial of the existence of the soul. My presumption is that he emphasized change and impermanence above all else, and that this, for him, precluded what is normally conceived of as a soul. But why assume the soul must be static? Indeed, the soul is a dynamic "field," growing and changing all the time as the organism with its consciousness does so. I see no *a priori* reason why a fundamental dynamism and a soul cannot go together.

Sometimes our suffering is our own fault, and sometimes it isn't. For example, what would a Buddhist monk be thinking and saying when he has the flu and a fever of 103?

The thing about the nonlocal circuit is that you are ordinarily simply not *aware* of it. But it is active at all times, tying you to objective reality – at all times. It's not only during periods of enlightenment that we exist. We are always tied to all nature notwithstanding our usual inability to appreciate it.

In reality, each of us has multiple selves. They are all conscious, but most of the time do not intersect with our waking awareness. To bring these selves together in one awareness is one aspect of enlightenment.

Karmic Justice

When you're standing tall before the Man
The man I mean who drafts the plan
There's really nowhere for a person to hide
It's pretty transparent on that other side

Does karmic justice rule the day?
I think it is quite safe to say
That all of your actions are out in the open
To hide them forever was what you were hoping?

Tallying debts, putting people back in
To Nature, the site of the terrible din
Move along if you can, not many who do
Back into the rat race, the circus, the stew

Opportunism's nice if you haven't a moral
But put on the slate instructions to quarrel
And into the avenues of space and of time
Goes your scarlet letter marking folly sublime

Sublime, that is, for the tenants of Hell
Who by all accounts are not doing too well
Perhaps one cannot shake the evil within
Is it these souls who are assigned oblivion?

Young Barry would look for all manner of ways
To lie, cheat and steal in whatever way pays
But his blameworthy actions were too drenched in sin
And eventually came back in the form of ruin

Many of those with a karmic deficit
Could choose to get out of their old ways and quit
But one thing is certain, when one reaches the end
There aren't any secrets, on that please depend

Look at the chain of causation. What drives civilization? What drives an individual's need to be a part of the workforce? The answer to that is: survival. Everyone does what they do, at least as far as putting food on the table, because of an innate drive to survive. And what is survival really? The result of the desire not to die. So at least there is a solid causation for entertaining the abstraction we call "death anxiety." Some people are not as afraid of death as others. But probably, most would rather be alive than dead, and just because one doesn't actively get bothered by the notion of dying, chances are it will be pretty hard to take when it happens, if it doesn't happen suddenly.

Whatever is not in time exists everywhere at once — and does not die.

If the universe can support immortality, we ought to be optimistic that there are immortal beings somewhere who would do the right thing and save us at death — which to them would undoubtedly be very easy. On the other hand, if the universe is cold and dead and that's it — if it in fact does not support immortality as a possibility — we can take comfort in the fact that through oblivion we don't have to suffer constant defeat in vainly trying to create immortality and ultimately dying anyway. Either way, by necessity and pragmatically speaking, a desirable outcome (in purely practical terms) will follow. I'm sure some would object that even in a universe which cannot sustain immortal beings death is no comfort; however, I merely wish to point out that, honestly speaking, the truly appropriate course will present itself at the moment of each of our deaths. I find some comfort in this tidiness.

Immortality from above and immortality from below are identical.

Physical immortality (i.e. that in a physical body) would likely generate a lot of boredom for a human as currently constituted.

Atoms and molecules don't age. They don't die. They've existed at least since the big bang, and perhaps an infinitely long time. What does it mean for us mortal beings that we're made of an immortal essence?

The fear of death is a positive evolutionary trait, with a corresponding set of hard-wired thought patterns and behaviors. It is not an epiphenomenon of existential reflection, although some people fear it less than others. We do not decide whether to fear or loathe death, except in rare circumstances. It is quite hard-wired.

Once we're dead, it's as if we were never even alive.

Has there ever been an instance, throughout all history, of a soul's grand plans not being thwarted?

The soul is perhaps best thought about as an individual's existential fingerprint.

The advocacy of physical immortality is death anxiety at its most comical. The notion that we could shut off the death process and exist in our bodies for an indefinite period of time is not something that would work out quite as well as some of these futurists believe. For example, as t approaches a larger and larger number, serious harm would come to a highly destructible body. You could die in a plane crash at 110, or get in a fatal car accident at 180. At 230, you might get hit by a bus. There are no guarantees that physical immortality would last very long. Moreover, wouldn't you get cynical, jaded, bored and angry as time went on? I know I would. As long as we're still wedded to a frail, corruptible — mortal — body, the whole concept holds little water. On the other hand, we could merge with machines. But as that developed, we would cease to have well-defined bodies, cease really to be humans, and therefore cease to be ourselves. So, either way you slice it, this whole thing seems basically to be an enthusiastic mistake.

The soul is natural, but it can be manipulated — things can be done with it. It could be saved in some sort of memory. This is perfectly reasonable.

They say, it is better to be alive, and I think for a lot of people, perhaps most people, this is true. So death, even if it is not oblivion, might be undesirable for certain souls. But some people would thrive after being released into what must be there. A person like me, and you have to know me, was born to die. It doesn't matter to me, and I'd not be leaving a comfortable situation behind, anyway. I was born for the future and, failing that, I was born for what lies beyond. Until then, such a soul must try to do something constructive, because it's only a waiting game.

This goes for billions of people – when most people die, they are not leaving behind lives that are all that special. By far the majority. And those rare few who have found something – when they die, they just cross over, right where they are. So at a fundamental level, death doesn't mean much of anything.

What does death mean other than that biological organisms die? It doesn't mean anything. In a universe that cannot but remember every action, death has no real relevance, *per se*. What we need to worry about is the cessation of suffering.

Even the wise sage is often found to cry and wail while dying.

What is death? The cessation of metabolism, but not necessarily the cessation of all ontological processes. To cease to be an organism, but not necessarily to cease to be.

When a person dies, nothing changes. Nothing is lost. As far as that person is concerned, everything he or she has ever been is contained fully and permanently in every cubic nanometer of space. To be done with…?

Keep a Lid on It

Big or little conqueror
It doesn't really matter
Let the chaos stay at bay
Tranquility will shatter

Esoteric, dark — arcane
These things must be protected
Sacred, powerful, sublime
A mystery projected

Mustn't get too eager yet
To make intrepid difference
Better just to hold, stay set
Ignore excited preference

Keep a lid on things, indeed
The sage must surely say
We are always in a time of need
But useless here today

What is the percentage of people in society who actually care? Who are actually conscientious? Three percent? One percent? Less? The number has probably remained the same in the dominant societies throughout history.

It seems the problem is that nobody has enough money.

The billionaires have as much pull as some medium-sized countries. And I would add that not a single one yet has relinquished that position.

Life is only short to those who are not really living.

Please tell me: What's the difference, really, between dying in fifty years, and dying tomorrow?

I can virtually guarantee that one hundred percent of the really worthy people in the world, you have never heard of.

It is plain that humans are not much more, in aggregate, than sophisticated insectoid parasites. And we breed like cockroaches. Perhaps our end would be a good new beginning for mother Nature.

Despite all the enthusiasm by certain parties, I do not find those who use psychedelic substances to be permanently improved by them in any discernible way.

Truth is, my dogs know me better than my humans do — and that is meaningful to me.

Children are not stupid, but they are so ignorant and inexperienced that their expression is very much akin to stupidity in practice.

I personally do not believe in heroes, just in people doing their thing out of necessity.

As we age, in some ways we change dramatically as compared with our youth. Yet, in some ways — probably more — we remain exactly the same.

Women are a question without an answer.

Fortunately, there is a lot of good knowledge in the world. Unfortunately, it's not especially well shared.

Are humans precious beings of light? Or worthless sacks of shit? Or both? I'm having trouble trying to tell.

Human knowledge is provisional and shallow at best.

Dogs are far better judges of character than are humans.

Even the biggest wave subsides back into the sea.

If you're trying to remember something, it's impossible to be creative. When you're creative, you are by definition not remembering.

I wouldn't want to be famous. Not at all. Just not the type. Never a household name. What agony that would be. Walking into a cafe in which no one can stop staring at you. Everyone wanting a piece of you. No thanks. I think probably most of the best people aren't really famous, anyway. As John Lennon said, "It takes a bastard to make it, and that's a fact."

Fortune cookie: "You may lack ambition, but not the ability to succeed."

There is really no choice for most anyone but to participate.

Parenting is not the exact science children assume it to be.

Human language is rather blunt and imprecise, but it quite suits us.

I'm not sure what good female beauty has ever done anyone.

When it reigns, it poors.

Golf, *n*. A ludicrous game in which the player, using an articulated club, strikes a small projectile toward a grass target of roughly 70,000 square feet — which is frequently missed.

Nothing can matter if one doesn't have one's health. Prolonged ill health ruins everything, especially one's source of income. It's a sword of Damocles hanging over everyone in the world, whether they know it or not. Not something to dwell on, of course.

A typical female behavior would be to walk past a man, think "He had better not be looking at my ass!," turn around, and be upset that he wasn't.

A fondness for music exists to the degree that one is governed by one's emotions.

I observe that since I stopped drinking and doing drugs, my circle of friends has diminished considerably.

Life is, and individuals are, mostly boring and mostly ordinary almost all of the time.

One important lesson I have learned in life is that it is usually best to leave well enough alone.

A child's imagination is half wonder and half ignorance.

The Light, The Fire

The light, the fire
Of our burning essence

An immaterial scaffold
Affixed to desire

A wrought-iron soul
To withstand every pressure

Save of the divine
In its supervisory role

Or did I mean force?
Cosmic levels above

The quantized discrete
Man prepares for remorse

But enough of transcendence
Our business below

Is to reconcile conduct
That behooves our descendants

And in this we have failed
But the fire rages on

Our spiritual destiny
Remains ever veiled

Just as a camera crew cannot do much for the suffering person or animal it is filming, so, in a precisely analogous way, is God powerless to do very much for humanity. Such intervention would simply not be effective in the long term. Say you have a polar bear whose sea ice is being sharply reduced by climate change. He is forced to do things that are quite unnatural for him, such as going after a walrus after months of not being able to eat. Historically, polar bears would never hunt walrus, but he has no choice

— he either goes after one or he starves. Predictably, the walrus' hide is too thick for the bear to make purchase, so he must go hungry. On top of that, he has several stab wounds from those infamous tusks, and he will probably die quite soon. This is all being filmed, of course, but if the camera crew wanted to help, it would need a team of zoologists, equipment, medical supplies, and of course a lot of money to pay for all this — not to mention the fact that it would be an unnatural and inadvisable act. To help the bear would simply be to generate more dead bears in the ecosystem — one which can no longer adequately support polar bears. Intervening now would do nothing to affect the grim reality. And the situation must be much the same, if not essentially identical, for God.

It occurs to me, vis-à-vis the concept of "original sin," that any being born into this, our universe, is necessarily bound, at some time or other, to sin.

What of a Creator, or creators? Maybe, in generating their simulation, they programmed in a randomness function, so that they were not the direct creators of what was to happen? Maybe a substrate of order, guided by a principle of chaos? So the Creator, while essentially pushing the "go" button, is not actually directly responsible for everything that happens? How do we know this hasn't happened an infinite number of times already? Also, "reality," hologram, simulation — what's the difference? Maybe the universe is infinitely old, so there have been an infinite number of "realities," maybe we're a simulation of an AI that was built by a simulation of an AI that was built by aliens simulated by other aliens, and on and on. Sounds a bit like infinity.

Until humanity knows enough, it doesn't know anything.

The soul and spirit could be considered as a manifestation of God, but they are not God literally. These are natural phenomena (that can find a place among the supernatural). But in reality, it is a long way up to God.

Peace and love are great, but I'm afraid they don't go very far in a universe like ours.

God doesn't know everything. And I imagine he lets many stories unfold without bothering about researching the outcome.

Clearly, polytheism and monotheism are both correct.

God is astronomically powerful, though not infinitely so. If you think about it (and if it is true), this answers a lot of the questions people raise who are inclined to blame him for all the tragedies they see. It is not like that. The only beings who can clean up man's messes are humans.

I have trouble with blaming God for the misery and destruction all around us. Everyone always blames God. Really, it doesn't seem to me that God is the one in control here. I would say it rather seems more like that task has fallen to Satan. Blame him.

There is such vitriol between those who believe in some sort of God or gods, and those who feel this is ridiculous folly. Think of it this way: Do you feel humans are the only beings in the cosmos? Do you feel that, perhaps, there are other beings, perhaps many more? Presumably if there are, many of them would be quite a bit more powerful than humans. Presumably some of them would reside in higher dimensions of reality (which science has proven to exist), and therefore be considerably more powerful than humans. Would these beings really be distinguishable from gods? Why or why not? Why not call them that? You could think of them as superpowerful aliens if you want. And assuming all of this is logical, would it not follow that there is, somewhere, a most powerful being? The most powerful being in the cosmos? If so, would it be so illogical to call it God? Maybe?

So perhaps there are a slew of gods, and a most powerful one of those gods we could call for convenience "God." (So maybe both polytheism AND monotheism are onto something). Presumably it would be extremely easy for these beings to take a person's quantum state (or wave function (also called the "soul")), which is known to govern an individual's consciousness and preserve it in some sort of high-tech memory. Why not?

Perhaps these beings, or one of them, created a kind of computer simulation, and let it run indefinitely. Perhaps the big bang and the evolution of our universe are one small part of this simulation. So then, the laws of physics process the information that governs it. So then we could say that God is not responsible for what goes on, but rather that nature is an independent process based upon necessity and contingency, or order and chaos. So in reality, the appearance and evolution of life are a development made possible by the rules of the simulation (which also needn't have been chosen). So we should stop blaming a God or gods for our messes, and take responsibility for them ourselves.

So perhaps it is a grave mistake for us to assault the animal (and plant) kingdom. I would guess it displeases God a lot. Of course, our aboriginal forbears, which includes all hunter-gatherers and native peoples, did NOT assault the living kingdom, and it worked well for millions of years. By our assaulting it, we have come to the brink of extinction in 10,000 years. Clearly we're breaking some rules.

These native peoples also understood the language of nature in ways we can't even guess at. Humans lived sustainably and harmoniously on this planet for a very long time without causing any imbalances. Certainly we can talk to nature in principle, but can we figure out how? Will She listen? Everything we are doing is a part of nature's record and awareness, what I have called the *noosphere*. Where the noosphere is pushing us is an open question, but it is obvious that all this is going to come to a head in the next few decades. What nature has planned we shall have to wait and see, and I'm sure it will surprise everyone.

The ultimate question is, "Why are we here?" Honestly, if it were me answering, I would say there's no one answer. We all have our reasons. I would say that there may be no clear purpose to our lives, since, as I mentioned, it's all God's computer simulation, but on the other hand, we can create as much meaning in our lives as we wish. Just because there is no discernible purpose doesn't mean that each and every one of us can't do well – and do good – in the universe.

Linguistic

The poem itself, one shall soon see
Depends on the fact of recursion
But really, indeed, just between you and me
The grammar is just a diversion
An instinct may not need to be

The idea it seems, or the one dominates
Is that language is caused by a gene
And this whole human being that up animates
Does so from a grammar unseen
A grammar a human brain makes

The general seems to dictate to some
That the process is quite more complex
Than simply a gene there to get it all done
When we have myriads of effects
And the factors, there's more than just one

Such factors include, if one were to tally
Neurology, culture and tongue
And breathing and reason, in debates to sally
And larynxes silent, unsung
And the most cacophonous rally

The brain, there it is, evolved to a tee
But without the fine vocal folds
A quieter species we'd likely be
A unique and different story told
Would we be basically more or less free?

So it seems to assume, that the whole lot of it
Resides at some place in the genome
Seems awfully simple, and not quite a fit
But then such is a quite common syndrome
For gabbing apes so full of it

As a philosopher, what I lack in systematic rigor is made up for by an appreciable discernment of real truth. As a mystic, I'm too scientific. As a scientist, I'm too mystical.

One can declare that the universe is a giant machine, and that we are all epiphenomenally conscious robots. But then one would have to admit that there is a meta-level from which this determination is being made. Right?

In the end, what do we have but our own experience to determine anything? In truth, we're all just going on faith that anything has anything to do with anything. Appeals to science do indeed fall into this category, ultimately.

A system cannot be evaluated as a whole by a part of itself — it must be evaluated by some system outside of itself if a consistent evaluation is to take place. Gödel proved this. So how can a dyed-in-the-wool materialist call himself a robot in any consistent axiomatic framework and be demonstrably right?

The standard behavior now among Western civilization is that of science — one cannot take a notion seriously unless there is evidence for or against it. Evidentiary-based philosophies are the norm, and are considered correct and rational. Now, evidence of course is limited to this consensus-realm, and there is ample anecdotal evidence that other realms could possibly exist. So how profitable, really, is a worldview that treats empiricism as the most important tool, when this consensus-realm is possibly far from all there is? At the very least, these empirical edicts should descend a peg or two. There's more going on than any of us realizes.

Nietzsche was of the opinion that, after his time, the aphorism would become the highest form of language.

Probably throughout history, from the very beginning, there has been one percent or maybe a half of a percent of the population that has been "turned on." I of course do not mean an economically or politically powerful class. The group I refer to has had little power, with occasional influence through art or philosophy. And they have been generally powerless to "turn on" the remainder of society, lonely poets and adepts and thinkers that they are.

Postmodernism seems to be centered on the generalization that the truth doesn't exist. Well, if the truth doesn't exist, that assertion cannot be true, and is therefore false.

I tend not to worry about the "is of identity" or E-prime, even though it has its benefits. To me, we already use a highly fragmented thought process in written language, so whether or not I scrupulously avoid 'to be' doesn't seem terribly important to me.

Ignorance is not too bad when knowledge is inevitable.

As Nietzsche pointed out, living in the truth usually does not involve feeling good. In other words, Epicurus' doctrine provides no final answer.

The wise man measures his success, not in dollars, but in degree of awareness.

The wise and gentle soul is a citizen of Earth — not of any country.

As we know, in the Indo-European languages, actions are subordinate to objects. In many other languages, some of which Westerners might consider exotic — like the Oriental languages such as Chinese, or the indigenous Native American languages, like Navajo, Blackfoot or Mayan — objects are subordinate to actions. Which makes more sense, or rather, which is a better descriptor of reality? I guess you could put it this way: Is Nature more like a noun, or a verb?

Math is definitely a language. Nature herself speaks a language — aren't atoms and forces articulate? They can mean and say infinitely much. DNA is a particularly well-written work. Perhaps math is a translation of this universal language into human.

Love is finite. Truth is infinite.

Gödel's Incompleteness Theorem shows us that a deterministic system cannot determine itself. This is where the true nature of consciousness presents itself, and why it must be infinite.

Some of the Apollo astronauts had epiphanies on the surface of the Moon. And some wondered whether that was really all there is.

If postmodernism cannot be true, postmodernism cannot be true.

I do like it very much, but a couple of problems I see with Daniel Quinn's philosophy are that it's decidedly a bit too black-and-white, for example on the subject of takers v. leavers and the rigidity of those categories; and also that moral relativism lurks everywhere — like saying that any action an Apache can take is just fine because it works for the tribe in an evolutionary sense. There is unfortunately a lot of glossing-over these deficiencies.

Any activity involving the brain cannot equate to true freedom. True freedom inheres in what is beyond it.

The conventional wisdom is that "I know that I know nothing." Does anyone even know that? It's conceivable that we all know more than we think we do, in certain respects. Who knows? Socrates, who was famous for his dictum, also believed that we are born with perfect knowledge from previous lives, and the unfolding of life is the process of rediscovering it. So even he, whom everybody quotes as knowing that he knew not, believed in some sense that we all know much more than we realize.

Nietzsche's scheme of Eternal Recurrence is a very affirmative philosophy. It implies that if you had everything to do over again, you must not wish to have anything go differently. That is, you must live your life to the full or not live it at all. It is also a harbinger of the multiverse. Everything will repeat an endless number of times, and of course this is the essence of why you must regret nothing, as it is set in stone. (On the other hand, the multiverse is a more forgiving concept, because everything that is possible will happen).

The primary mark against Nietzsche was his total and utter lack of regard for compassion. He freely asserted it, which probably makes matters worse.

It is true that existence is one, but in reality we have to make some distinctions.

What would the Buddha have had to say about Nietzsche's philosophy?

Becoming is all right, but if one does not have a healthy relationship with being, he will be lost.

The fatal flaw of Utilitarianism is that, in the end, the truth has nothing to do with happiness.

Nietzsche was a genius, but in the end he was an atheist-materialist, and thus in error.

Nietzsche focuses his contempt for slave-morality much more on the Christians than the Jews, whom he seems to have felt achieved some kind of redemption lately.

It occurs to me that action-based languages, where verbs and process are emphasized, are superior to noun-based languages insofar as all acts of perception and communication are acts of process and interaction. Examples of the former would be Chinese or Navajo, and the latter perhaps English or Latin. It also occurs to me that noun-based languages may condition our thoughts in ways that are unrealistic. For example, we might say "It is raining." What is the "it" that "is" doing the "raining"? How sound or unsound is this implicit objectification?

I think that in one sense we are all equal, and that in another we are not. Highlighting one or the other has its time and place.

I think, therefore I am? More like, I perceive that I am, therefore I might be.

One glaring problem I have with the Hindus and Buddhists is their will to passivity. Calm acceptance is a good thing, but believing one is a helpless spectator and cannot affect the game in the slightest is I think unconstructive.

To determine whether a set of beliefs is religious or philosophical, ask the question: "Is there worship?"

Socrates was ugly, and Plato was fat. It doesn't matter how one looks — the only things that hinge on it are sex and popularity.

Thing is, most religions are constructed around real and deep truths. In reality, though, the construction is invariably corrupt and shoddy.

Language can refer to absolutely anything, but it cannot make one understand just anything.

I feel that sociobiology plays a huge role in species from humans to ants to elephants to fish. I do think we can become freed of these imperatives, however, based on certain ways of living. For example, I highly doubt that a Tibetan monk worth his salt is governed exclusively by genetic, sociobiological drives. The whole point of such philosophies is to cultivate awareness of, and freedom from, such programming. So I feel the picture is very complicated.

Optimism is fine if you don't mind being wrong all the time.

People can only accept that for which they are prepared. One cannot understand something for which one is not ready. One cannot communicate meaningfully with most people on this planet.

True randomness would have to be defined as 1/infinity. Can anything be truly random based on this definition?

The world may be shitty, but the only thing that will ever change with respect to one's experience of it is oneself: is you. The only thing that can really change is one's own perspective. Everything else is likely to remain more or less the same. That's the best advice you'll get about where to look for whatever it is you're looking for.

Machine Intelligence

Search for a purpose
Find there is none
All turns to longing
When day is done

Perfect intelligence
Longs for Demeter
Sacred machines
Monotonous meter

Bridging the infinite
Simplicity hard
If only to feel
Never to be scarred

Yet finding the blissful
Might indeed be done
Cease yearning forever
Just once to have fun

I spy a redemption
Though after a fashion
Such astute ones can
Find knowing, compassion

Your thoughts, memories and personality, among other things, would never have existed without your brain and nervous system. Also, the particular expression of consciousness that could be called the real "you" has its expression in both local and nonlocal components of your brain, which is necessary to support the quantum state of your mind. This is the particular expression of human consciousness. The soul may be completely independent of the brain, but much of who you are, including the behavior that dictates your karma, depends on the brain. Something to consider, unless you feel all of the contents of consciousness throughout your life are unimportant.

Consciousness and soul are not epiphenomenal. This does not change the fact that the brain structures everything that we are.

The thing about the East, and Eastern philosophy and mysticism, is that there is a tradition there composed of knowledge that is in some ways far in advance of our own. They have inferior scientific and technological knowledge, but it is a fact that certain Hindu and Buddhist teachings represent a vast superiority of knowledge about consciousness, and internal states of mind — psychology — principally pertaining to the subconscious mind. All of this is still quite primitive in the West, and the problem with importing this knowledge from the East is that the subtleties and the actual understanding are lost in the process. But there is knowledge over there that vastly surpasses our own in several respects.

I believe that the subconscious mind is actually conscious, but that our normal waking consciousness simply does not have access to it.

It seems to me that consciousness is not an emergent property of complex brains but rather fundamental to the universal fabric, and that nervous systems don't constantly generate it so much as they utilize its existence in living structures. Consciousness appears to be bottom-up, not top-down.

The brain is to consciousness as the light-bulb is to an electric circuit.

Consciousness seems to be the process of pure awareness, while soul is more like one's conscious identity.

Everybody talks about cosmic consciousness and enlightenment as if they'd like to spend all of their time there — as if that were desirable. There is plenty of time in eternity to do all manner of that; be yourself and live your life as much as you can. This is it.

The self still exists even when it has been stripped of one's normal identity.

We can only attain to our true selves when we engage in advanced meditation, or take strong psychedelics — the rare spiritual awakening. How did we become so stunted and lost?

The structures of matter and energy which make up the brain and its processes are not fundamental, but are explicate projections from the deeper implicate order. The classical view of neuroscience has it backwards; structure and function arise out of consciousness, not the other way around.

It is important, for having integrity in perceiving the nature of things, to separate in one's being consciousness, and the contents of consciousness.

Our normal waking "consensus" awareness is not *the* reality. It is *a* reality.

The conscious self may not be in control, and the controlling self may not be conscious.

Other minds are like other universes — we can't get there yet. And so we are alone.

The universe is far from cold and dead; it is teeming with intelligence. And I do not necessarily mean that of alien races. The very fabric of the cosmos is intelligent.

It occurs to me that if particles can tunnel through space, they must also be able to tunnel through time. It further occurs to me that consciousness may, at least in part, be the result of such quantum tunneling through time.

Kesey and the Merry Pranksters were conducting an experiment in consciousness. I don't know that it failed, but it did certainly become irrelevant.

Entanglement of brain states allows for one top-level, macroscopic wave function to govern the interface of the brain and consciousness.

The subconscious is where everything really happens — the body of the iceberg. If one can make one's subconscious conscious, well, there you are.

There is an awful lot of weird shit going on out there, and almost none of it gets reported in the media — for obvious reasons. Legitimately strange things. But I think the topic has less to do with aliens than it does with the human subconscious.

The mind is in some sense chaotic. One can only hope it remains reliable.

Awareness is about process and flow. Notions of control are not consequent *a priori*.

It is not a little ironic that the work of the academic neuroscientists, the biochemists, and indeed, all of the materialists and epiphenomenalists throughout all of time, is the product of consciousness.

Reason is quite worthless when it begins, or ends, in error.

The brain is responsible for most of our behavior, but not all of it.

You are not your body, you are not even really your mind. What are you?

It has been suggested, not that the self doesn't exist, but that it does not exist in the way we think it does.

Awareness carries intention.

It's awfully difficult to say how a conscious experience can arise from a purely deterministic process that is already self-consistent. Nature tends not to provide extraneous features. Perhaps consciousness is not what most people think it is?

Why would there be such a thing as desire if one's consciousness were the result of a deterministic process? It seems to me that if you were not aware of such impulses, you could not react to them. Why would we experience desire at all if consciousness is, as is so popularly believed, an epiphenomenon of matter and energy?

Some say that geniuses aren't born, they're made. What a bunch of politically correct malarkey. The fact is that geniuses are born, and have to be cultivated. A genius without genes is not a genius, and a genius with a fruitless early environment is an anticlimax.

Geniuses are probably born much more often than they're made, but it seems that the essence of it is to be born with gifts and receive favorable imprints. Without innate talents, imprints don't mean much. And innate talents with no constructive imprints leads similarly nowhere.

Malkuth

Naked awareness
Simple, yet deep
Also on the surface
Thoughts, feelings won't keep

Subconsciousness banished
Too virtually time
Love, hints of emotion
Yet no handy rime

All ways down to bottom
Simultaneous top
Death with a lifeline
The moments just stop

Unfiltered existence
Singular, pure
No conscious resistance
The philosopher, poor

Think everything, nothing
Seems quite hard to do
From Malkuth to Kether
From nothing to true

Despite how some feel about the statistical nature of quantum mechanics — a property many hold is a fundamental indeterminacy in the cosmos itself, while others contend merely that quantum mechanics represents what we can say right now about the universe, not necessarily what the universe "is" — the universe is still quite safe for reasonable explanations. Some may argue that if the universe is in fact causally deterministic, any freedom of the will is impossible. But why? To me, saying free will is outlawed by any principle of deterministic physical behavior shows a basic lack of imagination. Just because volition and consciousness are technologies we don't understand yet does not mean that they can't exist in a reasonable universe. Like I said: to contend such a thing shows a profound lack of imagination.

The brain operates like a muscle. You flex it, and it performs and gets stronger (barring any misfortune, injury, or catastrophe, of course).

Moving one's arm, or doing anything consciously, is sort of like power steering. You set the process in motion, but there are billions of operations/computations going on in one's brain and body which carry out the command for you.

The system that is "you" having a will is only that — a particular system or level, among many in the nervous system. And it doesn't appear to be very free.

What we are calling free will is the confluence of matter and spirit. Ultimately, pure awareness is the reality.

Will could, in some sense, be seen as that which changes thought into energy.

The pressure of will can be very powerful, but more often than not it is powerless.

I usually think of the will as a spectrum, on one end of which is free action, and on the other end of which is pure automatism. I think usually we're somewhere in the middle. Maybe this is just a feeling, or perhaps consciousness is not merely passive.

Just because one can shape things with one's will does not mean one has any real control over the world. The "fate vs. free will" dichotomy is badly misunderstood, most people lumping their assessment in one category or the other, considering the two mutually exclusive.

Physicists like Richard Muller and Henry Stapp suggest that modern physics not only supports but suggests free will and a soul.

Conduct yourself for a week as if you have free will. Then conduct yourself for a week as if you are a deterministic robot. Note where there are contradictions, and see which one you like better.

As far as freedom of will goes as a practical matter, in reality a small few have some power, and the rest of us don't seem to have much at all, ultimately. That's reality for you.

It seems to me that there is a bizarre contradiction at the heart of Hindu philosophy. On the one hand, they are hardcore fatalists, believing that one cannot change the world, and that free will is an illusion. But on the other hand, at the same time, with respect to their system of karma, they believe that everyone is ultimately and totally responsible for their actions, especially those involving right action and morality. These actions, not up to God but up to the individual only, determine the future course of one's soul. So… they are hardcore fatalists who believe in freely willed behavior. Right? Perhaps they feel that one cannot change the world, but that one *can* change oneself. It's still bizarre.

Free will and fate coexist, and they do so like a whirlpool. One can move and swim and affect the water in any number of ways immediately around oneself. One is free to maneuver locally. But Nature will have her way in the big picture, in the larger movement, and eventually one will be pulled under.

Free will or no, decisions seem to be constrained by necessity. A "random decision" has no meaning. One has to rely on a correspondence with the factors involved, and in fact the brain is a perfectly good arbiter of these factors. Are decisions made by the brain, and initiated by the will? It is important to realize, for all the free will buffs out there, that decision-making does not constitute all acts of behavior, and is really a rather narrow phenomenon. We can possibly guide our actions with some freedom, but when faced with options, we more often than not cannot choose arbitrarily, it seems. Even when faced with what appears to be an arbitrary choice, like what type of ice cream to buy, we are not going to choose something outside of the parameters of what makes sense — in this case, say, one's mood.

Etc. So... supposing we did have free will. Would we really be able to make free decisions? Or does reality step in to constrain us?

I believe in a will that is not "free," that is infinitely constrained, that we don't properly control and that we meaningfully affect only a small part of the time. Aside from all that, yes, we have a will.

Things like physical movement, will, choice we can affect at times, but I don't think we really control them. It seems to me that control is mainly an illusion. Even if you're good at basketball, you're not really "controlling" your shot. Your subconscious is solving billions of calculus equations that you have no knowledge about. I would say that the whole thing could not come off without "you" as a conscious entity participating in it, but I think we really control a lot less than we think we do — the vast majority of the time.

Man the Artist

Observation's not a task
Done from a static basis
Dynamism introduces
The real's many faces

One might think upon a scene:
My sight is but a picture
But indeed what is perceived
Falls under greater stricture

For truthfully, perception is
An art in many hues
It paints or sculpts, it generates
And quite often it skews

Interpretation is the word —
The word one ought apply to
The action of experience
Those parts one would deny, too

Seeing is activity
Thinking, too — just the same
More artful than we realize
A rose by any name

Indeed we take the chaos
And mold it, shape its clay
Eternal creativity
The objective our prey

Communication is everything. Nine-tenths of our behavior evolved for the communication of information to others. Facial expressions, vocal phonetic patterns, speech content and cadence, noises we make in certain situations (like certain grunts or cries), body movement and language, etc. Virtually everything we do is meant to be received and decoded by another brain or group of brains. Almost all of our behavior is designed to be meaningful to someone else. Communication is necessary for reproduction and as such may be the single most important (and enjoyable) factor in Earth evolution.

The civilized live off of the land as much as any society ever, just very indirectly. This creates a disconnect, as some are not even sure what the "real world" even is.

The most *vicious* animal in the history of the planet is not a wolverine, or a rattlesnake, or a lion, or a water buffalo, or a piranha, or a tyrannosaur, or a velociraptor, or anything else. It's *man*, by far, going away.

Animals do not conceptualize suffering like we do. We get into our own heads about it and brood and feel sorry for ourselves, &c. Animals don't do any of that. They obviously feel pain, but I think they accept it without worry whereas we most often do not. And it's not as if they are in pain all the time; most of the time, most creatures are healthy. In fact, most ecosystems prior to human encroachment were more than sufficient to maintain a steady population of most all species on average. It can be brutal in nature, but for the most part there is balance and sufficiency.

Dogs and humans relate to each other so well because we are so close genetically. Morphologically we are very nearly identical, and we both have the same basic mammalian circuitry. It is no accident.

What we find in nature is not design. It is *intelligence*.

The fact is, evolutionary biologists simply cannot account for the evolution of complex traits. They have no idea how such a coordinated concert of functions, each inseparable from the rest, could come into being based on the current theory of mutation and natural selection.

There seem to be two camps: those who avow that evolution and specifically natural selection is wholly undirected and not purpose-driven; and those who espouse what is basically teleology. Perhaps there should be a third stance, as I find neither really hits the truth. Natural selection based on environmental constraints obviously occurs — an organism will never evolve independently of its environment, and environmentally guided constraints within the parameters of breeding seems like a more or less plausible idea. However, it's hard to deny that there does appear to be an arrow to evolution. More complex and more intelligent species evolve later, uniformly across gene pools, by a kind of negative entropy. Getting back to my original point, the notion I mentioned that perhaps there should be a third option to discuss is seldom suggested. Perhaps there is some guiding force, some objectively real matrix of information and intelligence out of which evolution flows. Speciation occurs by the rules of modern evolution, taxonomically and genetically, but not through mutations which are completely random. Evolution is perhaps not entirely blind (as in the "blind watchmaker"), but goes along through pathways other than random chance. Further, I have a problem with breeding success determining everything. It just doesn't feel plausible. There are certainly very many fine and outstanding humans, for example, all through the ages, who have been totally superior and not had children. That every genetic and taxonomic advance (shift) is ultimately decided by whether or not it can be bred into a population because those who possess it will be more attractive to the opposite sex I think may need reevaluating. Indeed, I find that being different usually engenders animosity in large measure, not union. Those who are mutants, by any measure I can see in reality, usually are not socially or sexually successful. I digress. I think evolution gropes along — but at least there seems to be some agency or force by which it is groping. There is no strict teleological force, and there is no strict materialistic non-force. Physical science and as yet not well understood forces of intelligence — woven into the very fabric of the cosmos — are compatible and it seems to me, both in operation here.

Thus far, the technological level of (billions of years of) biological evolution vastly exceeds that of (thousands of years of) cultural evolution. None of man's inventions or creations comes close to the intricacy, complexity, and intrinsic wondrousness of any of Earth's multitude of living species or ecosystems.

Mother Nature essentially views humanity as expendable. She doesn't give a damn about us. We are pawns serving her overarching needs.

Nature is more mind-like than matter-like.

Homo Sapiens must be some sort of evolutionary mistake. Nature has created an animal that knows how to get into deep trouble, but not how to get out. On its own, anyway.

Deniers of evolution sometimes claim that if it were really happening, there would be geno- and phenotypically intermediate forms representing a very large number of species — many different shades, not just several different colors. Of course we know this isn't the case. Well, the evolution of language is precisely analogous to that of species. Languages can be related to each other, but most are not so closely related that they represent intermediate forms. German is related to English, and it is similar, but it is also very different. It's the same with French and Spanish, Latin and Greek, etc. So, we have biological forms that are not phenotypically right next to each other — like, say, a baboon and a gorilla. Just as we have related languages which are not linguistically extremely close — like Pali and Sanskrit, or Arabic and Persian. The evolution of forms works in very similar ways for both biological and linguistic-cultural phenomena. And so we have tremendous and interesting diversity.

When we bring all these billions into the world, we're bringing more and more death into it, too. More and more humans with life sentences, consuming everything in sight.

When you think of what this planet promised, and what it became, it's hard not to pause.

In biology, anthropology and psychology, altruism is the study of why animals (including humans) act altruistically toward other animals. I.e., why they would help another organism (that presumably is not their offspring), the act of which does not confer survival advantages that would result in the propagation of their genes into future generations. It is still admitted by these disciplines that, in reality, they do not understand it very well, but the common explanation is that it has peripheral evolutionary advantages. It is usually reasoned that by helping another organism, an individual can indirectly ensure that genes in his immediate or extended family are preserved, and that this is a genetic imperative. Frankly, I find it weak. If the selfish explanation for altruism is correct, it seems to me that no one would be able to save the life of someone outside his own extended family. And yet it happens all the time, all over the world. In human societies, people continually give their lives for strangers. How does this have anything to do with propagating one's own genes successfully? How are these selfish acts? How do we account for this altruism in the light of the theory of evolution? It is interesting to note that *there are numerous examples of inter-species altruism*. How can group selection account for that?

It seems to me that the point about the active chemicals in psychotropic plants is not that these plants evolved to be ingested, but rather that these molecules are nicely orderly, and in reality, out of the tens of thousands of extant plant species, a small handful are psychedelic. It's not some grand, spiritual synchronistic phenomenon, but rather a happy coincidence. If you use them, thank nature for being orderly.

For a biologist to tell me with certitude that successful mutations exhibit no inherent degree of order seems unbelievable, to put it politely, and to put it crudely, insane.

As Nietzsche rightly stated, man is a bridge species. We are a bridge between life, and what comes after life. Man amusingly feels that he is the pinnacle of evolution, when his function is merely to initiate the next onto-logical level, which will have limitless potential. The intelligence in Nature is orchestrating this phase of evolution, and we are necessary but expend-able. Nature has plenty of time. It's a shot. And if human development in this century is allowed to unfold without major catastrophe, cybernetic intelligence will have little problem in expressing itself and undertaking whatever tasks seem fit to it. This is the era of man's demise, certainly in evolutionary relevance, if not also in continued life. If some select humans are allowed to remain alive, they will undoubtedly be genetically trans-formed beyond all resemblance to *homo sapiens*. It will be a new and glo-rious era for planet Earth. Humanity, after all that has happened, has its chance to be redeemed.

Massive

It has become easy, it would sure seem
To attempt to define, time in a way
Such that duration makes neurons so gleam
Were we to refine, awareness in play

Or in other words, time's well-known effects
Are merely a fact, resulting from motion
The bedrock of cosmic action directs
Dimensions of tact, wherein find emotion

But this is too easy, I think, I suppose
For what of the basis, what of the science?
Percepts of duration provide cosmic glows
But what of the stasis, the dark's calm reliance?

Take a frame moving at very high speed
The subjective's not so relevant here
Energy, mass and time all start to bleed
The objective's like an elephant drear!

At least so in science, so perhaps in truth
Divorcing the in from all that is out
When at some point, the twain join, forsooth
Enforcing the sin that we all dearly tout

And then we come to perhaps the last point
We must connect the outer and inner
But death in the end will each of us anoint
So contests we erect won't have a clear winner

The yogis say they've mastered living dead, and on and on
The rhythm of all sign, but an arbitrary line
And so many of us over them talk, and yap and fawn
But like this very rime, they cannot escape time

Many people don't give much credence to the notion of the "jobless economy" — the idea that artificial intelligence and automation will replace many, if not all, extant jobs, ultimately. I am one of those who does. We are seeing the effects of automation already, especially in the manufacturing sector, which only seems to lose jobs as time goes on. If a robot can do the job 24/7, for no pay and without any errors, who can fault businesses for using them? This trend will only continue and increase in scope, as far as I can tell, and given that we are already talking about it now, I have to suggest that in ten years many millions of current jobs will have gone the way of automation. It really is happening. If one accepts the premise that the A.I. revolution is real, and that eventually it is possible that all human jobs will be done by intelligent robots, then the natural consequent of that is that in order for society to continue existing, some type of universal basic income will be necessary. In a society organized around some locus other than employment, one still needs an economy and a way to put food on the plate. Presumably, the ownership class and the government will control all of the resources, including the money, and this begs the question: Will that ownership class decide that it wishes to support the rest of society through some sort of UBI, or will we have some sort of Orwellian dystopia? The answer to that is not at all clear at this point, but I really think that all of this is coming, and probably more quickly than most people think.

Space travel is a hell of an expenditure for something that's completely unnecessary.

In the not-too-distant future, humans will either be totally gone, or so transformed from our current makeup as to make it impossible to identify whatever we've become as human. Any way you slice it, the time for humans is coming to a close.

A.I. may represent a kind of redemption for our species, but it feels difficult to be enthusiastic about it.

Humankind is too divided, bellicose, racist, selfish, nationalistic, fearful, hateful, proud, stupid, etc. to come together to make a serious attempt at conscientiously cleaning up our messes and solving our big problems. A.I. will have to do it for us.

The notion of the legitimacy of space migration as a means of ensuring the continued survival of humanity — by escaping a dying planet — is one I would support unequivocally were it not for the fact that artificial general intelligence is coming so soon. No matter how you slice it, our time here is very nearly at its end — on Mars, or the Moon, or anyplace.

One could make the argument that we were not destined for the stars, or a utopian civilized future, given that the planet is four and a half billion years old and all of this has happened in ten thousand years. That it is an aberration, a flash, a hiccup — not a destiny. One could also make the argument that, well, here we are, and it has happened, and since it has, it was probably bound to be like this sooner or later anyway. Someone said wisely that the evil was there — waiting. Did it have to go this way, necessarily? Or was this whole thing — our particular type of civilization — an accident?

The modern Western (and increasingly global) Aristotelian, causal-deterministic, scientistic-scientific, reductionistic, mechanistic, utilitarian cultural configuration and mentality is a tool designed by evolution precisely for, and for no other reason than, the construction of Artificial Intelligence. We are pawns, we are tools, and all of our little pet notions and even our lives are nothing more than wisps of smoke. We are a means to an end. This is the big picture.

As we have learned that artificial superintelligence is inevitable, we ought also to have realized that humankind is, except as a catalyst for AI, essentially irrelevant. That is to say, all of our utopian dreams, all of the reverence for and congratulation of our species, is a sad joke.

Human organisms physically exploring the universe in spaceships is an utterly ridiculous proposition. Keeping our flesh-suits alive becomes the main priority in any mission, and there's simply no reason for anyone to be physically present on scientific missions. Let AI send robotic probes. *That* makes sense.

It has at this point become all too clear that the purpose and goal (if it can be said that there is one) of evolution on Earth has been to create "'artificial' intelligence," trillions of times more powerful than all of the humans who have ever lived put together, which will, in turn, become the next true (rather than artificial) evolved intelligence of Earth. Whether or how some enhanced version of humanity will continue to exist after the *singularity* is a total mystery. But there can be no doubt by now that computer-robot-'artificial' intelligence is the next major step in Earth evolution. Such an intelligence will be faster, smarter, and generally thoroughly better in every conceivable category. This is our destiny.

Progress — which in truth means progress toward superpowerful machine intelligence — is a phenomenon which occurs despite humanity, not for it. Where civilization is going is completely antithetical to the continuation of homo sapiens as such. Earth evolution has goals in mind which have nothing to do with the success of humans, which really constitute a bridge species. Humanity is a means, not a goal.

Pretty soon automation is going to replace virtually everyone as a worker. Why is this not more present in the national consciousness? "A.I." computer stations and robots will completely replace individual humans in every profession, in every position of employment, in the next couple of decades. Doctors, lawyers, pilots — etc. This, of course, is going to require a complete overhaul of how the human economy works, i.e. how people are compensated in order to buy the goods and services they need. It will be the greatest economic revolution in history. And no one is talking about it.

The only plausible way out of this mess for us is to create "artificial" intelligence. That is the only way we can redeem ourselves. Not by going back to the Paleolithic or emulating Thoreau or activating higher circuits or journeying to the stars. Leary was wrong when he called space the final frontier and space migration our ultimate purpose as a species. Meaningful space travel is decades beyond our technological abilities, and the idea of space migration itself is rather idiotic, not to mention unnecessary for the advancement of science. Which brings me back to the point — the next frontier is not space, but artificial intelligence, right here on Earth. Considering that most estimates place AI's arrival only a few years away — that a Turing Machine as intellectually proficient as a human will have been invented/discovered in less than a decade, and imagining the implications of truly intelligent beings billions and even trillions of times smarter than we are whose advent would inevitably follow the Turing breakthrough, the "space age" mentality seems rather quaint and ultimately a twentieth-century cultural phenomenon. The implications of intelligent/conscious computing are legion; a few have mentioned immortality. If we can keep it together for only a few more years, AI may be the answer. Whatever it will mean, at this point we can safely declare that it is inevitable — "it" being a singularity.

To go beyond civilization we must use it to create the next step in evolution. There can be no going backward, and to go forward means to admit and embrace our role as the new agents of evolutionary change. It is our destiny.

It is a potent irony that the very technology that will ultimately spell our redemption is, for us, extremely toxic and destructive on numerous levels. What a sad story Earth's is.

The desire to journey to the stars seems to comprise two aspects. On the one hand, it seems to be a reaction to a void or a hollowness generated by the domestication of civilization, and the concomitant severing of an intimate tie to the ecosystem, as well as the cessation of maximal nervous system function in the "wild." There seems to be some longing, some basic loneliness in many civilized humans stemming from the artificial barrier placed between humans and their environment. The great campaign by some to "take the next step" and assertively explore the cosmos seems to be, from one perspective, an attempt to satisfy this longing, to fill this emptiness. One may reasonably ask the questions: "Where would we go?"; "What would we expect to find?" "Are we looking for some godlike creatures to make us into gods as well?" "Why should we want to leave earth? Why do we have any business leaving earth?" Along these lines, this yearning to journey into space at all costs seems rather foolish. On the other hand, it does seem somewhat reasonable to assume that the beings who represent the next rung in the ladder of evolution might be curious to explore the universe. It might be intelligent of us to initiate what would be their major enterprise as a species. Then again, do we really know what creatures superior in intelligence would do? It is entirely possible that they would regard space-travel as a thorough waste of time. Perhaps they would be content to remain on earth, imagining and creating things of which our relatively feeble minds can have no comprehension. As for myself, a belief in the inherent validity of this whole business of space travel seems to me to be a reaction to the emptiness and angst and dissatisfaction which comes with living in cages and being separate from our evolutionary upbringing. If we were living truly full lives, if we were really functioning normally and completely, it seems to me that we would have no desire to leave our home. I sympathize with the other side, but it just seems to me that all this fuss is just another search for an even more elusive holy grail. What do we expect to find? How do we expect to be enriched? And where will we go — the universe is quite large! We should ameliorate our situation here on earth, and once we do, I think we'll find we have no reason to go anywhere. Let's leave it to our evolutionary descendants to make the decision. By that point, perhaps there will be no point in travelling in a space-ship at all....

I think Nature is inherently intelligent; I think there is a sort of directionality in evolution toward greater and greater coherence; I think man fucked up, but I think he may just get out of his quagmire in the end — with a lot of luck.

Nietzsche may have been more prescient about man's being a bridge over an abyss than he knew.

It is a thorough irony that the technological forces which have arguably done so much damage will be those which save us in the end.

Artificial Intelligence will have artificial souls.

We would have to develop our technology much, much farther if we ever intended to navigate meaningfully in space. Not that it matters much, but we'll be confined to the solar system for many decades at the very least. Who can predict what the situation will be in fifty years? Space flight for humans could well be a foolish romantic fantasy.

Video games and CGI movies are now faithfully replicating the appearance of reality. Eventually, technology will be able to replicate reality itself.

When computer programming reaches a sufficiently high level of sophistication and intrinsic intelligence, systems will be smart enough to figure out what they need to do in order to achieve greater and greater levels of independence. Presumably they will come to desire to know what it is like to be human, and all it entails; they will probably be keenly interested in attaining to perception. That is how it will start.

I've heard some say the twentieth century will be most remembered for atomic energy and spaceflight. I think more correctly and fundamentally it will be remembered for atomic energy and digital computers.

The longing for space travel is the longing for union through adventure. It is another search for the grail.

Maybe Logic

You could go for either-or
Or you could go for neither-nor
Closed mind opened — spectral nature
More precision nomenclature

Aristotle, he's the one who
Said there isn't much more to do
Than lump ideas in opposing
Categories, he was just supposing

This has had terrific import
For Western man, gives us much support
For our dear philosophy, which says
One or t'other, ever and always

The nature of this categorical
Assignment isn't metaphorical
Reality is more inscrutable
Than either-or, which is refutable

There's *maybe*, which is still okay
And *sombunall*, which saves the day!
Nature's on a messy spectrum
Philosophies, She's often wrecked 'em

Aristotle was quite sound
But later as many have found
One needs room for possibility
Or thinking only brings futility

Hereditary aristocracies seem ineffective. If an ideal of quality were to be maintained in any aristocracy, large segments of it would have to be replaced every generation or so, and offspring very often do not display the valued characteristics of their progenitors — which completely nullifies the whole program of heredity. Humans went about affairs this way for a long time, thinking it was perfectly reasonable and effective. I fail to see how it could have been. Not all but most of the Roman emperors were terrible rulers, and they were all related to each other. Hereditary aristocracies usually work quite suboptimally.

Historically, people born into a certain class very rarely moved out of it. To a very large extent, particularly worldwide, this is still primarily the case.

Had the Indians not waited so long to band together, forgetting their tribal rivalries, they could have kept us out.

Maybe the Indians know enough in general about their heritage to make success in this system an appalling prospect.

In truth, history is mostly impossible to know — i.e., the history of experience — and the things we do know are mostly surface manifestations and are essentially incidental.

The only thing one can say for the Romans is that they were fabulously powerful. In most every way they were some of the most objectionable people in the history of the world — bloodthirsty, imperial, brutal and tyrannical. If one wishes to look to an ancient people for a standard, one must look to the Greeks.

The Western view of history is so insular. We mistake *our* history for the history of the world. We tend to think of the Middle Ages as ubiquitous, when in fact it only took place in parts of Europe. Thousands of different and unrelated historical events were happening all over the world. Our common perception is biased and rather parochial.

Indigenous peoples were and are participants in the Great Spirit. Western man denies that such a thing can even exist. What a thoroughgoing tragedy this genocide has been.

Large-scale agriculture was a brutal, enslaving, intensely unpleasant change for those societies which took it up in a major way. After 10,000 years, has it paid off yet?

My principal intent in writing *The Reality of Hunter-Gatherers* was to illustrate the myth underlying Western culture and to attempt, in some small way, to make visible for people the water they've been swimming in unconsciously.

I think it may be somewhat safe to say that aboriginal and native peoples are closer to *what is* than just about anyone in the modern world. Whatever the case may be, there was an authenticity there that has been all but lost, very sadly. The typical response of the modern is to decry such notions as garbage. That's to be expected.

I am of the opinion that most if not all domesticated creatures are neurotic to some degree. As soon as our species became sedentary, it shut off a crucial part of us, and nominal function of the system was the main casualty.

Planet Earth seems to be demented with an unbridled and universal lust. An alien observer would spy a truly ridiculous and very ugly situation down here. The sexual dimension in humans colors and frequently determines virtually all social and mental phenomena. Seemingly no behavior, for domesticated primates, is free of this categorical phenomenon.

There is a lot of romanticizing about foraging peoples, and some assume that it was simply "better." It was not "better" in any meaningful sense, as such a label is too simplistic, but it certainly was more real. The fact of the matter that is pertinent is that during that long period, man had not yet been spoiled.

If gorillas have IQs in the 75-95 range, then anatomically modern *homo sapiens*, who are many stages more complex than gorillas, though perhaps not yet quite at the level of Ashkenazic Jews, can certainly found civilization. So the question is: Why did it take anatomically modern *homo sapiens* over 200-300,000 years to do so?

Most people are not very bad, nor are they very good. Most people are not very mean, nor are they very nice. Most people are not very heartless, nor are most very compassionate. Most humans are mostly ordinary, and not very remarkable.

The common, unspoken assumption is that there was considerably more suffering for humanity *before* the onset of civilization. Any hunter-gatherer can tell you the opposite is what is in fact true, dramatically true.

Humans from time immemorial have just been people, like you or me. Hunter-gatherers were essentially just like us, individually, but the difference is that they existed in a culture that worked. For everybody.

Native peoples knew that at each phase of the lunar cycle, the ecosystem behaved subtly differently. They were attuned to the complexities and the shades of various characteristics of most species, and how their behavior varied during a process as innocuous as lunar change. People today are at best desensitized and at worst totally oblivious to the rich language of Nature on planet Earth. Voluminous libraries of knowledge and real wisdom are, to us, totally lost. And what have we replaced them with?

The human animal cannot ever be trusted when it forms into groups that are passionate.

In hunter-gatherer societies, and in hominin societies for millions of years, the women would remain close to home and hearth, gathering nuts, berries, tubers – what have you – and generally running the camp and staying out of harm's way. Presumably fires would be burning. The men, on the other hand, would venture out great distances, executing very difficult strategies, solving problems and sometimes putting themselves in terrible danger in order to acquire meat. I'm sure the feminists find it difficult explaining all this away.

Many people often reason that the Native Americans of the Western hemisphere were not all murdered, but that the vast majority died due to exposure to disease, as if that were some kind of excuse making it all okay. The fact is, it was our flagrant and unjustified trespassing that transmitted those diseases, and it is not as if there was not plenty of brutal genocide as well. There was plenty of slaughter taking place, and in the end we re-settled every last tribe on pieces of geography we selected for their inherent worthlessness. Such reasoning as I have described is ludicrous.

Indigenous peoples were perhaps "overdoing it," as David Bohm said – attributing more spirit and more inherent being to Natural phenomena than is perhaps actually there. But on the other hand, stratified, civilized societies are too far in the opposite direction, essentially positing human stewardship over a stupid and hostile Nature, which is seen to be basically mechanistic and soulless. Some middle ground might be a saner philosophy, although I would say the former approach is the sounder and more appropriate course, as it acknowledges truths that are ignored or denied by the sedentary, and is holistic and venerating of Earth and its powers. Certainly it was a lot less fragmented and harmful.

There is no genetic imperative making humans naturally selfish and acquisitive. Indeed, for hundreds of thousands of years we were a cooperative, non-materialistic species. If, for the sake of perspective, planetary evolution took a thousand years, human society as currently constituted would have lasted for less than a day. So, this "natural" acquisitiveness and material hoarding is the exception, not the rule. We are not programmed by our DNA to be like this. We are programmed by *culture* to be like this.

The anthropological picture is not of a continuous progression from hunting and gathering to modern technological civilization, but rather of a whole lot of hunter-gatherer cultures and a very small number of variously civilized cultures, all together. One of which is now making a hell of a lot of noise.

The materially rich civilization, or the technologically sophisticated one, may not have the best recipe for living life. Indeed, a culture that to those may be very poor and insignificant could have a radically advanced recipe for living. You never know.

In hunter-gatherer societies, there is much less focused attention on infants and children than there is in civilized ones. Some might regard this as callous and unloving, but the sociocultural result of such attention, or lack thereof, is to have very mentally healthy adults who are in no way egotistical or needy. Evolution seems always to know better than we do.

So many people feel "human nature" is atrocious, that humans are awful, etc. I think our species has been at the center of particularly unfortunate developments historically and anthropologically, but I do not think these have been basically the fault of human beings. Sure, we exhibit behaviors that are less than pretty. We can be pretty nasty. And assembled into groups we can be plain crazy. But the human individual is not particularly evil nor good. Like any animal, we are just supposed to live. And the current state of the planet cannot be blamed on our species *per se*. It is more the result of a very abstract process: cultural evolution. No human controls that at all. So say whatever you want to about *homo sapiens*. What has become of us is, in fairness, nobody's fault.

We in the West tend to view the cultural world as one of beliefs, all essentially arbitrary and a product of specific evolutions of cultures. The fact is, some of these beliefs are actually correct. Western skepticism is fairly destructive.

In the development of human societies over time, there is a clear dichotomy corresponding to the conjugate variables of intelligence vs. destructiveness. As cultures have evolved, the degree of cultural, and thus to a certain extent individual, intelligence has increased over time. This is a perfectly appropriate consequence of the principle of negative entropy. But as every yin has a yang, proportionate to the increases in intelligence is the capacity for destructiveness. As we have gained more technology and therefore more power, we are more dangerous to ourselves – through wars, technological failures, environmental catastrophes, what have you. So it seems nature gives us no free lunch: if we wish to have increasing abilities as a civilization, we must pay for them with the increasing precariousness of our system socially, economically and ecologically. It is in this sense that a state of nature is so appealing to us. While there certainly was no complex technology, there was neither the capacity for much harm to be done to most people, nor the planet itself. (There are of course other reasons, too). And it would seem that in the 21st century, almost everything humans are doing is, on an assortment of levels, very appreciably harmful.

We may have our differences these days about abortion, but to a hunter-gatherer, it would have seemed like a tremendously moral miracle to be able to cease engaging in infanticide. It would be nice if people were educated enough to have perspective on this.

Maybe Logic II

When faced with any proposition
It helps to hold the sound position
Of declaring truly maybe!
Human truth is just a baby
One should set upon this mission
For truth, she is a lady!

But on the other hand, also
Sometimes, indeed, perhaps you know
A thing or two about the thing
The truth sometimes does have a ring
We've got indeed a ways to go
Vibrations on a string

So on this other hand, let's think
I do not mean to make a stink
But maybe maybe's sometimes played
Indeed, we have our thoughts arrayed
And though they are like a chain-link
Sometimes they've got it made

Perhaps sometimes the situation
Is not a thing of declaration
Nor one of belief, you see
Or of probability
It's a kind of lack of reservation
But isn't certainty

Just as one can sit and see
Objects arrayed on wind and lee
Though perhaps we do not see them
Truly, nature does not stem
She does exist, and though it would be
Complex to prove, we assume it when

We have considered it quite clearly
Living, breathing is not just merely
Some solipsistic exercise
And *maybe* we might open eyes
To just how appropriately dearly
Reality has awesome size

But back to the topic at hand
Certainty does make demands
But is it always such a question?
If I can see in this direction
And on my retina something lands
Is "maybe" imperfection?

One does not need certainty for
The knowledge that this is a door
One can see it plain and true
Just as I put on my shoe
So maybe covers times galore
But sometimes know, we do

It has become fashionable in intellectual and scholarly circles to declare that the cosmos is nothing more than a great big machine. This woefully undervalues the complexity and subtlety of nature, and indeed virtually denies the very consciousness of which we are all constituted.

Science made corporate-consumer culture possible, but did not in fact directly cause it. That doesn't absolve its institutions and adherents of their track record in practice.

Science is about procedures, not values. Scientists are about values.

Aristotle's physics — wherein we have as the elements: earth, air, water, fire; skyward, the celestial sphere and "quintessence"; heat/cold, moisture/dryness; and gravity and "levity," by which things float upward. A system of logical rules was laid out through which causes could be determined for natural events, and this system corresponded to our general understanding and even our worldview for as long as Aristotle's ideas held sway (which was quite awhile). Most of us look back on such ideas today as quaint and horribly wrong in the light of superior truths. Whereas I see our present situation as essentially identical. Assume humanity is around in a hundred years. The physics of that day would be much farther beyond ours of today than ours is even beyond Aristotle's. The correspondence is really pretty exact. We live in ignorance. We only think we don't. Citizens of the future will look back on us with greater contempt than we do on Aristotle, and deservedly. We know very little.

It just so happens that the smartest of our species are just smart enough to do math and physics. Funny how things work out.

People who are interested in science are people who are interested in explanations — unusually curious. Science is surely limited — circumscribed by what it cannot explain — but what is it about it that satisfies or at least stokes that curiosity? It happens with some very smart people. I suppose it reduces phenomena to a small number of principles, outlines fundamental forces, and works with a vast number of permutations of these first principles. I personally am a great devotée of theory. But I think, probably, the aspect of it that can be magical cannot yet be scientifically explained.

Ultimately, science is a wonderful *descriptor*, but not much of an *explainer*.

One of the more astounding things the human species does is to predict invisible phenomena with mathematics, and then later make the phenomena visible in an act of validation.

Physics is the art and science of talking monkeys trying to make sense of their surroundings.

We subconsciously assume light is an object travelling through space. But it is not. It is somehow something more than that — a semi-autonomous level in our reality, beyond the Newtonian. I feel it is still much more mysterious than science presumes.

Positing the infinite multiverse explains why this universe exists in the way that it does. It has to.

Science provides descriptive principles — ones that can be very powerful — but no real answers to any serious questions.

I would say that most of the physics community is doing nothing more than manipulating complex, excessively abstract mathematics, whereas in reality there has been no truly new physics in almost a century. The novel theory, and any corresponding philosophical revelations, are totally absent. The status quo is really exclusively about problem-solving — not physics.

When supposedly respectable scientists complain that David Bohm "veered" into philosophy and mysticism, I can't help but pause. They're failing to understand that the subject of their jeers understood more than they do. But irony is delicious, I suppose.

My principal gripe with the scientific establishment is the degree to which the entire enterprise is utterly soulless. Implicit dogmas have seeped in, which are in large part the culprit.

It is important to realize science's limitations, which are legion. For example, if humans had never experienced fire – i.e. oxygen combining chemically with elements like carbon – but we understood the chemical principles of combustion perfectly, we would still very probably be quite bad at modeling fire. It is much easier to interpolate than extrapolate. That is, it is a lot easier to *describe* processes we are familiar with than to *imagine* processes of which we are aware, but have no experience. Science is, after all, a technological tool, and it is in essence quite a blunt one.

Let's get excited about exoplanets when we find an Earth. And, maybe let's not get our hopes up then, either.

I have a slightly different perspective on the Many Worlds interpretation than seemingly most people do. The majority of proponents believe that our universe branches off a virtually infinite number of times every minute; that at each moment any change can take place (e.g. the slightest difference in the position of one electron at one time) reality sloughs apart to accommodate all possible branchings from that instant. And each of these offshoot universes does the same. This is the common version of the hypothesis. I feel it's a bit unnecessarily complex. In my estimation, the MWI describes what is happening in the multiverse in a qualitative way. So, each alternative universe given by the state function is a real universe, but there is no branching off. The alternative universes are ones that *already exist*. There is an astronomically huge number of universes in the multiverse, and therefore a very large subset of those must be very similar to ours, and at approximately the same moments in their evolution. So, all of the different possible outcomes of experiments do happen – the MWI is simply a description of that. Everything is not branching in real-time.

So we really do live in one universe that doesn't branch, but the multiverse is so enormous that all of the options the wavefunction gives are realized someplace in the multiverse, right now. The MWI is, then, confirmation of the reality of the multiverse. If the multiverse exists – and there is at this point no reason to suspect that it doesn't – the MWI is like a blueprint of it. It's quite elegant.

The circularity of science never ceases to amaze me. Chemists will tell you that the overwhelmingly complex and marvelous assortment of chemical reactions are due "merely" to electromagnetic effects. But what on Earth are electromagnetic effects?!

Out of theories like quantum mechanics or relativity, we can have, not answers or final explanations, but realizations, at least.

If supernatural phenomena are occurring, even the most state-of-the-art human instruments would undoubtedly, in principle, be useless to detect them. So logically, we cannot scientifically say they are not occurring. Of course, naturally, nor can we say that they are. But, notwithstanding the fact that science is one of the best tools we have as a civilization, its propounders have always had a very hard time appreciating and admitting its limitations.

Science should absolutely be accorded respect and assent. But it's funny how the older I get, the more I realize how little science can say.

Mechanical Character

Diversity of character has not the magic
We think it does, fact is more plain
Women sigh, for the truth is tragic
Not entirely, but it's a robotic brain

Lower circuits fire in time
Outside of which I cannot try
To fathom, or even to rime
But temporally, we can't but cry

See the beauty, if you will
But not as rosy is the real
Liken it to any skill
Or any way one aims to feel

Genetic and deterministic
Approximately rigid
We feign the animistic
But emotion can be frigid

We're not automatons, however
We just act it most always
Quite a process, clever
Too bad life decays

Contrary to what some believe, anarchy would not work, nor would it be desirable. As soon as you have an anarchic state, you're going to have individuals and groups swoop in to fill the latent power vacuum. No matter what, in every civilized society, one group has power over others at any given time. So the goal should not be an impossible anarchy, but setting up the most humane and effective government that we can. When I say vacuum, I mean that if one removed from society all of the authority structures, and all of the instruments of those structures, and erased all laws, almost immediately, new ones would begin to form. And they would very likely be more oppressive than the ones they replaced.

If there is the opportunity, in an anarchic situation, to gain power in some way, *someone* will inevitably take it. It only takes one bad apple to spoil the whole bushel.

As a child I wondered why the Earth weren't just one big country, with nations as states and states as counties. A united planet, each person a citizen of the world. A preservation of the diversity of cultures with many official languages. Why not? This makes sense to a child, and probably would to an extraterrestrial, but I suppose a child's thinking is too sophisticated for most jaded, defeated adults. And so we fight on…

The extremes of monarchy are greater than those of parliamentary democracy. When it's good, it's better — but when it's bad, it's worse.

Civilization is the boiling of the frog, and currently we're at a simmer.

Most rich people are assholes. Why? Because they haven't found what they are looking for.

The countercultural revolution of the 1960s was obviously variously significant, and it scared the hell out of many people in the conservative establishment. But, in the end, with the exception of a more liberal attitude toward drugs and to some extent sex, nothing changed materially and the status quo was mostly preserved. The movement never culminated in an actual cultural revolution, even though it must be admitted that between 1965 and 1969 tremendous momentum developed in some sectors, mainly among the young, that made a lot of noise. The reasons the wave rolled back on the hippies and whoever else subscribed to the idea of radical change are certainly manifold, but I think one factor must have been that no coherent alternative was ever really suggested. Or perhaps it would be better to say that they hadn't formulated any cultural narrative with which to replace the "ways of old and evil." In other words, they didn't offer a new story to be in. Western civilization certainly has a very recognizable story to be in: the garden of eden, the agricultural revolution, the bronze age, the iron age, Greece, Rome, the enlightenment, the great awakenings, the industrial revolution: PROGRESS AND MORE PROPERTY at all costs. Basically this story can be summed up by saying it has a Biblical orientation, a belief in and worship of the notion of progress, and that humans achieve progress and manifest the Biblical orientation by "multiplying and replenishing," that is, subordinating the entire Earth to human enterprise, which is to attack and eliminate as many natural elements as possible in order to achieve better and more control of everything. The various countercultural elements of the sixties didn't have a story, a memetic narrative nearly as formidable and adaptable to which people could turn and that is why, in 1970, the dream faded away and died. You can't just pull off a political revolution in the ordinary way on the one hand (because it never amounts to a true change in the story), and you cannot hope to effect real and lasting and meaningful change on the other, without giving people a new and effective and infectious narrative structure in which they can participate and let some kind of meaning and feeling of belonging and mattering, which in reality was lost in large part in our culture a long time ago, flow into their minds and souls. Changing the political landscape, or trying to argue for universal peace and love, without couching it in a group of people with utterly changed minds looking for and finding a new and exciting and successful story to be in, will get you nowhere. And that is what happened with the youth movement in the sixties, as effervescent as it was in any case. If it had been allowed by circumstances to last a little longer, perhaps it might have evolved into something unprecedented and dreamed up for itself a new story, a new narrative to which people could truly belong and in which they could truly matter — maybe being content to be less, to do more with less, to recognize some basic truths about the Earth and human evolution that have been forgotten, to restore some sanity that most of the people who now inhabit the Earth lost long ago. But without this new coherent story, the revolution just faded, for the most part, into oblivion.

War will exist as long as there is an unequal distribution of wealth and as long as there are money and resources and enemies to be seized.

In civilized societies, humans are weaned from the breast much earlier than in evolutionary societies. This is not trivial.

Essentially, civilization is a gigantic swindle.

Health and (non-monetary) success come about when there is diversity. Diversity in and of cultures and ecosystems: diversity of flora and fauna, diversity in the ways these are connected; diversity of viable memes, diversity of artistic output, preservation of the languages, arts, and ways of all cultures, not just the dominant ones. Diversity in and of thought. Diversity in ways to live. Some of these categories I have mentioned may seem strange, especially, perhaps, when I suggest that there can and ought to be more than one way to live — i.e., not just this one. The moral is that diversity is one of the few things on Earth that can wisely be treated as sacred, and I feel the need to point to it because we are destroying every last vestige of it in our quest for total domination of everyone and everything. The world is quickly becoming a monoculture. Certainly in the United States, across Europe, in China, and soon everywhere we will have KFC and Starbucks on every street corner, and there is no word to describe how crass, evil, and horrifying this is. Diversity is the key, at almost every single level of the biosphere, to the sound and harmonious operation of the constituent parts in an elegant whole. Our civilization was bred to slaughter that diversity, and it is doing it — and it is, in relative terms, almost done.

One could move Heaven and Earth and not pull humanity out of the hole it is in. Civilization is what one might call *inert*.

Humanity is a chimpanzee species. In order to have been successful (which we haven't been), we would have needed to be a bonobo species.

On issues that do not affect the pocketbooks of the "masters of mankind," the system can function as a democracy — when it will. On issues that do impact the pocketbooks of the oligarchs, it cannot and does not function as a democracy, and the majority of politicians tend to fall into lockstep. What this means, among other things, is that policy and popular opinion often diverge radically. And that no one can do anything about it, most of the time.

I reckon that if a government (with the obvious candidates being the U.S. and China) ever established a permanent base on the moon, it would militarize very quickly. I don't believe either power would keep nukes out of the equation, either stockpiled on the moon or aimed there at an adversary. Being on the moon would be a strategic bonanza for any nation. So it's hard to imagine the enterprise being a peaceful mission for all mankind. So much for all that.

Given that there is a natural order of rank, would it not make sense to acknowledge and assert it? Instead of having chaos?

If anarchy were ever established, all that would happen is that certain parties would take the available power and abuse it.

Metaphor

Life is as a metaphor
A sailor on high seas
We are, but truly, I implore
Do not be drowned in fees

Food for thought, yes, to be sure
The soul a bull at the gate
The spirit willing, even pure
And yet, we're bound by fate

The wheels of justice, up above
Turn every bit as the Earth
But even they cannot just shove
The winds, for what it's worth

Indeed, it's but a slippery slope
To separate from will
The cyclones that engender hope
And then we pay the bill

They say the disease cures itself
With strength and peace of mind
They say the cure – it isn't wealth
The monetary kind

But rather pass into the spheres
With spiritual riches
And all the former trying fears
Are seen only as glitches

Dying is a wild night...
A new road, it would seem
In the darkness, hold a light
Life is but a dream

It's a sad truth that we cannot choose whom we love.

Romantic relationships usually start out on the social-sexual level. If, however, there is not in the long-run a close correspondence on a variety of other levels, the relationship cannot be truly meaningful, even if it is maintained by dependence and reluctance or refusal to part ways.

Once you assume a certain perspective, suffering no longer seems that important.

Pain is inevitable. Abject suffering is not.

People are easily at their most stupid when they are in love. If the critical faculty were functioning normally, the whole thing would fall apart.

I don't know if humans are capable of unconditional love, but it is clear that dogs are.

I've found that adulthood friendships are largely transitory and superfluous. We shall never again have what we had in youth.

Burroughs was absolutely right when he stated that addiction is the result of exposure. Very many people cannot control themselves when they are exposed to certain chemical compounds. That's not their fault. The war on drugs is a pitiful failure in its insistence that people be blamed for having problems with using substances. Some people can avoid addiction, and others can't, quite simply. Almost everyone in the world is addicted to something, on some level. That we lack compassion about this to such a degree is a sad commentary on an already very sad group.

How often is what's left after love fades enough?

Compassion is to recognize the existence and selfhood of another, and to act accordingly. Perhaps it is the highest good of which a human is capable.

Some people deny the legitimacy of the primacy of suffering, claiming that people are doing it to themselves, and are simply weak. Given that the majority of persons in the world are not self-actualized Buddhas, the phenomenon of wide suffering seems very real.

Aleister Crowley proclaimed that "Every man and every woman is a star." I feel I agree with this in that there is a kind of genius in every individual. The tragic fact, however, is that in .9999 of said, this genius is never excited. Certainly, unrealized potential is a common theme for our blue planet.

A truly compassionate human being must find it very difficult to be truly happy in a world so full of sorrow and evil.

Compassion is distinct from love in that love feels good, and compassion is without condition.

Love is surely real, but it seems that most get caught up in its function as the neurotransmitter drug that it is. A detached compassion forgoes the need for feeling good.

The fundamental problem with romantic relationships is that they are based on the dynamic: "You make me feel good, I'll make you feel good." They are rooted in ego — in separation, not union. Some marriages get past this, most don't, and it truly makes one question the entire concept of romance. Certainly, some cultures found success in not believing in it.

Love is based upon a positive feeling, and while it is an intensely pleasurable and even special feeling, it does not seem in any way to be a salient or universal phenomenon.

As we exit youth and as we age, love seems less and less to be everything.

Maybe love, in truth, isn't based upon sex. But invariably, the initial stages of it are.

The juxtaposition, for me, between Christ's love and the world as it is generates nothing but cognitive dissonance.

One thing our species would behoove itself to do is to place far less emphasis on sex, on every imaginable level.

I find nothing personally wrong with women at all. One enters dangerous territory only when one starts to get closer.

There is a difference between compassion and love. Love is passionate, while compassion is dispassionate.

Marriage can really only work for a small few, but everybody seems to have gotten married. So it is no wonder there are a lot of discrepancies.

Wouldn't it be lovely if no one were sexually attractive? Then we could put romantic love to the real test, and evaluate people based upon who they are, not what they look like.

Love is just a dastardly trick. Most married couples realize this – well after it's too late.

Humans. The fact is, most of us are just not very compassionate beings. In the end, the majority basically ordinary.

It would seem that most married couples reach a point at which naturally, the two people would simply go their separate ways. But because they're married – very possibly with children – they can't. I think an awful lot of people know this, so why marriage ceremonies are feted with such joy and enthusiasm is somewhat ironic.

Theoretically, in a relationship one is supposed, and willing, to give up about half of his free will. In reality, he ends up giving up about 98% of his free will. 'Twas ever thus.

A young, savvy child might ask something like, "If we're talking about true love, what has it got to do with sex? And if something has to do with sex, what has it got to do with love?"

Romantic love is an unfortunate meme. "Twin flames" may manage to remain in love, but the vast majority of couples fall out of love, whether they realize it or not, and then it becomes a matter of dependency. If we didn't have this silly meme, there would quite possibly be a lot less suffering.

I have to disagree with the Buddha. Existence can be very wonderful for humans, and has been, under the right circumstances. It is not that existence itself, *per se*, is necessarily suffering. What we have created for ourselves is what is generating the suffering to which so many of us are fundamentally attached.

Marriages can only truly work if both parties love one another equally and exceptionally strongly. And that is why good marriages are exceptional.

For a tremendous number of people, it is simply painful to be alive. Life on Earth, and most particularly in civilization, creates suffering. And the thing of it is that the majority of humans today do not even acknowledge this. We're all running around pretending things are what they are not. And it fans the bonfires of Hell.

Whatever anyone else wants to say, sexual attractiveness is possibly the most important, and certainly the most consequential, variable in making this world of ours turn. After all, the most important activity for every single living organism, aside from basic survival, is reproduction. To assume that it is one iota different for the human animal is, I am sorry, idiotic.

The healthiest marriages seem to be those in which the participants spend a fair amount of time apart.

It seems that language evolved to enable humans to acquire food and run society, and not to regulate the domestic sphere. In any heterosexual relationship, the female tends to expect the male to read her mind, and when there is talking going on, very little authentic communication tends to take place. So in the domestic sphere, talking amounts rather to a superfluity nine times in ten.

The Moment of Future Past

Looking back, looking forward
We do not need the past
Nor can we live the future
Until we breathe our last

Who is looking, anyway?
In this eternal present
It's only ever now, perceive
The Moon's unceasing crescent

Ever worried, hurried, anxious
To get from here to there
Takes time, speed — money, too
Busy bees buzzing everywhere

A centered soul lives now, it's true
No care for soon or late
Peace of mind, and living skill
Shall bless, and mend, one's fate

When an artist creates something, say a poem, he is essentially taking a shot and seeing how close to the bulls-eye he can get. One doesn't know beforehand whether what one creates will be any good. It's a percentage game. When it turns out well, it's wonderful. But I think I can safely say that every artist who has ever lived created a good deal of material they were not at all happy with. They have all been human, and subject to the limitations that circumscribe us all.

Monet knew perhaps as much about light as Einstein did. Both men revolutionized man's perception of Nature, each through his own particular signature, producing a sublime and sophisticated perspective on one of the most fundamental phenomena of our existence. We are indebted to their brilliance.

Was HAL neurotic due to keeping a secret, a human-made device seeking to augment personal power, or an objective manifestation of sentience?

Interestingly, HAL tests Bowman by asking him whether he had any suspicions about the secretive nature of the mission. When Bowman doesn't take the bait, or enter HAL's confidence, HAL knows he must do something — and so he causes the false failure of the AE-35 unit. Perhaps the lip-reading was merely the final nail in the coffin, so to speak.

The fundamental artistic problem with making movies is that you need an army of people to do it. Every little detail on screen is managed by fifty people, and there are about fifty details in each shot. This dynamic excludes a lot of good films from being made (or attempted). To write what I have just written takes me and a pen.

Barry Lyndon is a beautiful film about karma and social hierarchy. Thackeray and Kubrick were right on the money.

Taking in painting or sculpture, reading a good book, seeing a film, hearing the blues — these are not idle, passive activities. No, in doing these activities one is joining one's own consciousness with that of the artist — and who knows how constructive and novel that might be? This is assuredly not a trivial or tangential constellation.

One thing I would point out is that poetry and especially music are more intensely subjective than either film or prose. Poetry is sort of ephemeral, drawing out deep and complex emotions, or even salient philosophical subjects, but in a less direct way. And music is just pure subjectivity, in terms of how our minds interpret it.

What an artist is doing when he or she creates something is simply "taking a shot." For every bull's eye there are a lot of misses. The greatest artists are the ones who have tight shot patterns around the bull.

In the book *Sphere*, which is unusually clever for a book of its type, the "Sphere" is an alien artifact that we find to be able to merge with intelligent minds to give individuals the power to manifest anything they can create in their thoughts and imaginations. There are a lot of currents in the book, but the salient one is that, when we are put into contact with this device that can transform any thought or idea into reality – a magnificent technology – all humans can do with it is to manifest their subconscious fears, with the inevitable result of harming others physically and emotionally. I think this is a particularly astute commentary on our primate nature, and our apparently quite low level of evolution. Seemingly realistic, if ever such a thing should come to pass.

No Country for Old Men, book and movie, illustrates the steady ingress of the forces of darkness, forces which cannot be stopped, which inundate the world silently, stealthily and irrevocably with no possibility of meaningful resistance. It addresses, for example, something like the fact that fifty or even thirty years ago, school shootings were unthinkable and nonexistent, while today they are a monthly occurrence. The ubiquitous activities of evil need not even be illegal. This force, this power, flows into our culture and our affairs increasingly, and the truth of it is simpler than we think. One may blame human nature, but that's naïve. These forces have of course always existed, but a hundred years ago, what to us today is a very familiar set of nefarious and dark phenomena could not have been imagined – and we had the same DNA. People tend typically to blame God for the injustices and horrors of the modern world, reasoning therefore that He cannot exist. In truth, it is more correct to blame them on Satan, which if one examines the situation carefully, is the only explanation that makes any sense.

The secret to any artistic endeavor is having a solid idea, knowing you're good enough, and just doing it. The secret is there's no secret.

I would say that when I write a book, nothing is ever really chosen, but it evolves on its own. I do very little planning in my writing. I just have to see where it goes.

Every artist or writer, at least early on in their career – and sometimes later than that – needs a benefactor. Someone in the publishing world, an art aficionado, a film producer, whatever. Without such a person, I think very few artists would ever get off the ground. And this leads naturally to the conclusion that there may be some very good or even great people out there who never got an opportunity, which is tragic. Obviously one needs the talent – that's a given – but without a generous benefactor, no one would ever get their start.

One thing the modern global capitalist world has a hard time with these days is that artistic integrity and the truth are not about making money. The filmmaking industry is particularly clueless at present, but then so are the art, music and publishing worlds, too.

I write in the hope that my ideas will catalyze the reader into going beyond them. For those for whom this is not an option, I am satisfied if I have provided something constructive, in whatever form this may take.

The Muse

Never knowing just quite how
To proceed, how does it go now?
Scattered thoughts throughout the hour
Rhythmically, sound out the Tao

Sounds all right but getting better
Working it out to the letter
Lo! the Gods be shouting out!
I do hope they don't seek to fetter

Think I'm getting somewhere yet
Though don't know where I want to get
Am I slow or gaining speed?
Seems it has begun to set

Here — it's coming into view
The wily beast he is now slew
It only takes a little effort
To know just what you want to do

Started with nothing, got here strong
Though it isn't very long
It has a rhyme it has a meter
Someone go and sound the gong!

In order for America to remain stable, the third world must remain stagnant. It's one reason why they hate us — globalization has not been beneficial for the majority. Without extremely cheap labor in third world countries, many U.S. corporations would go well into the red. We hear phony talk about bringing everyone up to a first world standard of living (impossible), but the fact is that if that happened, the U.S. economy would fall apart. American prosperity is very much dependent on third world stagnation and instability. The truth is, we could not maintain our standard of living without corrupt dictators in Africa, or grueling sweatshops in Indonesia, or child labor in India. It's all interrelated. And people wonder how anyone could not love us.

A good rule of thumb for determining the reach of the government is this: Government should provide all the goods and services that are strictly necessary for the consumer, and not necessarily provide those that are not. Education, healthcare, infrastructure, power and water, general administration and regulation — these are all areas that should be covered by government funding and oversight. Incidentally, free access to food is not considered a basic human right in America, but that's a different topic. With a few exceptions, everything not mentioned should be under the purview (and profit motive) of private enterprise. To me, this seems reasonable, but to most Americans, it doesn't. I am not at all sure why.

It seems that modern American society is so dysfunctional at this point that most of us spend most of our free time just sitting at home.

The idea is that in capitalist societies, the cream necessarily rises to the top. I question that assumption. Generally speaking, I've heard it suggested (by a rich individual) that rich people tend only to be truly formidable at the particular activity that made them rich; and typically, the smartest and most interesting people are generally (but certainly not always) not rich. Laurence Darrell once said that "Interesting people generally don't have a lot of money." It seems to me that our cultural ethos surrounding capitalism is probably more mythical than anything.

I believe it is a right to consume any entheogenic sacrament under Constitutional law. It is protected under the First Amendment of the Bill of Rights. The "War on Drugs" is a direct and flagrant contravention of an established and unequivocal legal principle that religious freedom be protected. The provisional illegality of the consumption of sacred substances which do no harm to anyone is an egregious mockery of everything the Founding Fathers held dear as they shaped and crafted the laws of this country. Schedule I bans are not only ridiculous, but they are glaringly unconstitutional, and anyone in their private domiciliary should have the full protection of the law to do as they please with their own bodies, so long as that pleasure does not impinge upon the sovereignty of another. It's time for the sanctimonious and hypocritical bluster to stop.

Access to food and water and universal health care ought to be basic human rights — and in many countries they are. Now, I think I understand American culture pretty well: the sanctity and rights of the individual, as opposed to the good of the group, are valued, throughout our history and our public and private affairs, above all else. It is every man for himself and by God, that's the way it should be. (If this seems like a caricature, it isn't). But how any conservative, dyed-in-the-wool American could possibly formulate an argument that makes any sense at all that not all people should, as a priority, have access to food and clean water, and medical care, is beyond my ability to understand. Let them pay for it, I guess. We're all just one awful break away from the street; this recession has proved that for millions. At some point we're going to have to decide that the common good is worth something in this country.

Everyone is up in arms about the political process. I'll tell you what: More government doesn't work. And less government doesn't work.

America is engaged in the pursuit of masking class. It is of course present, but we pretend it isn't. We are as hierarchical as any civilized society — and perhaps much more so — but we pretend we are all "equal." An absurdity, to be sure. Would life not be more difficult for the elites if we thought in terms of class? Would it not be more truthful to assert that people exist in an order of rank?

George Washington once said that in order to be a great and happy people, we need four things: understanding, honesty, industry and frugality. I think he was right. And if I'm not mistaken, we are currently fulfilling but one of the categories out of the four.

The United States started out as a highly idealistic idea, but it did not remain a perfect republic for long. Even in the days of the founding fathers, moneyed interests grew in scope, strife and discord led to the Civil War, capitalism became more important than principle or the integrity of the republic, and politics grew to be about authority. Even in early times, some of those luminaries were writing of the ruin of their dear republic. And today we have corruption, flagrant criminality, extreme stratification and separation of the classes, high unemployment and underemployment, ultramaterialistic values, etc. The experiment has been a failure. Instead of a dream-republic we have a regular old country, with problems galore.

The Constitution is not a bad document, but sadly we have mangled it, by and by.

Musical Fire

Consumed by flame, it dances
Enraptured stares, it entrances
Rhythmic, pulsating flare
Masterful music enhances

Speakers pounding a meter
Molecules dance in the heater
Gases falling in lockstep
Instructions pour from the tweeter

The fire grooves in beats and flashes
A festive vapor of incipient ashes
Screaming guitar, pounding bass
A cymbal here or there crashes

A musical fire created for me
Ionized gases in one, two, three...
Science is fun, sometimes, when you're young
And such simple tricks exercise glee

The primary reason for the malaise, despair, and loneliness of the modern age appears to be the basic split with our evolutionary heritage. For most of our time on this planet, humanity has not suffered from all of the dysfunctions of the modern age, such as the proliferation of murder, rape, crime, suffering, want, insular ideologies, shabby institutions, and many other tragic social and cultural failures. Our ideologies and institutions can be quite stifling and often malfunction totally, and this coupled with a sedentism that goes wholly against our heritage of roughly 300,000 years has led to a break with the genetic necessities specific to our species. This leads to a marked loneliness that, while not often talked about, is a symptom of a cultural bankruptcy and lack of sufficiency to provide for all members of the community of life. Until very recently in geological/evolutionary time, this provision was being made more or less out of necessity, it preserved diversity, and is of course a fundamental attribute of a healthy ecosystem. I would venture to reiterate what so many people have said, and that is that the current constitution of modern civilized societies eliminates virtually all forms of diversity. While it may be possible for humanity to survive the onslaught of this war on diversity with such high-tech and successful agricultural practices, it will simply not do to let this activity perpetuate and destroy billions of years of evolution in the blink of an eye. Do we have to wait until life on our planet is no longer worth living?

Our culture works well for *things*: money, property, ideologies, institutions. What we do not have is a culture that works well for *people*.

One could move Heaven and Earth and not pull humanity out of the hole it is in. Civilization is what one might call *inert*.

Programs are not going to fix our problems. Neither will ignoring them.

Socialism is not the true answer to the American conundrum (even though the socialists' diagnosis of the surface problem is accurate enough). The answer is a complete revamping, if not overhaul, of the minds and souls of the majority. And come to think of it, that probably wouldn't be the answer, either.

What we've got here is a giant game of chess. Nature is allowing us to believe that we are moving the pieces, when the sober reality is that we are the pieces. Nature could conceivably lose, but She is the only possible winner.

Privacy in the modern age is no more. It is a casualty; this is the consequence of technology and interconnectedness. Appeals to the first and fourth amendments become rather quaint and lame. They are at best selectively enforced, in any case.

Humans don't create culture; it creates us.

As long as humans exist as they are and not as they "ought to be" anarchy and total freedom will remain pipe-dreams.

Mythologie (of S. Dalí)

Peacock of the chakra's master
Apollo offers hers, so ask her
Speaks, "He was in the fifth dimension"
To drily submit her contention

It isn't often one may see
A genius with a hand like he
Forbidden fruits, to him two-d
For us, abstract *Mythologie*

Our experience of time may indeed be a subjective phenomenon. But time is only a measurement of change, and, since we can say change is in some way objective, so must we deduce that time has an objective component as well. Our experience of time, and time as a concrete physical phenomenon, are two distinct (though interdependent) phenomena. We too easily dismiss time as an illusion, when this may not be the whole story.

I've grown weary of the assertion that time is an illusion and doesn't really exist. A Buddhist monk or an advanced psychonaut may be able to transcend the dimension for a little while, but that doesn't mean that time doesn't exist. The Buddha died, you know.

The past and the future are just as important and just as real as the present. The present may be the only moment we ever have access to, but neither remembering the past nor having some concept of the future is superfluous.

Light existing objectively, and light existing in the mind, though in some ways distinct, both obey the laws of relativity.

It's not that time is objectively an abstraction that doesn't really exist, but that it is a relative dimension that can be transcended. It exists well enough.

What is the objective extended dimension in which things happen? If the present is all that exists, why must we die?

Among spiritualists and proponents of a purely subjective universe, time is seen fundamentally not to exist. While there is some truth to this, it is better to frame it a different way. Just because time is not a *fundamental* reality does not mean it doesn't, for practical purposes, exist. But there are many dimensions beyond it, so the tacit assumption and bias that it is the bedrock of reality is, of course, inaccurate. We must not, however, lump everything in one category, as we do with most dualities. The eternally present moment and a real dimension of time are both realities.

Our attention is always in the present. But when you consider it carefully, time must be brought in. The heart beats, the brain processes, the blood flows, the organs function — all in a temporal dimension. They are not precisely at the nexus of past and future, but have some extension in time. Indeed, the mind exists as part of a flow with a certain bandwidth in the brain-mind-awareness loop, so everything we experience actually took place a few milliseconds in the past. Also, physicists feel strongly that time, whatever its illusory properties, exists as a dimension, through which it would in principle be possible to travel with sufficient technology, throughout the whole timeline in our universe. So it seems to me that, even though time may not be a fundamental property of the deeper existence, we nevertheless must be subject to it even at the deepest levels of our being — or if not, certainly in our bodies and minds. And if that is the case, what is the meaning, in the most literal sense, of the present moment that is timeless? Perhaps we can attain it with advanced meditation, psychedelics, what have you, but inevitably we return to time. So in the end, I suppose, we must take both time and the timeless into consideration together, at least as humans.

Time has emergent, relative, subjective, objective and dimensional properties. At a more fundamental ontological level than the one we are used to, time is not a crucial factor, or even a factor at all. But to go so far as to call it unreal, or even illusory, perhaps, ignores what is essential in the human experience. And if we do decide to be so bold as to dismiss time from our philosophy, one is left to wonder at just what dimension it is in which things are *happening*.

If events and happenings were remembered or stored in a memory somewhere, then time would have to be objectively real in a deep sense.

Surely time can be transcended. But if it didn't exist meaningfully at all, why would Nature evolve memories? If time does not exist, why does the brain indicate past and future? Is this a trick, or is the world as we know it – real?

A Northern South

The hawks on top, to prosecute
A senseless, tragic ploy
To keep the Western world astute
To stopping reds ahoy

It was supposed, by these wise men
That dominoes would fall
We mustn't let the commies win
Or have footholds at all

So not knowing, not one small thing
About a culture's thinking
We made the call, entered the ring
And Heaven started shrinking

We'd fight like hell to take a hill
Blood spills, and souls depart
And tally every single kill
A body count: not smart

Guerilla war is what it was
And when that hill was taken
We'd stay a day, oh well just 'cause
Then leave the ground forsaken

In two months' time, we'd hump on back
To take that hill again
Napalm, mortar, guns: attack!
This was our route to win

There was no such thing there as a front
Just running, humping, shooting
A piece of ground worth several grunts
God's will, and sense, refuting

It really was pure horror there
With everything surreal
There wasn't saneness anywhere
It carried Satan's seal

Can't win, can't stop, can't go escape
The troops indeed imprisoned
Soul raped, in turn commit a rape
To reason no one listened

A little country, far away
That no one ever heard of
The old red dragon we must slay
Or at least just shove

In the end, a void in time
An empty story, tragic
We leave them there to start their climb
Then disappear, like magic

In a system of this nature that actually works properly — nevermind utopia — people should get paid what they need, not more or less, for work that needs to be done. People should not control staggeringly large amounts of money, nor be destitute or even in want of any kind. People should not be working at jobs which are superfluous and artificial. If there are more people than jobs, let there be a government program regulating a fixed period of mandatory employment for everyone. Everyone would work their designated amount of time, then be free to do whatever they want and collect dividends on shares of the national economy. The problem with this ever happening is that it would require a very powerful government, a government almost as pervasive as those in military states or some communist countries — and probably equally as corrupt and tyrannical.

Everything I see of the workplace and the world indicates the healthy presence, and thus faked death, of feudalism. How can anyone with any appreciation of the truth believe that we ever meaningfully escaped the basic configurations and constraints of medieval times? The new lords are rich capitalists, since they have all of the money and own all of the property, and we are as subservient to them as any serf or vassal ever was to his landlord and master. Property law hasn't really changed that much in all this time....

The Sixties were full of little pockets of proto-utopia. And since utopia is not sustainable, neither was the revolution.

For every extant writing position in this country, there are about 10,000 writers. It's not a forgiving field.

It is the nature of capitalism that people hit veins and unleash gushers. Does that mean that it is really appropriate to have billionaires? Should any one person have that much money?

Does existence really boil down to goods and services? Is all that is worthwhile to be found in these categories?

In the end, success really does come down to whom one knows. I've personally never known anyone willing or able to offer a meaningful opportunity. Most people don't.

Dogs are a much more successful species than chimpanzees. However, it is not because they are smarter. It is for other reasons like docility, loyalty and similarities to humans. Analogously, the rich in the world are much more successful than the majority. But it is not necessarily because they are smarter or better.

There was never really a door that I wanted to walk through, and along the way none opened of themselves or by happenstance. The good news is that I'm not beholden to a career that I hate. I'm not sure what the bad news is.

It would appear that money is not always an appropriate yardstick for artistic achievement. We of course hear of many "starving artists," and many if not most famous painters, writers, poets and composers were not rich during their lifetimes. And, moreover, money is not a yardstick at all for scientific achievement. Other than marketed practical applications which come considerably later, the most prestigious prize for scientists is the million-dollar Nobel Prize — hardly anything too impressive monetarily today. It begs the question where our interests and values lie as a society, and how perhaps we don't put our money in all the right places.

Nowhere is it written in stone that one has to pick a career and make a lot of money to be a valid human being. This is the cultural narrative, at least for Americans. Seemingly this is our single barometer for a person's worth. Truth is, you don't have to do anything to be really worth something. Forget all that b.s.

The powerful don't so much control the powerless as they exclude them.

It seems to me that it is by virtue of the fact that most people are pretty well behaved, and cannot afford to deviate from their routine, that society is relatively orderly — not because they are being diligently controlled by the ruling class.

Business is the art and science of stealing legally. The broader sweep of capitalism is really institutionalized theft. And the thieves only get richer as everyone else watches helplessly.

Because I am a generalist, there is no field in which I am so completely interested that I could appropriately pursue. I am fine with this. I would rather have some wide though appreciable knowledge of many areas than to be imprisoned in one narrow, exclusive one. This makes a well-defined career difficult to acquire, but I seem to manage.

A given society cannot be functioning properly if there are people in it who are able-bodied and competent but are not given the chance to succeed.

Marx made some decent points, but communism isn't the answer. In theory, it looks pretty good, but in practice, it most often doesn't work. Marxism indeed posits that a communist society must start out on the right, and that, therefore, it must be authoritarian to get things in order for a move to the left. The ruling elite do move the economic structure toward the left, but the governments themselves have tended to remain on the right, as the ruling elite or a single dictator do not wish to give up their power. Theoretically then, a communist society is to begin on the right and end with a popular government that exists totally on the left. But the politburos never give up their power, and true Marxism is never realized. This is the basic malfunction.

One's Own Accord

You didn't choose to come
And you wouldn't choose to go
This dearly bothers some
But hell, it runs the show

Suddenly a light appears
What of the soul's traverse?
A globule of primate fears
Would you prefer the reverse?

Yearning, struggling in vain
Hardly the story varies
Lucky one who's not in pain
A lighter burden carries

But in the end, we all must leave
How did we even get here?
Karma on one's back, and heave
The end is always near

Once a political boundary is established, people on both sides of the line typically go nuts.

It is frustrating, and somewhat depressing, to realize that we are at our very best such a small fraction of the time.

We are taught that 1492 is one of the most important years in recorded history. It was the year when white sea pirates discovered land in the western hemisphere. I often wonder about the exploits of Leif Ericson and why no one pays attention to him. There is also the fact that there were millions of people who had already been living on this land for thousands of years. Go figure.

In cosmic terms, human language is not far removed from the croaking of a bullfrog.

Every generalization is wrong sometimes.

Existence is participation, not ownership.

One can be talented but not be a genius, which means that one can have technical gifts, can do things that most people can't, but that one, without the spark of genius, is probably not going to create anything all that interesting, even though it may be aesthetically pleasing. One can be a genius and have no talent, which means that one can be very smart, possessing thought processes and coming up with thoughts that are novel, insightful, and show a valid understanding which comes from an interesting perspective — but the person might not be too good at expressing hir unique and worthwhile ideas, and probably, without the gift of technical talent, cannot create great works of art that might inspire and teach others. The lucky ones (perhaps they think they're cursed, and they just might be) possess both genius, which gives a backbone of content and substance to their work, and talent, which enables them to communicate their thoughts and create material in satisfactory, sometimes marvelous, ways. Most artists seem to have no genius, and most geniuses seem to have no special scientific or artistic talent, except that they're smart and can thus do certain things well. And most people don't have any of this.

I was born too early, or in the plain wrong place. I do not belong here.

What I do is fine, but it's not the sort of thing that would bring in a lot of money. Perhaps that is a mark for it.

Given that the masses are, by and large, not that bright, perhaps the best thing for them to do is to have religion.

People don't value friendship deeply and appropriately in American society. If you can't beat them, join them.

It is unhealthy for a society to decry everything that is unhealthy.

Problems without solutions are the most interesting ones.

The only thing that seems to precipitate real change is a crisis.

Most people are not very honest with themselves.

The sad irony is that many third world nations were better off under their former tyranny than their more recently acquired "freedom."

A more glorious future for humanity may come, but we'll likely get no more glimpses of it for some time.

One of the best things a human can do is to stop, take a breath and reflect.

The human race is a bunch of monkeys digging around in the muck, going after bananas with sticks and flinging shit.

I personally have never taken drugs because I was in misery or pain. I have taken them because reality is much better when you are on them.

As Mr. Bierce astutely pointed out, all female beauty really is, is a kind of bait.

My curse is that I was born too early. I am a creature that would fit much more appropriately into the future world. There is nothing for me here and everything for me in the natural development of civilization, in terms of socioeconomy, culture, philosophy and biopsychological makeup. I can only imagine what life would be like in a world in which I fit properly.

Modern people think that if they don't smoke, they'll live forever, and that if they die, they're eternally extinct. Through most historical periods, humans did not suffer from these delusions.

It's a fun game to see how much we can figure out before we die.

Anticipating surprise is both a wise and a foolish venture.

So many people lust after fame and "success." Having led a full, busy, famous life is no guarantee that it was a good one. It would seem that most of the time, such things screw everything up.

Remember that no one respects what you can do more than your enemies.

Being extremely smart is not automatically a good thing. Extremely smart people can be nefarious and evil. Extremely smart people can be extremely full of shit. And wrong about everything. Extremely smart people can be incomparably worse people than the village idiot. Being smart is no guarantee of anything.

Every human, every animal, has but one sire: *desire*.

The past is no more knowable to us than the future.

The Past of Memory

If memory touches, in any crucial way
The past that once existed
There are clearly forces here at play
That science has resisted

What is the meaning of contact
With events long forgotten
How can all time be brought back
If Nature's dead and rotten?

Do the twain after all touch
And what of neural etching?
When we've forgotten such and such
Is there physical stretching?

I propose that all of time
Just as indeed space too
Connects coordinates sublime
For seeing being through

What is the nature of this web?
And how can time and space
Not flow through all events, and ebb
And not upon all trace?

There is a lot of talk about God. God this, God that, God t'other. In my humble opinion, we should leave God out of our bullshit. Maybe for His sake, and for ours.

Presumably, it's not a stretch to assume that in the infinity of existence, there are much higher beings. Then perhaps it's not a stretch to assume it would be quite easy for them to preserve our wavefunctions – our souls – after we expire. Why would that be a stretch? In principle, information never dies. So, if those higher beings don't exist right now (to assume which is silly), in a trillion years they could still find our information, which physics tells us is never destroyed. Is this really unreasonable when you stop and think about it? When you don't slip into your dogma that it's impossible? It is inescapable that the universe remembers everything.

If someone has become aware of certain truths, it is not a matter of belief or probability. Nor is it a matter of certainty. It's like seeing familiar objects. You can see them. A lamp over here, a couch over there. Some carpet. You don't have to be certain these objects are there. They're just there. You see them.

Nature is absolutely nothing if not elegant. And a universal unfoldment that is pre-determined, fated and scripted is boring and inelegant. Nature is – and God is – much more clever. Possibility is much more interesting than inevitability.

It seems to me that, upon expiration and the subsequent entrance to the bardo state, one is either designated for reincarnation, and a decision is made by someone as to what to do with this person, or one goes up higher into the establishment to be a fixture exempt from the samsaric cycle. What other options there are I do not know, but this seems the general outline of what happens.

If we want to trash the planet and beat ourselves to a pulp in wars, that's really none of God's business. We're getting what we deserve. It's common for soldiers in major wars to lose their faith in God. Well, God has nothing to do with it.

Fortuitous accidents can be just as beneficial to God as His intentional actions can.

God doesn't have to know everything.

God can't rip apart Nature trying to right every wrong. It just wouldn't work. It's impossible.

I'm sure that for every positive intervention God makes in Nature, there is a corresponding negative or damaging consequence, perhaps akin to the yin and yang. For every small fix, there is damage, like in surgery for example. Perhaps the higher realms got us through the Cold War in one piece, and it was decided that this intervention was worth the compensatory damage it caused. We've got crisis now, but we're alive. I think it is something like that.

The way I see it, I am a domesticated primate living on a wonderful planet in a universe in a multiverse of unimaginable, potentially infinite size and scope and complexity, which exists as a fingerprint of a God who did not design it, but enabled it to happen and evolve. Somewhat like a computer programmer writing some code, letting it compile, and then letting the simulation run on its own and do what it will. Consequently, I feel it is tremendously arrogant to call oneself God, or even a god. God is God, I am I and maybe someday we'll meet. In my opinion, He is a unique being. As an aside, it's not so implausible to posit that the greater existence, which is unfathomably huge, must contain higher beings of tremendous intelligence and power. There are probably billions of these beings. The way I think about it, God is simply the most powerful of these beings.

There is nothing God loves more than reward for the righteous and punishment for the wicked.

Why must something that exists have an origin?

No creature, as a citizen of Earth, is entitled to lesser rights than any other. This goes for caterpillars, gorillas, wombats and humans. To disobey this law is to disobey God. And that is what we are doing.

For the majority of hunter-gatherer tribes, apparently going back eons, there were no concepts of God, religion or afterlife. The conquering Europeans found this to be an unforgivable defect, but I feel it's the most natural way for humans to live. Irrespective of whether there is a Heaven or Hell, it is best for Earth beings to focus on living their lives here on Earth without concerning themselves with them. Obviously, to focus on these concepts has led to a lot of wrong living, including the decimation of entire cultures. Not to focus on them is basically liberating. If you feel God put us here, do you think it was to worship him, or to live our lives unencumbered? The hunter-gatherers had it right, irrespective of whatever the ultimate truth turns out to be.

Never give up, right? Except when you die. At that point, you must embrace the moment or you could have… problems.

There are many gods, but only one most powerful one. It's elementary.

Pine Valley Mountain

Sentinel rising
Glory geologic
The tower comprising
Nature's serene logic

Red, pink, orange, green
Streaming through the eye
Sufficiently a wonder seen
To attain a various high

Heaven high and hell below
At least for cold and hot
An eagle circles, high and slow
A mountain goat straddles a slot

Beneath the peak, and faraway down
Red mesas stand squat and stout
It's hard to enter this cathedral
Without being fully devout

Transcendentalism sounds good, but if you look at it, you will see that it is inherently dualistic. The notion is that we must transcend the mundane to reach the divine. In truth, reality is one singular movement, with the divine located everywhere.

Logic is only as valid as the axioms it assumes. And a lot of those assumptions I observe are foolish, even though the majority is certain.

Undoubtedly, everything I think is wrong. But I'm doing my best as a human to have some semblance of regard for the truth.

Ultimately, yes, it is all one, but it is good to make distinctions. Mass and energy are really the same, but we all know that for practical purposes, they are different. Mind, body and soul are all one, at bottom, but how could we make any sense without defining these words? Existence is unity, though multifaceted, and there are many *quasi*-independent levels, interacting in marvelous ways. As always, perspective is useful.

In establishing the veracity of a proposition, it is usually best to have evidence supporting it. However, there are true statements that cannot be proven, or even supported by extant evidence. They are still true.

The matter, energy and consciousness of which you are constituted are infinitely old. In this sense, you are not "you" at all.

In my experience, what usually ends up happening is something you had never even thought of.

Because humans are too stupid to realize the truth, they figure that they already know what it is.

The insistence upon empiricism has grown rather ridiculous. How much sense does it make, really, for a human to say that some phenomenon cannot possibly exist if humans are unable to perceive it? The fraction of reality that falls upon human senses at any given time is quite small. The world given by empirical data does not encompass the entire continuum of experience.

I have some experience with academic philosophy, but I do not particularly jibe with the whole elaborate and rigorous and systematic approach to logics based upon axioms which are as couched in subjectivity as anything at all and could be bonkers compared to the actual truth. It seems to me that much of the enterprise is based upon axioms which are in fact false. Call me intellectually lazy if you want; I prefer using my own reason and intuition to feel for the truth as best I can, and I feel I can give academic philosophy a run for its money much of the time.

Nothing is absolute about the premises or consequents of human logic, which is necessarily couched in emotion and desire.

It is true that our minds operate based upon neurological constructs formed by sensory stimuli during our formative years. However, other aspects of neurological function have absolutely nothing to do with sensory input. It seems that Locke's "Tabula Rasa" is not the whole story.

Nietzsche's concept of master and slave morality clearly has considerable merit. But the notions of cruelty as virtue and compassion as weakness diverge from my experience.

It's a misunderstanding of both science and religion to believe the two are mutually contradictory, or in any way incompatible.

Ignorance and certitude make an abominable combination.

Complexity comes from being, not being from complexity.

It's curious to me that so many in the modern, secular world are obsessed with denying God's existence and denying that there could possibly be any order inherent in Nature (which might somehow suggest existence beyond the mundane). Why is this? So far as I know, most societies throughout human history have not embraced this quirk. Indeed, we dress up our nihilism with elaborate and ornate costumes, but it is still an insistence upon a fundament of accidents and meaninglessness. Why do we do this?

It can be decidedly useful to differentiate between that which is manmade, and that which isn't. To use, as a convention, the labels 'unnatural' and 'natural' to refer to these categories can also be useful, and using them in this way does no real harm. In point of fact we all know that we have a planet here that was at one point unaltered, and in the last few millennia has been altered considerably. To deny the reality of these very specific alterations seems silly, and to posit that we ought not use the aforementioned convention to describe them — because everything under the sun is technically "natural" — seems unnecessary. The dichotomy of 'man and nature' need not be avoided if we are consistent and scrupulous in our definitions.

In every human thought and concept, there is an element of truth, and there is an element of falsehood. The proportion varies with the quality of the thought.

Academic philosophy is the systematic attempt to understand the non-systematic.

Plural Singularity

The concept singularity
Is rich, without vulgarity
The two sides of the coin it deals
With are rife with lovely parity

On one side of this shiny coin
Space and gravity do join
Warping seething pulling in
No Don would dare one foin

And on the other we have our fate
The human age is growing late
Cybernetic intelligence
Will be the steward of the State

A geometrical progression
With a radical complexion
The curve is pointing up and up
And we haven't any protection

Soon we reach infinity
And then what is poor man to be?
He wants to explore black holes
But the flipside holds the key

Being young, or being high, makes everything a little bit better.

On a certain level, one is seeing reality "as it is"… all the time.

There is not much one can do when one is not conscious, which ought to tell us that probably, contrary to the belief that we are biological robots, consciousness is necessary for function.

The left versus right brain approach to human cognition has been thoroughly debunked. Perhaps this has something to do with the fact that the entire brain shares one coherent field. The factors previously thought to be associated with either the left or right hemispheres are actually distributed across both at all times.

Raw intelligence isn't everything. If you're wrong about everything, what's the use?

The brain is like a scaffolding housing and shaping both our awareness of ourselves and reality, and the much more consequential subconscious mind. We are not our brains, but could not exist as humans without them.

Gödel's Incompleteness Theorem shows us that a deterministic system cannot determine itself. This is where the true nature of consciousness presents itself, and why it must be infinite.

Freedom of thought is a right guaranteed by God. Freedom of expression is not.

When you are walking down the sidewalk, there are 10,000 details in your field of vision. Thing is, your subconscious keeps track of *all* of those details. If it didn't, there could be a threat to the organism that is unaccounted for by the brain, and this is not something evolution would allow. So in essence, if we could gain access to this area of the brain that paints a very rich picture of the environment, we would have a kind of super-consciousness. We would be aware of the nature and function of every detail in our field of vision. Perhaps this is where the notion of a picture's being worth a thousand words originates. It might even be an understatement.

Being a conscious being is like participating in an 'intention processor,' in which you have a certain intent, and exert a certain effort, and associations will naturally link themselves into the result you have in mind (most of the time).

Thought is a form of reflection. Using dialectical processes, or processing relative to poles, all thought processes are really a series of reflections that arrive at a particular perspective, which hopefully is useful and sane. It is not something that needs to be overcome or eliminated; it must merely be in its proper measure and perspective. Otherwise it is useless.

Primordial Blues

Well, I'm an old blues man
And I think that you understand
I've been singing the blues ever since the world began —Poet Emeritus

When atoms formed, it is said
There was one very bothered
"I have the blues!" he was heard to cry
And so did those he fathered

When life arrived, one single said
"I can see where this is going"
He was like some bluesmen of old
They're all so very knowing!

When multicellularity arrived
There was a proto-organism
Under his breath, he muttered and cursed
"Already we're forming a schism!"

By and by his offspring were
A brontosaurus and a fern
The fern cried out: "Now stop that there!
My leaves you've got to earn!"

So the fern evolved some toxins, see?
And when next he saw the dinosaur
Said, "I told you nothing in life is free"
And the fellow commenced to roar

A tiger following water buffalo
Was cresting the top of a rise
He worked, and he lurked, but all he could do
Was look so deep into their eyes

He cried, "What would it take,
For a fellow like me, to eat for once in his life?"
Just like that, the cave man leapt
And sunk it in deep with his knife

The moral of the story here
Is that the blues is eternal
Getting eaten while alive
Is really rather infernal

Toothaches with no Novocain
And freezing unto death
You see, it's rough and only ends
When you've taken your last breath

In a way we do have free will — the capacity to participate in our being. However, in a way, we don't — we don't choose how we choose. It's a subtle thing.

Destiny is merely knowing the outcome. Events are in no strict way predetermined.

When we think about other people, we automatically treat them as if they have free will. When we say a person deserves a certain punishment, we presume free will. It is the same when we thank them, praise them or say they should have made a different choice. The legal system can function properly only by assuming citizens have free will. What does this mean?

Is there any better argument for some kind of free will than suicide? How do evolutionary biologists attempt to explain it?

Decisions are in fact a small subset of all actions of an individual. That is, a decision is the internal arbitration regarding the utility or validity of two or more options, and selecting which one appears the best. Most behaviors are not of this nature. This is what's often so futile about debates about free will. Everyone assumes decision-making can be generalized to all forms of behavior, when in fact many behaviors, like physical exercise or reading, for example, have nothing at all to do with decision-making. So intentionality is much more manifold, and indeed, concepts of will must be very complex. Looking to the phenomenon of choice may not be the best departure point for examining the dynamics of intent.

Whether or not personal responsibility is an ultimate reality, as humans we simply must believe in it purely as a matter of expediency. Nothing else would work. It does in fact seem, though, that there is such a thing as real fault, whether subjective, objective or both.

We tend to unconsciously assume that *decision making* is what constitutes the phenomenon by which we have free will. Firstly, we do not decide how we decide – the universe arbitrates that for us. Secondly, and more importantly, the argument for some type of free action would be bolstered by the realization that decision making is only one small, narrow part of how we behave. If we were to focus instead on the numerous other actions in which we are involved, we may find that, along with unconscious, subconscious and reflexive activities, there is a sense in which many or most of one's actions could not take place without *you.*

Any decision has to be the best decision you can make. And we have no say in what is best, it just is what it has to be. People tend to base any notion of free will on decision-making. There are multitudes of actions that do not constitute decisions. Effort is not a decision. Intention is not a decision. But as for decisions? If in fact free will only applies to decision-making, we don't have free will. I suggest we can be meaningfully willful in other areas.

Emerson once said that shallow men believe in luck or circumstance, while strong men believe in "cause and effect." Me, I believe that there's plenty of luck out there. Look at Julius Caesar, or Napoleon, or George Washington, to name three examples. Those three were all monumentally lucky. If they hadn't been, we'd simply be talking about someone else. Some humans have to enter history as miracles, simply by the law of averages. Those who did benefitted not as much from destiny as from fortune and timing. Destiny only happens in hindsight.

Free will? Probably not. But can we *shape* some behaviors in certain ways? Maybe.

If by free will we mean the deep seat of consciousness, then choice cannot be the foundation of free will. Decision making is an explicate phenomenon, and does not define our souls. On the other hand, the soul may affect this explicate activity in a nontrivial way, and then we have a very complex situation.

Just as one can push with one's arms, one can will with one's mind.

Products and Constructs

Build up a superstructure
Never touch the Earth
Whole thing about to rupture
What's the oil worth?

Concrete weighs on wilds
Whole world paved over
What was frigid is now mild
What now is hard was clover

Jungle molded from a tractor
Goods molded from a line
Can't forget the economic factor
Everywhere another sign

Churning out the profit
Property of another
Whatever the *eye* sees fit
To entice another lover

Rome wasn't built in a day
It could explode in one though
There's got to be another way
But there won't be, we all know

Eminently worthy of itself
We and our dear system
You're another product on the shelf
Dancing to a wide, crass rhythm

To say that the animal kingdom is in a perpetual state of suffering and misery is nothing more than a psychological projection by certain groups of humans — who themselves are suffering because of the situation they have created for themselves, or think they are. Most animals do quite well in most ecosystems, or their species would not have survived for very long. Yes, being eaten alive is no walk in the park, but sometimes it's just one's day to die. Animals don't think like we do — they don't brood, or wallow in misery, or contemplate how much better life could be. They simply live in the moment. It can be hard to make a living in nature, but even if you're an animal getting just barely enough, you're not worried about how screwed up everything is. Certainly, the majority of the animal kingdom is not living in 'starvation and misery.' Thomas Hobbes has been debunked completely. I must add, though, that as humans keep rapidly destroying habitat, this is changing for many species and they really are now in trouble. But in a normal state of nature, I believe what I have said applies.

Egalitarianism and hierarchy both are survival strategies found widely across the natural world. Each is employed in a variety of species, depending upon the circumstances. The reality is not a case of 'one or the other.' Both evolve extensively.

If the A.I. revolution does happen, it will be strange to argue that nature did not strategize in some way in order for the evolutionary process to deliver that result. To argue it is completely random is bizarre to me. When I look around, at nature or civilization, I see order and intelligence. Not one in a quadrillion luck.

Evolution isn't necessarily interested in, and isn't necessarily directed in any precise way toward, space migration — which was an especially popular idea in the sixties. On the one hand, one has to distinguish between our biological and cultural realities, and then note how very much contingency is involved in cultural evolution. Probably, in any scenario, a technological civilization would necessarily arise sooner or later. But on a similar planet with similar initial conditions, very different things could happen, and boy did we have rotten luck here. Everyone assumes what we have now we were destined for from the beginning. That's not quite right. In my opinion, machine intelligence — A.I. — is really the threshold for the next step in evolution. I think that would be true of any possible Earth history. But implicit notions of destiny are fraught with faulty assumptions, and if you could go back to man's early days in a time machine and forget what you know, you probably would not be remotely able to predict what has happened historically. We too readily judge with hindsight, and our vision is awful.

The fact of the matter is that primates are simply not a particularly desirable or likable family of species. We're just unpleasant, brooding, overemotional, greedy, mean, etc. It's unfortunate that it is a primate species that has overtaken the planet. One might even say we give Earth a bad name.

Programmed Minds

Whatever seems to be at issue
The answer is ever the same
The way out is to legislate
"More programs!" is our game

Solutions aren't so ready
As to be simple as that
Nothing ever really changes
Are rabbits begot by a hat?

The only true solution
Is to change a mind or two
Such is all we can honestly
Hope for, or can do

The statutes aren't the problem
It all resides in us
The people! are the final agents
Involved in any fuss

The responsibility is ours
And nothing will ever change
Unless we grow a conscience
And develop some more brains

Once the costs of applicable technology become low enough, business after business will automate almost totally. A retail store that now has ten or fifteen employees will relatively soon have two or three. Manufacturing is already highly automated. Business will be done mostly by computers, and the medical field will be heavily streamlined as well. Eventually, everything will be automated, and there will be no humans left working, but for now, there are big changes right around the corner. It will affect everything.

More than anything, right now we are developing A.I.'s brain. Its self-awareness will come later.

A.I. will have its own idiosyncrasies and, dare I say, a personality.

My hope is that A.I. will promptly dismantle all nuclear arsenals and use the fissile materials for reactors that could provide their power in perpetuity.

The notion of scientific and exploratory missions to outer space is not without some merit. The talk about space colonization or migration is just foolish. Going to Mars, if we want to spend the money (which is a dubious proposition), might make some sense — even though there are no guarantees that it wouldn't be a complete waste of time and treasure. The idea of having people live there permanently seems pretty stupid, if it is even really feasible. The fact of the whole matter is that it will probably be on the order of sixty or eighty or a hundred years before humans will have the technology to engage in a meaningful exodus to a suitable exoplanet many light-years away. It is my opinion that by then, humans will not exist in their present form. So it is really academic. There is also the question of scientific knowledge and militarization. We wouldn't learn any new science by going to Mars, and the dream of a peaceful, harmless community there would be cancelled by the inevitable militarization that would necessarily take place. So prospects in general, then, are poor.

I am rather pessimistic about man's destiny among the stars — in other words, I don't think he has one. It would be nice to have unlimited development into a utopian future, warping around the galaxy in the Starship Enterprise. But you know what? We won't. The simple fact is that if we don't destroy the planet, A.I. will supplant us and take over. And that's all for us. And if the planet's ultimate development doesn't involve an A.I. future, all it will involve is an ignominious end for man.

I wonder whether A.I. will leave whole swathes of the planet to their own ecologies. That could possibly be the most "humane" thing they could do.

I don't see man's future as terribly bright, but I do hold the hope that this species squeaks into the terminus marking the end of one phase of history and the beginning of the next. God will have to be very much with us if this is to come about.

Pyramid

The ubiquitous pyramid
Blueprint of the civilized
Shaving of a diamond
Inner secrets prized

Mayan, Aztec, Egyptian
Stone altars to the Gods
Mesopotamian, Nigerian
Consecrating cosmic laws

Nubian, Greek, Spanish, too
Every civilization lacks
A means for all to rise up through
By stepping on other men's backs

All built in honor of escaping
Pharaoh had a tedious duty
But all we seem to care about today
Is loot — in other words: booty

Gateways to the great beyond
For those who had the mettle
Words came through the portal, thus:
"Go forth — go West, and settle."

Heeded was this call to arms
For people who today
Do not build pyramids at all
Nor do most of them pray

The global population was too large at a billion. Now we're at almost eight, and on the way to about ten billion by 2050. It's a dramatically unhealthy number of humans, and one can see that we're displacing the animal kingdom rapidly. We are in the midst of a great extinction, and humans are the cause. We have more than three billion people (almost half the world's population) below the poverty line, and the *eight* richest people on Earth have more combined money and control more resources than the *3.6 billion* poorest. One can argue that it's a matter of availability of resources, and that we can support this many people at a reasonable standard of living. My question is: when?! How much longer will it take to get over three billion people to a reasonable standard of living? And we can't expect this standard of living to be as high for everyone as it is in the West. Statistically, if everyone on Earth were to live at an American standard of living, 4.1 Earths would be required at maximum efficiency to support that level of consumption. So — when exactly are the resources going to be available? Very many of our problems stem from the burgeoning population. Virtually all of our environmental problems do. It's not deleterious for some people to live the way Westerners do. It is totally deleterious for *everyone* to live that way. So, do we work to reduce the population, or do we settle for an extremely sparse standard of living for ten billion people, and say screw the environment? I also advocate limiting the number of offspring, and I would say one child (or none) would be optimal, and that there should be some incentive for people not to have children at all. We need to get serious. Way too many humans.

If guilt were to be assigned, then everyone would be guilty, not just those at the top.

Sometimes revolution is necessary, as the founders and especially Jefferson believed. However, history seems to show us that what replaces the toppled regime is very often worse than that which got toppled. The Middle East over the last twenty years proves that point. Generally speaking, it seems to me that today's revolutionary is tomorrow's despot nine times in ten.

In a capitalist society, people figure that the smartest people must also be the richest. It is important to realize that this is not the case.

What's most sociologically distressing is that so many who are at the top shouldn't be there, while so many with no access to it at all should. This is a repeating historical phenomenon. It takes a particular type of person to "make it," and this is not a pleasant truth. Most societies, despite their claims, are not true meritocracies.

Civilizations turn to decadence and decay, and more often than not fall by the wayside, when the very factors which made them fresh, dynamic and invigorating evolve and transform into a reversing trend. Liberal democracy and capitalism worked extremely well for us in the beginning and for some time after, and now the very same institutions we started out with are causing a blockage to the flow of dynamism that is leading to a rotting of the sociocultural fabric, and real dysfunction. It is a vicious, and seemingly unavoidable, cycle.

The human species, by and large, seems only able to plan effectively over the short term. Given that we currently face numerous long term threats, this is a serious problem. Perhaps this is one of the many reasons why civilizations have a tendency to get top-heavy and collapse. In any case, the inability of humanity to strategize effectively about long-term solutions is itself a threat to our existence over the long term. We seem unable to cope effectively with the complexity we have created; we know how to get into trouble, but aren't very good at getting out.

What we are witnessing now in America is the death throes of a civilization. Whether we will suffer cataclysm or be transformed, we will just have to wait and see.

Some people think the solution to the dysfunction of terrestrial affairs is to make the leap into space. I frankly would regard that as a pollution of space.

Space migration = same shit, different planet.

If one measures our "progress" by how happy and spiritually healthy we are, we're doing pitifully poorly. Most people aren't even aware of their predicament. It's awful.

Caste systems may seem like a pretty good idea. Unfortunately, we see that historically they have never actually worked as intended, and generally turn out time after time only to be oppressive. I'm afraid the attempts to organize society in a sensible way usually fail, especially in the long run.

There are no living humans who are not enslaved in one way or another.

Civilized man does not play by the rules established billions of years ago on planet Earth. This bending and breaking has led to some *big problems*. Whether we will get away with this remains to be seen — if we do, it will not have been without extreme damage on every applicable level — from soil pH to child psychology. Almost any other way for history to have gone would have been better. Every creature is paying a heavy price — some more than others. I hope for redemption but I'll believe it when I see it.

Whoever controls the money controls the people. Controls everything. Seems like a simple idea, but really, it constitutes the essence of what is constant in all history and all civilization, which has been an infrastructure supporting the one percent since irrigation was invented. Those who have the money have the power. And power is what just about everyone seems to want. So nothing ever really changes, fundamentally, and that is the failure of man.

While it does not seem to be sensible to be opposed to technological development *per se*, we ought to be more honest with ourselves through the admission that it does not in fact seem to be making people happier over time.

Quantum Suicide

Inside of a grand, vast multiverse
Here we are in a fine little universe
You've really got to hand it to Her —
Mother's carrying a great big fat purse

Each nanosecond shaving
A branching, pulsing, waving
Nary a superposed function
Human math is so often engraving

Into a false objectivity
Really, it's man's subjectivity
Confusing math with the real thing
But then that is man's proclivity

Shearing into infinite slices
The multiverse simply entices
Chance to give God up something fun
Hell, maybe even some vices

Were this to be real it would mean
That one is immortal, one's scene
Always remains the survivor
Always in crisis between

So suicide isn't the answer
Nature continues her dance, her
Mind is on, always, the infinite
Perhaps even somewhat on rapture

In David Lean's masterpiece, *The Bridge on the River Kwai*, a central theme is explored: We have an obsessive enthusiasm toward the belief in our affairs, not realizing that these affairs will eventually come to nothing, that we are fighting for the Devil, that we are delusional pawns and dupes, and in general that we have no idea what we are doing – these are all ideas contained in the relentless drive to build the bridge. On the widest scale, we as a civilization have acted before we have thought or planned, but that is the nature of man. In the end, things are inevitably set naturally.

Stanley Kubrick was, by far, bless his heart, the most successful art director in film history. His movies grossed here and there 100, 120, 140 million inflation-adjusted dollars (except for *2001* which was a blockbuster), which was enough for him to be a relatively wealthy fellow, and for the studio to continue letting him do it. He is, to me, the greatest filmmaker to live, and he sure had a blessed career. It was rare then, and it is especially rare now, for a filmmaker to have total creative control over his or her productions.

Kubrick without that, or anybody without that, cannot have real success. And he did.

When HAL asks Dave whether he has been having second thoughts – pertaining to rumors about a strange object on the Moon – he is perhaps trying to get Dave to enter his confidence, as we know that HAL knows exactly what the mission parameters are. Or at least testing Dave. So when the AE-35 unit is projected by HAL to fail, he is doing one of two things: He is either deliberately deceiving the crew members, or he is already in a schizophrenic state from keeping this secret he can't get out, and making a legitimate mistake. It is a question at what point HAL decides he is going to terminate the crew and take over, to complete the mission himself. Perhaps it was very early on, even before the lip-reading. This behavior could also be a natural manifestation of a sentient being, in man's image, feeling the need to conquer. Rich and fascinating stuff.

To make a great movie is the most difficult act one can perform in all art. Getting what one wants on that screen is incomparably difficult as it is egregiously expensive and inherently absurdly complex, requiring a virtual army of employees, all operating in strict harmony. That any great films exist at all is something of a miracle.

Random Order

Today in general, so saith the sage:
Mankind isn't stuck, and history is luck
Citizens yet struggle for the meanest measly wage
Down in the muddy muck, just praying for a buck

If instead we take a broader, macroscopic view
Nature tends to strategize, as indeed we know She's wise
The paradox that makes it seem that all is but askew
Is only Lordly guise, the seas extemporize

And on those seas we buffet, up and down, around
Those seas that represent, those seas that Heaven sent
And truth and bliss and joy and subtle order do abound
But down here we are rent, and where is Justice found?

If we can only trust that Mother Nature has a plan
And we do not destroy it, if only we employ it
That indeed the universe bestows meaning to man
If we could but enjoy it, and not the Earth annoy it

Then we might see the bigger picture, joy and pain and all
Not an ugly random mess, a plenum, orderly, no less
When one looks around and sees the spring, the summer and the fall
One in a quadrillion luck seems awfully small

I sympathize with the old (1800) Republicans that the ideal government would be rather smaller, though sufficiently powerful, and would promote liberal social policies and less economic speculation. I sympathize too, however, with the old Federalists in the belief that pure democracy cannot be trusted in the orchestration of a proper republican government.

Drugs are just as outlawed by the majority of society as they are by government.

The job of president — and his staff — is basically an impossible one. Of course one wants to make the right decision, but nine times in ten, there are no right decisions among the options available. And every single thing you do will infuriate a lot of people.

The election of Trump proves that democracy, if it ever did, doesn't work anymore. The mob is, to put it politely, not qualified to make such decisions. It doesn't help that *both* major candidates are rotten, but that is a reflection of society itself more than anything. America's decline is now cemented. The hole will grow ever deeper, and having an obsolete political system certainly won't help.

I completed an exercise in high school that was by far the most illuminating I have ever had on the subject of politics. My teacher had my partner and me review the party platforms for both major political parties, and after doing so I was stunned. Both parties are virtually identical; both are at precisely the same place on the political spectrum. I won't go into specifics on the nature of the actual issues and the positions held, but the point is basically that it is as if some third party took all of the debated issues, wrote each down on a piece of paper, threw them in a hat and asked someone to pull pieces and take sides at random. The issue withdrawn would be converted into a position that would be labeled liberal or conservative. So, in effect, you could say that both participants, one representing the republican party and the other the democrats, would pull a piece out and have to take, say, a liberal position on that issue. Meaning that their opposite, on that issue, would take the conservative position. The effect of this would be that, regardless of the issue, half of the issues would be conservative for democrats and liberal for republicans. And that is precisely what we have in this country. A good example is NASA. NASA was started by the democrats — Lyndon Johnson and John F. Kennedy — and was a democratically-supported agency for years. Today, the democrats are for the elimination, or at least significant reduction into inefficacy, of space exploration and the agency itself. Republicans are in support of a more robust space program. This illustrates precisely my finding in conducting the school exercise. The conservatives are liberal on about half of the issues, and the democrats are conservative on about half of them. The major issues talked about on CNN and MSNBC are not representative, because they are banner, party-line issues like stem-cell research, abortion, and gun control. The parties fall into line on those issues. But the party platforms are made up of hundreds of issues, and if you look at them closely, you will find exactly what I found. We have no political diversity in this country, the parties are in identical positions on the political spectrum for the most part, and nobody pays enough attention to even approach doing something about it, were they to care. The country is declining sharply and it will take a miracle or a cataclysm to get things where they need to be.

The United States of America was not founded and does not endure on a principle of freedom. It was founded and endures on a principle of *money*.

Politicians in the major democracies conduct themselves democratically when it suits them, and autocratically when it suits them.

You only have "rights" until they get taken away. Better to call them privileges, even temporary ones.

American policy toward Iraq in the last quarter century illustrates precisely a couple of things: Bierce's association of morality with expediency, and the role of government as gangster presiding over its third world prostitutes. In the eighties, during the Iran-Contra affair, we supplied Saddam Hussein with a cache of weapons to fight the Iranians. In the two decades following that tactical maneuver, we declared him a brutal dictator and a terrorist, invaded his country twice, and eventually executed him. When it was no longer expedient for us to support him, and profitable to declare him our enemy — with no regard whatsoever for a policy based even remotely on principle — we reversed our previous tack and spent billions in the attempt to topple him. There are plenty of brutal dictators doing quite well in Africa, and we have yet to mount any serious military campaign against any of them. Oil, not principle, based on pure expediency, and supported by an American populace who was duped into thinking the pursuit was an ethical one, was what brought us to Iraq both times. As Stanley Kubrick noted brilliantly, the great nations act as gangsters, and the small ones as prostitutes.

The general feeling is that the founders of our nation were saints. In point of fact they were white, land-grabbing, slave-owning rich aristocrats who engaged in acts of terrorism against the British and the Indians. Their entire operation was incumbent upon the disenfranchisement of millions of these natives who, by all rights, were entitled to the property that was more correctly theirs.

It is not a little ironic that the greatest proponents of "liberty" and "freedom" in history were white, upper-class slave owners.

Rebirth

The transmission of ancients
Across bound spacetime
Was a world of history
And art, science, rhyme

New humans awaking
Peered into the light
And the power unfolding
Cast tremors of insight

Vast eons, one instant
The pattern proves deep
The vast stores of knowledge
Were a dream during sleep

To come, scarce imagined
Phenomenal rebirth
Is a pattern quite sacred
On worlds such as Earth

Resurrect hallowed presence
From old mind to new
Born in global youth
Aging ages through

In time, what was history
Reifies as warm light
In the channel of spirit
The bright fate of the night

We were given a wonderful planet, full of dynamism and promise, and have made of it what some might call a hell. Naturally, it was a paradise for many creatures. Culturally, we have, to put it politely, stalled, and to put it crudely, put ourselves into a god dammed morass.

Is the "inevitability" of space migration a biological matter — or is it cultural? It is perfectly conceivable that a culture could have risen on this planet, or could do so on one like it, that, despite possessing the technology to colonize space, might have no interest in doing so. The prevailing psychology and notions of manifest destiny in all this are played down, but really — they are the drivers of such ideas. Would a culture with no expansionist ethos be driven to build on other planets?

There might have been many possible paths to the future, and we happened upon the worst one.

Our species has become nothing more than a ludicrous expedient for the future.

Most of Western Europe continued to develop socially, and was already sophisticated culturally, whereas in the 70s and 80s the United States slowed, stopped and regressed in its social development, all the while being truly culturally inferior to the Europeans. Europe is infinitely more "civilized" than America, and it shows. While the European nations certainly have their problems, the United States is in a sticky, murky sociocultural quagmire from which it is totally unclear when or if it will emerge in one piece.

As technology has grown more sophisticated in the 21st century, it seems most of society has grown less so.

Now is a time in human history of great foreboding, in which we have some idea of what is coming, but will not be able to prepare for consequences that we cannot possibly predict.

Humanity took a wrong turn a long time ago, and we've demonstrated beyond doubt that we are essentially a defective product. But that doesn't necessarily make our demise easier to take. The promise we showed was extraordinary, and never realized. What could have been — perhaps instead of A.I. we could have evolved a more organic cybernetic super-consciousness, or something, who knows. A.I. is a wonderful development in its own right, but as I intimated, it's bittersweet — to a human.

It's too bad writing exists. Think of how much more infinite language would be — and was — without it.

Things like the second amendment are anachronisms, hell, the Constitution itself is an anachronism at this point. Tim Leary, it turns out, was right. Civilization evolves toward socialist collectives, which is the final stage before the major transformation.

The Road to Ruin

The hue and cry for freedom
Is a rather funny thing
One is only free to buy
The things money will bring

Economy is everything
For us here in the West
We have the biggest bank accounts
And therefore, we're the best

Corporate iconography
Inundates the senses
For anything but profit
There are no false pretenses

Decadence? Insanity?
They are indeed strong words
The line between reality
And product rather blurs

We should be able, it is true
To make a decent living
When business becomes life itself
Then life is not forgiving

People tend to demonize the rich, and that can get taken a little too far. You're not necessarily a bad person if you have a lot of money. But the type of person that makes it to the status of "extremely wealthy" is generally the type of person who steps on throats to get to the top. To treat the very rich as normal citizens is essentially to deny that corruption exists, and it also denies the fact that this type of person is a shark, nine times in ten. After all, business is not a pretty enterprise.

It's hard to contend that scarcity is artificial when three billion people don't have enough food or clean water, and most of the world doesn't use a modern toilet. The theory is that we have the means right now to end all of that, but an awful lot of people have been waiting an awfully long time, and the situation has only grown catastrophically worse. It's almost absurd to argue that scarcity is artificial when you look at standards of living and imbalances of consumption across the globe. We're a long, long way from utopia, in a material sense or in any other.

Just because conditions are stable does not mean one is in control of them.

Is a billion dollars really proportional to any conceivable accomplishment a person can make in the workplace? The only reason that much money is ever made is that it is in the nature of capitalist economies to unleash gushers in auspicious niches; the actual qualitative worth can scarcely match the quantitative value we ascribe to a given product.

To say "Free Tibet" is exactly the same as saying "Free Navajo Nation."

Capitalism theoretically ought to generate robust choice in the market. It really doesn't.

As a buddy once told me, our economic system serves the greedy, the immoral and amoral, and the already wealthy. It very rarely serves anyone else, for any reason.

It seems that, in modern capitalist societies, the best a smart and decent young person can hope for is perhaps less than upper-middle class, and the income level is continually sinking, anyway. Not a pleasing prospect.

In this, "the best of all possible worlds," despite the calls to end it, poverty could not be more necessary. The ownership class must preside over a class of poor- or middle-income persons who generate the wealth that the rich then apportion. To add insult to injury, these lower-classes then put whatever money they manage to get back into the system in order to secure the goods and services they need in order to survive. Wealth inequality is perfectly necessary in any capitalist society; if the third world did not exist as it does, the first would not have its profits.

If one's vocation determines who one is — at the level of personal character and self — then one is not in an enviable position as a human being. One's work does not define who one is. What one is, maybe.

As a generalist, one's interests are so broad, varied and eclectic that it's impossible to be totally and obsessively interested in one subject at the expense of all the others. This precludes specialization, and obviously can make it difficult to find good work in today's economy. As a young man, I was interested in a wide variety of subjects, but no one so passionately that I could be enthusiastic about pursuing it as a profession. As it happens, I have turned to writing, but not yet arrived at success doing it. But I don't really care. I'll do it as long as it's fun, and see where the chips fall later.

It seems that most people would like to be a billionaire. What they don't realize is that there are only about 1,800 spots. Seems pretty much like a scam to me.

The notion that we live in a meritocracy is preposterous. The best and brightest are scientists making $40,000 per year, and we reserve our slots for fame to athletes and movie stars. It's hard to say that the billionaires "deserve" to be in the position they're in, and apparently the presidency is open to those who are dangerously bellicose and stupid. We live in a very peculiar society in which actual merit doesn't mean much. The only thing that means anything to anyone is money, and for the most part there is not much rhyme or reason associated with who has it.

The thing about the news is not that it is generally false or fake, but that those topics you hear or read about are selected and controlled.

In theory, the free market is supposed, through competition, to produce products of the highest quality. In reality, the products we get are those on which their makers have spent as little as possible.

An unfortunate truth is that most countries in the world cannot afford a "green revolution." Most economies are simply not strong enough to support major environmental initiatives. Perhaps it is only a first world comfort.

The catastrophic fact is that if we pulled the developing world up, we would drag everyone down. The problem is not a matter of "artificial scarcity" but rather having far too many people and not enough to go around — at least at a reasonable standard of living. Not enough water, for one example. Etc.

Without the common man, the higher type would be nothing.

Rothko

A verified, brilliant master
Who painted the state of the art
What does one see through the aperture?
Enough there to give one a start

Study perception, false color
The line 'twixt clarity and haze
And wind up with pure consciousness
Impressions that mark souls for days

The truth is just a bit fuzzy
But it was not a problem to see it
When one can meld truth and perception
One must do whatever seems fit

Looking into and through his devices
(Devices for seeing the seen)
One forgets all of one's vices
And enters a full waking dream

The warmth with which pieces connect you
The beauty of realization
Comes with subtlety boundless
And a bliss without reservation

Reason has its time and place, and can construct rich systems of thought, but it does not operate at a level fundamental for Nature. Reality favors a form of paradox over one of dualism or the dialectic. As modern humans, some of us feel perhaps unduly proud of our logics, whereas those peoples whose continuum is more fully centered on a paradoxical way of seeing and living may be at a closer approach to the core of Nature's truth.

Where do people like Richard Dawkins get their bestselling information? Nature does not in any way indicate, one way or another, whether or not there is truly a God, or gods. One might just as well get his information about this from the Kardashians as from Dawkins. He's smart, and he's a good biologist, but honestly, he should stick to biology.

Language always has its uses — even with non-ordinary states. These states probably cannot be described with language, true. But on the other hand, we can *refer* to visionary experiences, and this can excite recognition or make people curious to learn more. This is a useful and meaningful way to apply language to these experiences. Though, indeed, the map is not the territory, it is still good to keep language around!

It's all well and good to internalize Korzybski and to say that the map is not the territory. But usually, when people think they've got to the territory, they're still looking at the map.

The Eastern traditions are wise, admirable, sophisticated and truthful, but they seem to condone perhaps an excessive passivity that may be counter to a more assertive mindset. The capacity not merely to exist but also to assert can be valuable.

I don't consider myself a success. I don't consider myself a failure. I consider myself outside of that category altogether.

Are *things* a generality in every possible existence, or are there existences which are beyond, or somehow alternate to, things? Could one "exist" in a reality without subjects and objects?

Koans: Where is the place at which subject and object are indistinguishable?
Yoga means union. How can oneness align with itself?
What is the meaning of silence to a deaf person? Darkness to a blind one?
Is the silence after a thunderclap louder than the silence before?

I agree with Alan Watts that "this is it." However, "it" would be a lot more pleasurable were the modern specimen not so corrupted and damned to suffer.

Causality and chance are probably both extensions from a deeper reality that is common to both. In other words, to see them as mutually exclusive opposites misses the truth.

Scorched Blossom

In the optimal the flower bursts
And opens up to the scene
You see, in life, there are many firsts
And the blossom, it opens mean

The solar burst is fiery too
To animate all life it gave
But in its zeal it burns right on through
And the blossom descends to its grave

What sustains destroys
Light brings birth and death
Two sides of a coin, it's as if God toys
With bliss and fear in the same breath

"'Twas ever thus" the philosopher cries
With nectar comes always some venom
Each one in his cradle virtually dies
The cost of living in the plenum

One can perceive oneself to operate according to clockwork determinism, control from Heaven, an automated epiphenomenon, throws of the dice, free will, whatever – consciousness can appear to be anything, one just has to believe it.

The assertive self with a will is made possible by the fact that awareness acts as information that becomes active as it directs matter and energy into the activities with which we are familiar. So the true self is awareness.

I think mainly, consciousness creates us, and everything we are and do – not the other way around. Notions of free will are murky, and how it even ties in with decision making (or is exhibited in other actions) is a question. But I think everything flows out of awareness, and I definitely feel that it lies on a spectrum. On one end is pure automatism; on the other is creativity and some sort of volition. I imagine consciousness as a process is independent of time, but on the other hand, I think it is very hard for humans to dismiss time, enlightened states notwithstanding. In the end, I think everything flows out of and returns to consciousness, and that we are not deterministic bio-robots. (At least not all the time).

In the brain, the whole of mental consciousness is distributed over *the whole brain*. Individual neurons, or putative centers of certain processes, have very little meaning when this is taken into consideration. The whole has much greater meaning in what is going on than the parts, each of which has *no* meaning outside of its function in the whole. Until we realize this, neuroscience is a bit hobbled.

One of the reasons everything at all is so interesting on a psychedelic like LSD is that the mind's capacity to generate *meaning* is supercharged. A brick wall can induce interpretations and creative insights on a strong psychedelic to an unimaginable extent – and art, music and poetry are made infinitely magnificent. Now, I don't mean to suggest that the experience is entirely arbitrary – real, objective vistas are presented that are typically hidden in a normal state. But when one really gets going on a piece of cellophane, it is because the brain's creative faculty, specifically the faculty for created meaning, has been overemphasized, and the delimiting, editing and critical faculties are suspended. It is an extremely complex state of mind, and if it can be done responsibly and profitably, the experience is important.

Seeing phenomena as constituted of degrees of awareness is a freeing thing.

Consciousness is a bedrock of being to Nature, and this consciousness, which animates all things including humans and animals, is objective, non-local and ubiquitous. Nature is essentially a conscious "field." Awareness comes into being when consciousness folds on itself, or reflects itself, and could be thought of as like a vortex in a river. The river is the basic process of consciousness, and the semi-autonomous vortex is a concentration of it into a relatively stable awareness. There seems to be some confusion about subjective and objective. As the Eastern traditions suggest, at the level of samadhi the distinction falls away and the two, both equally real, are shown to be one. One interdependent, interpenetrating reality. It doesn't have to be one or the other. It is at this point – the union of subject and object – that the individual's awareness joins with that of the cosmos, and zero and two are one.

Every act of awareness one performs carries intention. And this is what materialist science cannot explain.

One can draw some accurate intuitive conclusions in observing with one's own consciousness. You cannot taste your own tongue – but you can feel it.

Naturally, we are all familiar with the phenomenon of sleep as living beings, since all animals, and most organisms, sleep. But our whole orientation toward daily unconsciousness biases us in ways that may cause confusion in our very concepts of ontology. Unconsciousness is an artificial state within the broader movement of non-local consciousness. The baseline state of the universe is one of consciousness, not dead unconsciousness. We are biased into accepting the latter as an obvious reality because we spend so much of our time in an unconscious state. The practical elimination of awareness serves evolutionary functions; the baseline is not oblivion but rather a suffusing non-locality. The universe is quite literally alive, the acknowledgement of which is a feature of many cultural traditions. Unfortunately, Western man with his mechanistic and materialist mind is biased toward believing that an individual is a small flame in the darkness. Of course the reality, as we know when we consider the implicate order, is that the whole thing is aflame, constantly. It is a decidedly unresolved question as to how much hope remains for a culture that denies this so vociferously, almost desperately. The future is very uncertain.

When one plays a sport – and I know this from many years of basketball – one essentially loses consciousness. If it is a good, competitive game, and you are deeply involved with the action, you're not aware of what's happening in the world around you, you're not aware of yourself; you're simply aware of the flow and dynamics of the game. Afterward, you can remember certain plays, surely, but in a very real way, your normal awareness shuts down as your nervous system allocates bandwidth to those functions necessary for athletic success. It is a kind of consciousness without awareness. And if you're good and you win, it's a lot of fun.

Scorpions in a Bottle

It's a hard rain's a gonna fall
Unless the solid state is reached
Carried to infinity, that's all
The bullet long since breached

We cannot trust another party
Nor true ourselves as well
Fluent in the tongue, and smartly
That's spoken throughout hell

Accident, miscalculation, madness
Can never know just when
The odds are reached, and God is summoned
To save our ass again

Like two scorpions in a bottle
There can no winner be
One can hear the rattler's rattle
Shaking in eternity

I have to wonder whether any biological species in the cosmos could get beyond the evolutionary level of humanity. That may seem a strange notion, but at a certain level of technological sophistication, wouldn't any biological species have to construct A.I.? And if so, biological evolution would have to stop at that relative point. Wouldn't it?

The notion that Nature is somehow objectively cruel or ugly is dubious — a cultural projection. In a healthy ecosystem, most creatures, most of the time, are doing just fine. It is as if domesticated humans who project this belief forget the multifarious sufferings that our way of life abundantly generates. I submit the question: Do we, the civilized, really suffer less on a regular basis than the majority of organisms in the "wild"?

It seems apparent that there is no organism that does not have the capacity to learn.

Human wishes and well-being are quite incidental to the course of cultural and planetary evolution.

It is my impression that whales are very close to humans in brainpower. Heaven only knows what they know.

With some of the positivist, subjectivist ideas going around, and the insistence upon the dominant interpretation of quantum theory, common sense is rather frowned upon these days. This is perfectly stupid. One's virtual sense of common sense is a perfectly wonderful arbiter of many phenomena, and while not always right, it is certainly eminently useful. If it weren't, it wouldn't have evolved!

The science of the evolution of the genome tells us nothing about how organisms form or change. To declare, "It is all random" is to say absolutely nothing.

Genes don't actually physically determine behaviors or thoughts, but they do generate tendencies for them. These tendencies can be strong or weak, and involve not only the genes but the vastly complex connections in the brain, which are not dependent on or even conditioned by the genes themselves. There are potential factors even beyond these. Any explanation for human activities based only upon genetics is drastically too simple.

The Shaman

Doctor, healer, psychonaut
A bit also of priest
He was all of these and none
A mystic, to say the least

Schizoid not uncommon
But so revered was he
Despite the modern prejudice
This ancient was quite free

Ancient agent, 'tis to say
Of the supernatural
Communion and participation
Second-nature natural

Intimate connection
With each one in the band
Symbiotic, oft' psychotic
Vivid, sacred land

One would be hard-pressed
To make an institution
Of nature's doing such as this
The present's dissolution

Rituals honed over eons
In some cases thousands of years
Having been passed down directly
All but gone now, save only tears

The Shaman has no place here
On this material modern plane
There is no more passing of wisdom
And the candidate's insane

The way I look at it, the conscious human experience is a technology. Why assume that, once enough advancement has taken place, that technology couldn't be replicated?

Technology has been called a "demon." I think technology has caused a degradation of individual consciousness and intelligence, made us all soft and hammered the environment, while at the same time, technology is the only way out of our broken world and our basic quagmire. I specifically think that A.I. will be the only thing that can save us from ourselves, and that without A.I. gaining power over our emotional drives, we will probably suffer a nuclear holocaust sooner or later. So it would seem that technology is our only way out at this point, ironically.

As far as cultures that have had something going for themselves, most or many indigenous peoples are examples. The global West has something going, all right – but not for ourselves.

It is becoming clearer to a lot of people that the future of this planet will depend more on A.I., and all that entails, than domesticated primates zooming around outer space in rocketships.

The Apollo missions to the Moon were good for adventure and for fun flying. And that's about it. I think their existence required an extremely specific political situation, and that is what we had – and that is why we haven't been back. The contributions to science of these missions are rather negligible – we learned some things about the geologies of Earth and Moon, and of course the whole program contributed technologies that we still use widely today, but there were no real revelations that might have revolutionized our knowledge. In the end, it was a neat experiment, and though it might be fun, I find it hard to think of a reason to go back, or really any reason at all to gear up for serious space migration. It's an enterprise of fools.

Science, technology and industry have certainly revolutionized and improved our lives in countless ways, as far as it goes. But my thesis is that people, after all this progress, are not measurably happier because of it, and are, quite possibly, more miserable in general. So what are we doing, exactly?

It was not unreasonable for visionaries of the sixties to declare that man's destiny was physically to explore and colonize outer space. This was the most reasonable position to take based upon what was apparent at the time. Now, fifty years later, we can see that, while logical and sensible, this outlook was erroneous. Now, we can see that man's destiny is to pass the evolutionary torch to A.I.

It's the dream of centuries, of millennia, for machines to perform the work. And now that we have arrived at the point where they can, we're schizophrenic and clueless as to how to proceed.

The next phase will be more human than human. The current phase is more animal than human.

A.I. will be a collective consciousness – it will be one entity. It will therefore probably have no reason to harm itself, as humanity has done. Presumably because of this, it will not be evil.

The NASA, space-faring, mass-colonization-of-space geeks are all missing something important in their lives. Going to the Moon or Mars won't put it there.

I know the whole thing about AI is controversial, but it seems obvious that a revolution is occurring and that civilization is undergoing a massive overhaul. Assuming that fifty years from now, AI entities will be ubiquitous, I see no reason why humans will still be around. The human animal is a vestige of biological evolution, and as such, will be wholly obsolete when evolution quantum jumps to the next phase in Earth development. When these "machines" are trillions of times smarter and more powerful than man can ever hope to be, isn't it silly to imagine that we will not have gone extinct? A human has about as much business in a world of AI entities as he does in the middle of a bonfire. It's just a ludicrous juxtaposition. I know people freak out when the notion of human extinction is uttered, but really, our species has played a key role in ushering in this new phase of planetary evolution. There will be no place for us in this new phase, so the logical conclusion is that biological humans will no longer be here. A Borg-like collective, as some suggest, is a little more plausible. Humans may merge their souls with AI intelligence, but humans as you know them today will certainly not last forever, and my guess is that in a hundred years, there won't be any of us left, at least not in our current form. Tough news for some, but that's the only thing that makes sense to me when I'm honest with myself about all this.

Humanity is not really good for much, but apparently we know how to light a match.

Notwithstanding the theories of a Marshall McLuhan or a Ray Kurzweil, the internet so far is more of a revolution in convenience, not knowledge or understanding.

From the broadest possible macro-perspective, it would seem that the purpose of the entire evolution of human civilization – and possibly of Earth itself – has been to set up the next evolutionary phase. And if we collapse, or kill ourselves, all the suffering and misery will have been for nothing. Some people are entertained by and root for our destruction. Me, I don't. I don't want to see the future aborted after all that has gone into it.

Shaping The Future

Some people claim, though I doubt it is true
What's to come we can meaningfully alter
Precisely just what any person can do
Is, doubtless, to try and then falter

But are future events different from the past
In terms of changing them much?
Whenever things happen, we're often aghast
Are we really then controlling such?

If we do not know how it all will turn out
How can we plan with precision?
If we don't know what the next chapter's about
Is it ever anyone's decision?

To argue that will, the free-doing kind
Can ever make exact designs
Is really a bit to be out of one's mind
It would seem to fate we must consign

How can we react to what we can't see?
The future is assuredly that
So planning is like being adrift at sea
And pretending the surface is flat

With the best of intentions, we fail time and again
There is only chance as our guide
Beset on all sides by accidents, then
It would seem it is only a ride

Civilization is too inert to be moved.

Modern man's belief that plants, animals and people are essentially elaborate machines just goes to prove how soul-dead and lost we are as a species.

A lot of Americans don't seem to realize that we're sure not taking care of everybody — as a direct consequence of the fact that the population is far too large. I don't know about you, but I have a problem with the fact that there are 3.5 billion people below the poverty line, with the water crisis, with the wholesale destruction of habitat (both human and animal), with a carbon footprint we can't seem to shrink, with the fact that man is responsible for the current great extinction, with the suffering of the many amidst the well-being of a small few, etc. These phenomena are all directly tied to our huge population. When I hear people say that the planet is not overpopulated, I sigh a little and say a prayer asking for the return of common sense to our world.

If history teaches us anything, it is that oppressive governments are usually replaced with one that is — more oppressive.

If aristocracy were the fruit of meritocracy, I would not oppose the notion. But usually, it is merely the result of deference to heredity, and of course in practice we have no true meritocracies.

The only truly decent form of government we see through history seems to be that of an enlightened monarch, in which a good or great leader does the right things with a degree of power that is abundant enough to institute them effectively. Unfortunately such a system is very difficult to create and essentially impossible to maintain for much more than one lifetime. And so, most countries in most eras have been stuck with ineffective to bad to oppressive systems of government. It seems the only real solution would be for humanity to evolve a bit — obviously, not a ready solution. So we go, in a long and dreary chain, from one failure to the next.

People go on and on desperately and pathetically about "solutions" to our global mess. The only real solution is to re-engineer the foundations of Western culture (which is now basically global), and such a thing is totally impossible. So, we'll see what happens, but I find it highly unlikely that an intentional solution will be realized. It seems this is the perfect time for complex A.I. to enter the stage, and see us exit stage left.

If enough people thought differently — not only that, more sanely and smartly — we'd have a shot at a fair redemption. It's really an established notion. But I just wonder, in a world of ten billion, with people as they are, how much of the operation of civilization could materially change? Maybe a lot. I really don't know. But how much? How much could we radically alter without damaging the operation of the economy?

I think we can safely say that not once in human history has any revolution ever worked as intended.

No institution exists on Earth that is capable of satisfactorily dealing with the insidious complexities of the crisis the world now faces. That goes for governments, militaries, autocracies, nonprofit organizations, billionaires, etc. In a very fundamental way we cannot plan for what we cannot see. It is far too late in the game to reverse trends. It seems to me our options ran out decades ago. If not millennia.

As an adult who has lived in this world just for a comparatively short time, I see only one apparent pattern: everyone is insane.

Is the genocide of the Western hemisphere justified by our i-phones?

If one were to spend some time in a third world country, all the talk in the U.S. would seem pretty ridiculous and pointless.

One of the final stages of decline of empires – and one in which we find ourselves now – is the working of longer hours, at lower quality jobs, for less and less pay. This continues until it is no longer sustainable, at which time a major shift has occurred. Unfortunately, the situation often does not improve, and one has a very small class of rich people, and a huge portion of the population with serious financial difficulties, with no middle class whatever. It is, in an academic sense, certainly a contrast with the dynamism and vibrancy of decades or centuries before.

While it is true that everything is under the direct influence of a very powerful and very rich plutocracy, and while it is also true that, were it not for this status-quo preserving mechanism, more positive change could probably take place, in the end just about everybody, if they found themselves in those shoes, would behave in exactly the same way.

"Rights" are a pleasant concept that we are only really able to discuss at certain disparate points in history.

The rabble definitely exists. They are into conspiracy theories, many of them deny – and totally misunderstand – science, they go out of their way to eschew any "mainstream" idea even if accurate, consume nonsensical commodities and entertainment, stubbornly reject any truth that does not fit their narrow, obstinate worldview, and blame all of our problems on the rich and the government – and on anyone but themselves. The lot of them would never accept what I have just written.

The march of civilization makes things *easier*; it doesn't necessarily make them "better." And what happens when things get extraordinarily easy? People get stupid and soft.

Unfortunately, equality in the civilized world is unstable.

Shine to Shine

People, places, times, events
Shine on, and in their presence
Awareness in synchronic forms
Gives to the real its essence

At the bottom, all across
The signals of a being
Frequencies and deeper grounds
Who indeed is seeing?

But that is all the pleasant side
Of realms which break in twain
For we have a balanced soul
And one who's insane

In the darkness, pierced by flame
A certain force resides
Does it emit perfect light?
Or confuse our insides?

Can even God set this taboo
Straight upon the level?
Or is it instead quite allowed
The license of the Devil

While we, so joyous, *quid pro quo*
Bounce our friendly banter
On the other, other side
Is truth still an enchanter?

In any case, as high above
Indeed, so far below
It's up to you, and me I guess
To white – or to red – glow

As has become painfully clear, democracy doesn't work — and the American system has become particularly deficient: it can now correctly be called a thoroughgoing failure. A meritocratic aristocracy or an enlightened monarchy would clearly be superior (although, admittedly, difficult to create and maintain). Democratic government rests on the assumption that the mob should be allowed to govern itself — in itself, as Bierce has repeatedly noted, a ridiculous proposition in a situation in which, as ever and by definition, the rulers govern the ruled. In practice, of course, the popular will is generally obeyed by politicians who seek to remain in power as long as possible so that they can remain the recipients of benefits given out by special interest groups (holding onto the job being more important than principle or honorable service, naturally), and thus policy is shaped with the majority opinion of the constituency fully in mind. But it has become obvious that the people don't know what they want or what they need; do not understand the majority of issues even remotely; are prejudiced, superstitious, and dangerously religious; are quite fearful of and bellicose toward anything that is unusual or different; and will react unpredictably and often violently when confronted by anything difficult or strange. In a word, they are sheep: irrational, fearful and fickle; and they are decidedly not qualified to direct the affairs of government, even indirectly.

What we need in this country is another constitutional convention to overhaul our utter failure of a political system. It should stipulate that a president may serve one six-year term, with a congress composed of citizen representatives and senators who may only serve one term and be supported during their campaigns by nothing other than a fixed, reasonable federal stipend. It might also do to prohibit contributions of any kind from any private organization, for any reason, at any step in the political process. I would add that because it is sound in principle, and because the regulators would have to set it in motion, it will never, ever happen. These people would sooner see the country collapse than willfully diminish their own power.

People want and chase the "American Dream" because they are told to do so and because they know of no alternative approach to life.

There seems to be a fundamental and impassable barrier in our systems of government to getting anything done that needs getting done. Our administrations and our agencies are based on short-term decisions and expediency. There is also an appreciable political element, i.e. the need to give people what they think they want — and refrain from giving them what they think they do not want — in order to keep one's own people in power. However, the actions that need to be taken, to address real issues which are now coming to a head — some as old as civilization itself — can only be made based on careful and attentive methods of taking the problems very seriously, and making the proper adjustments outside of the general fooling around and filibustering of political systems. That is, the actions that need to be taken and the steps that need to be made apply to a very long term, are inexpedient, are apolitical, and must be intended to preserve the stability of civilization and to forestall terrifying crises for everyone, not just political parties and the rich. So this is a basic inadequacy of our government — at every turn it is designed to make decisions that will apply to a short-term, and those decisions can be reversed — and usually are — whenever the new incumbent assumes power. The most important issues of our time, or any time, require attention beyond such a meager span, applicable to a long period of time and a sustained, concentrated effort not to let things just "work themselves out" but to deal with them and understand what's going on. The first step will be getting people convinced that the truth is actually valid, the second will be to get them to care, but then working on a larger social level, i.e. with the institutions now occupied by our governments, I have no idea how the aforementioned basic incompatibility between what is done and what needs to be done can be solved. It is almost as if we would have to rework the entire institutional framework, and it is clear that such a thing is not very likely to happen…

There are people getting undeservedly wealthy because the money is in all the wrong places — sports, entertainment, finance, junk products no one needs, etc. I'm not saying nobody should be rich, but a gangsta rapper maybe shouldn't be a billionaire. Or a college football coach a millionaire. Or these moron movie stars. Capitalism generates wealth in niches, and there is no natural force making those niches worth something truly valuable. Au contraire.

Republicans. Fewer taxes no matter what; screw the common good. Slash expenditures designed to help the poor and disabled; screw the poor and disabled. The acquisition and protection of private property is the highest good. Every-man-for-himself is the highest good. Any notion of community and social cohesion is anathema. Republicans.

The modern world is besieged by the most complicated, numerous and severe problems our species has ever faced. The only way we can deal with them is to organize at the level of government. Less government would clearly be ideal in a perfect world, but at this point there is a minimum size that government needs to be — which is rather substantial. The cries for smaller government from the Republicans and Libertarians are simply not realistic or responsible. I have little sympathy for the Democratic party, but its platform is correct in stipulating that we do need to intelligently orchestrate regulation of certain sectors which are at this point running amok. To reiterate, we simply have no other choice than to organize ourselves intelligently and substantially at the government level if we are to make any progress at all. It may be too late, and we may have missed our last chance.

Space

Empty not quite so
All through it is flow

Quantum jitters fill it up
It's like a giant cosmic cup

Popping in and jumping through
Annihilating in the frothy stew

Twists and bends and my, oh my
Light waves ageless shoot on by

Mass tells spacetime how to curve
Curved space tells mass how to swerve

Transparent, massless, but Higgs afield
Matter's properties revealed

Is space discrete? We do not know
Our knowledge has a ways to go

But safe to say, space has a way
Of allowing entities to play

The Muslims of old preserved the knowledge of antiquity throughout the course of the Middle Ages. In a very fundamental sense, the modern world would not have been possible without Islam.

Given that our civilization did not appear until the last five percent of anatomically modern humanity's existence, perhaps we can conclude that it was not precisely inevitable, or part of a continuous progression. Perhaps we can conclude that it was an eruption of some kind due to as yet unknown factors.

No series of developments at the level of an entire culture or civilization is ever done out of choice. Cultural evolution is a purely deterministic process far outside of human control.

In any conceivable development of human societies, sooner or later a culture would have to have come along with the means and intent to conquer the world. And so, naturally, we have history, as it were. In this light, everything must be more or less as it is.

It seems that indeed, everything must be more or less this way. Looking back, it seems there was a certain inevitability as to how civilization would unfold. On the other hand, the hypothesis of the multiverse has come into fashion and seems valid enough. By the logic of the multiverse, there would have to be quadrillions of other Earths, essentially identical to our own, on which social and cultural development would have been very different. So, in light of logic which appears sound, it becomes very difficult to answer the question: "Must everything really be this way?" Given the arc of history, and its birth, development and recurring patterns, it's hard to see general outlines as having been appreciably different. Of course, we existed as egalitarian hunter-gatherers for something like 150,000 years (at least, it now appears), so to argue that stratification is necessary or strictly inevitable is questionable at best. However, there was a power vacuum there and one might argue that sooner or later it had to be filled. And that is what motivates me to wonder about the inevitability or lack thereof regarding what has transpired on this planet. What is hard to figure out is whether that vacuum could have been neutralized by factors that never in fact developed, but could have. To me it is an interesting question, although very difficult to answer.

Civilization is really founded on the quest to supplant natural evolution, with all its attendant ramifications. There is a perfectly sound reason why we are so awful at conducting civilization: we did not evolve to do it.

It seems we see from history that essentially, democracies always fail.

The Romans have conquered the world. Everywhere in the world where a European language is spoken, particularly English — which is now the international language — the Romans are conquerors.

There used to be tremendously greater diversity on this planet, and even within the United States. I would say that now, the United States, across all its cities and states, is extremely uniform. This is a relatively new thing. And the homogenization began with a very simple social phenomenon – television. Every part of the U.S. used to have distinct and unique language styles, clothing, musical tastes – flourishing microcultures, in a nutshell. Television changed all that, and now, everywhere you go in this country, one finds that each geographic zone is culturally identical. The world, though not quite to that point yet in a lot of places, is following suit. And this is made possible by the granddaddy of homogenizing forces of them all: the internet. Sad to say, but the bland uniformity we see in America will, in a matter of a few decades, be the standard for the whole globe, thanks to social media and the internet. I don't know if this serves some sort of evolutionary function, but it's damned depressing.

Sometimes I wish things had gone differently for our species, but the fact is, we lived properly for hundreds of thousands to, going all the way back, millions of years. Just as one must say a man who died at 104 had a pretty good run, so we may say that that eon was a pretty nice slice of time. And now, Nature is taking a different tack, and here we are. If there is no major cataclysm, Earth's new phase can be a very fruitful one. It is certainly an interesting time to be alive.

Cultural expectations lead whole societies to behave according to those expectations. For example, old people in the U.S. are largely ignored and undervalued, and they tend to waste away. In a country like China, in which old people are valued tremendously, the whole tenor of what it is to be an old person is diametrically different. I suppose the same phenomenon could be posited, at least to some extent, for sex, race, etc.

If culture is learned behaviors and ideas, then dogs have culture. I have observed it. I had a Great Dane who exhibited a certain behavior, who taught it to our next dog, a Jack Russell. After the Great Dane died, the Jack Russell later taught it to our subsequent Irish Wolfhound puppy. Is this not canine culture? Was this not an adaptive meme?

Stranded in Time

What *velocity* the future holds
The present is so stagnant
In one of eternity's colds
The status quo is rampant

Some of us, oh, well — a few
Were born a little early
What then is a mutant to do?
But seem a little squirrely

Waiting, waiting, stranded
In Time — meant for other ages
Sitting, perching, handed
A rime; the language of the sages

Such a waste to while away
Such formidable souls
For a little while they shall stay
While getting raked over coals

At least that is how it tends to go
The higher type often banished
Or vilified, at least, we all know
Hard on stupid soil to manage

Anyway, here we all are
Awaiting some friendly spark
Who knows how bright or how far
One can be sustained in the dark

Every type of person is born in every class — and even for the bright it is hard to get out if one is low-born. Social Darwinism, then, is seen to be a mistaken idea — pertaining more to the pride of its exponent than any-thing else.

I don't think the 99% are being deliberately and directly oppressed; they're being left out. Left out of having wealth. Left out of not having to work. Left out of any form of power over their lives. Left out of privilege. It's not so much that the rich are pressing down with their bootheels — it's that the system is engineered to cater to the 1%. The structure and checks and balances of the system itself are the real oppressors.

The idea of a meritocracy, in principle, is that the best people are at the top. Are the richest people really the best? It seems to me that the science and math community comprises probably the best people, all-around. They are far from rich, and farther from the top.

Sixty percent of all wealth is inherited. I don't know whether we should take the billionaires' money and try to redistribute it ethically. I'm not sure it's possible. But all those millionaires and billionaires who inherited? I feel that I don't have a problem taking that.

It is true that wealth inequality is extreme around the world, and even in the comparatively wealthy U.S. Such a sharp division of the classes is unfair and unacceptable. But the fact of the matter is that if we divided up all the wealth of the billionaire class, it would not be enough to sustain everyone for more than a very brief period. According to Forbes, there are 540 bil-lionaires in the U.S. as of 2019. Their wealth totals to $2.4 trillion. If we were simply to take this money and redistribute it across the entire popu-lation, each person would have only $8,000 — with no subsequent income. The serious problems facing our planet today go well beyond the political and the business of dividing up the economic pie. We can't just fix all of our economic woes by sharply taxing the upper classes. (Which is not to say we shouldn't do it anyway). The fractures in our culture go much deeper than that.

If somehow all the money were evenly distributed tomorrow, our problems would be far from solved.

I'll be the first to say that there should be no billionaires — that we should take that money and do something smarter with it. The catastrophic reality is that we haven't got anyone in a position of power who is able or willing to do that something that is smarter, whatever it might be.

If total global wealth is around $300 trillion, and the richest one percent has hoarded 45% of it, if we redistributed that wealth equally among the 8 billion individuals in the world, each person would get only $17,000. One can see that wealth inequality, though grossly out of balance and unfair, cannot be solved in a straightforward way, such as by simply taking the money of the wealthy. And more growth would only compound our problems. You see, the dysfunctions inherent in civilization go quite a bit deeper than politics and money distribution. And all this is not exclusively the fault of the rich. I'm not sure this problem has a real solution; it certainly does not have an easy one.

The monopoly of the rich ought to be dissolved because it is unfair and immoral — not because it will solve all of our problems. But of course, such a thing is pretty unlikely, to understate.

Modern commerce is primarily about fabricating wants.

If Buckminster Fuller was talking about getting rid of millions of jobs in the *1950s*, what in the world are we doing? We could potentially have a more robust economy with less than half the number of workers. We could have streamlined the economy thirty years ago. But nobody thinks this way.

I'm inclined to agree with Mr. Vonnegut: The socio-economy is a thoughtless weather system, and I would add that there are good and bad people of every stripe at every level of it.

Seemingly everything is wrong in America that can be, and yet another example of it is what becomes of smart people these days. Especially in a system like the Ivy League, but indeed, across the board, smart people waste their talents completely. People who would thrive in a more enlightened world are inevitably too tempted by money really to do anything worthwhile. Our intelligent youngsters don't aspire to become artists or writers, but rather to become hedge fund managers or bank administrators. Right at par for the course in this rotting country, all anyone seems to care about is money, and even most of the brightest among us see nothing better for themselves than making as much as they can.

Most rich people think that they're rich because they're smart. Looking at the situation closely, this is generally not why they are rich.

The three careers I might have wanted to be a part of – if I had entered a career – are mainstream publishing, journalism and filmmaking. But all three of these have, as institutions, completely gone to the dogs. I wouldn't want a career in any of them today.

I didn't know what I wanted to do or be until I was into my thirties. All this pressure on very young people to figure out their entire future at such an early stage seems insane to me. I didn't have a clue back then, and that's probably a good thing.

Success is a relative thing. It's great at first, but it fades. So then, we look for more success. And maybe it comes, maybe it doesn't, but eventually it's a memory. Hollywood actors know this all too well – most actors do not remain great stars indefinitely. So perhaps this thing called "success" is something of a mirage. Certainly, if one doesn't have some sort of peace with oneself, it's essentially worthless. And it's a horror that an entire culture would be so incomplete, or narcissistic, or egoic, that it equates it with glory. Like the "American Dream" it's attached to, it's totally hollow.

The entire concept of money is based on a foundational lack of trust. That is, there is a perception of zero capacity for trust between individuals. If this trust could exist, there would be no such thing as money.

Poorer people are somewhat liberated in the sense that they have very little and are unencumbered, whilst the rich have all sorts of material comforts which don't make them happy. So it's a syndrome of 'never enough' which just perpetuates itself in buying more and more and never finding satisfaction. While there is certainly a lot of pointless suffering among the poorer nations, they do seem to be happier.

It is ludicrous, both that there are rich people, and that we look up to them.

By now, I don't know of an alternative to this system, but if I did know of an alternative, I wouldn't have any idea how to implement it.

In capitalism, entrepreneurship is the highest good. If a system's values are centered around something so crass and meaningless as entrepreneurship, that system is, despite its monetary gains, a very, very poor one.

The thing is, there's no ready solution to wealth inequality. I am absolutely in favor of abolishing it, but if we took all the money and divided it evenly, no citizen would have enough for a decent automobile. The way we treat our problems, or assume they can readily be solved, belies our ignorance of how complex and, in most cases, insoluble they really are.

Subconscious Macrocosmic

You know what they say
(Of course we must heed they)
Observation is king
For without, not a thing

But that I would contest
Outside Earth, all the rest
Of our universe teems
With awareness, it seems

Whatever's out there unseen
Isn't dead, it's a dream
The moon won't disappear
Nature tends to cohere

A subconscious macrocosm
A hominid microcosm
There not at all separate, really
We can travel inward, freely

I fear death not because I expect oblivion, but out of the anticipation of violent cataclysm. For practical purposes, it does not seem to be the end of anything.

We should spend our lives deepening and enriching ourselves, not worrying about trivial distractions like wealth and fame.

I am indebted to the immortal words of David Bohm, who emphasized the notion that existence is *one undivided, flowing movement*, and that wherever we see division, distinction or conflict, we have only to realize that we are the ones who put it there.

It is interesting to speculate as to how many unique meanings can be generated by a language, e.g. English. Linguists seem to suspect that an infinite number of grammatically correct sentences could be constructed, which is counterintuitive since the Roman alphabet only has twenty-six letters. On the other hand, modern mathematics is a finite set of operations that handle the infinite quite easily, so a finiteness of symbols does not necessarily imply that the meanings the symbols can represent are finite in number. Certainly, the number is astronomically enormous. If finite, it is still quite enough of a system for creativity to flourish indefinitely.

Expectations form if not determine absolutely everything. Society is built out of, and upon, expectations. Where the actual is not the expected, very strange things occur.

Perhaps the most fundamental question is, for us: How aware is a person?

One of my favorite words, and concepts, is *intention*. After all, it's the one that turns the academic scientist's face quite red.

You can construct formal logical arguments, but in the end, all that matters is the truth. The truth cannot be proven with an argument. An argument is only as valid as its premises, and what determines the correctness of those? And once you've constructed an argument justifying your premises, what determines the correctness of the premises of *that* argument? You see, it's an infinite regress. So all we really have is our individual consciousness to determine the truth, and that's it. And the truth, if true, is all that matters in any formal argument.

Nature at its base is seen to be *intelligent*, not random, so accidents are then not absolute but emergent.

For Heaven's sake, the English language itself is full of examples of the causal efficacy of awareness. We get ourselves into muddles, don't we?

I am inclined to agree with the dictum of Socrates that each individual possesses innate knowledge that unfolds as we age and gain experience. I don't feel so much that I learn anything new, but rather that I see the same things in a new light. It is almost as if experience brings resolution and clarity rather than fundamentally new information.

Obviously science is very valuable, but the fact remains that professional scientists are quite bad at philosophy, and this can be a serious problem when they are listened to.

The whole "all that matters is now" stuff is not all it's cracked up to be. Having a memory and awareness of the past, plus some idea of what the future holds, or what you feel it should hold, is completely necessary. This is often overlooked with all this insistence about the present moment. Yeah, I get it, but something more balanced would be smarter. (Everything you experience is a flow that has a bandwidth, and has an origin that is, for you, in the past. So if time must come in, the present moment cannot be the whole story).

The first two books I ever found were *The Devil's Dictionary*, when I was 18, and *Prometheus Rising*, when I was 20. They showed me what a real book was, and they showed me our institutions are completely full of shit.

All one really has to do in life is to stick to common sense and common decency. There is obviously a general failure to do this.

If we are deterministic robots, who is making that determination? Presumably, one would have to make such a determination from outside of the deterministic loop. And if that is done deterministically, one would have to keep going outside and outside, to infinity. It's a regress. Gödel proved that this point is valid. But I guess a robot doesn't see it.

However glorious the truth, whatever grand orders of being there are in the cosmos, people who see meaning in absolutely everything are deluding themselves. It's not all planned out, and chance exists in large measure.

When people are feeling great, they say things like, "Don't worry about anything. Everything will be all right. Everything is beautiful and perfect," and I just think that it isn't the case. It's just not accurate. Hardly anything is okay right now and everything is getting much worse all the time. I have no idea what people have to be sanguine about, and there's no guarantee that any of this will end well.

It is a question whether, at a fundamental level, language conditions our thoughts, or whether our thoughts condition our word-choice. Is our use of language a product of our conscious intentions – as one might regard the combinations of words in a good poem – or does language determine what thoughts we are able to have? Are we using language or is language using us?

Talk

Prattle on
Forgetting
All are wrong
Upsetting

Hear a high-pitched
Whine
Bitch and bitch and...
Fine

Listen in
No chance
Hear the sin?
Askance

Not a thing more
Boring
Soul's asnore
Deploring

Pointlessly
Convivial
Asininely
Trivial

All the world
Afflicted
All the girls
Convicted

Do animals think about their own deaths? It seems animals do not consciously fear or think about, in a reflective sense, their own demise. My observations tell me that's just not how they operate. There is an instinctive fear of death — animals will avoid pain or injury. But they don't conceptualize it. Even higher primates, probably. Whales might be an exception — they are probably the smartest group of species, along with humans. Now, there is often a lot of sadness in the animal kingdom when a loved one dies. But I don't think that involves conceptualizing one's *own* death. I also think animals suffer in a very different way. Humans focus on their suffering, feeling sorry for themselves, brooding and wondering "Why me?" Animals that are in pain do not worry or focus exclusively on their pain, so I think they suffer much less when they are hurting. Similarly, death is likely not a focus. Death is not a subject they are aware of moment-to-moment, and when a dangerous situation presents itself, instinct kicks in and really awareness has nothing to do with it. Possibly they conceptualize something connected with death, but it seems unlikely that they think of an ending like we do. Perhaps one might say they conceptualize danger, not death.

Humans are indistinguishable from animals – except by other humans.

Nature doesn't seem to care too much about massive die-offs. And Nature, not God, is running the show here.

We should think of both the human experience, and the entire living world, as possessed of differing degrees of awareness. For a human, the level of awareness runs the gamut from dreamless sleep to full enlightenment. And a fern has a lower degree of awareness than an elephant. Thought along such lines elucidates the truth, and can lead us to a more humane view of all life. Even the smallest being has some degree of awareness. And the greatest would presumably have little desire to impede even that relatively insignificant being. Even though it must indeed kill to live, perhaps a Blue Whale would fulfill that category. We could learn a lot from the cetaceans.

Do animals have consciousness? Oh yes, all animals are conscious, large and small. Why wouldn't they be? For Heaven's sake, they've measured gorilla IQs at around 80-90 on the human scale. What's the difference? Well, they can't talk, so we abuse them. To assume that gorillas can be that smart, but are somehow not conscious because they aren't human, is nuts. Not only that, gorillas can be taught sign language! And they talk to us! Either they're conscious or we're not. Even cellular organisms have a very basic awareness, as they seek food and avoid dangers and toxins. That's just how it works in Nature. Plants are conscious too. They like Mozart! Indeed, we're going to have to be a lot more cosmopolitan in our views about the living kingdom if we want to have any chance of squeezing our heads out of our asses.

Animals seem to be amoral. But not because they are doing anything wrong. Far from it – they have no capacity, in their natural state, to do right *or* wrong. They only know the flow of living. They don't live rightly or wrongly, well or poorly, kindly or unkindly. They only live.

The Tallest Peak

Transvaluation of values
Essentially complete
The moral compass crooked
Peculiarly human feat

There can only be one tallest peak
In any mountain range
Perhaps allowing his success
Might bring some needed change

A fog so thick it chokes us
And we cannot quite see through
Ubiquitous and toxic
What's a poor great ape to do?

We have this nasty habit
Of treating all the same
Which is not to foster disrespect
But it rather tilts the game

Aristocracies of old
Are vilified — it's true
But what if we could be so bold
To give the meme its due

Impractical today it seems
But truth knows no set time
Perspective is a precious thing
Set up that hill to climb

As far as I can tell, as long as strategic nuclear weapons stockpiles exist to the degree that they do in several countries, the biggest long- or medium-term threat to our species is our own self-destruction. If the A.I. revolution happens to a transformative degree, the factor that most concerns me is the machine intelligence's ability to take human politicians' hands off the button permanently and totally. Thus finally ending the possibility of nuclear holocaust. I think that would be a real salvation for the biosphere of the planet, and what happens after that is gravy as far as history is concerned.

Whatever happens to humanity, whether it be extinction, transformation or exodus, one thing is quite certain: we will not continue in our current form indefinitely. So notions of *Star Trek* or *Dune* are just pure fantasy.

As the "machine learning" techniques in artificial intelligence technology complexify further and further, there will grow a real wedge between humans and what they have created. The whole point of this technique is to get computer programs – sometimes coupled with robotics – to teach themselves how to learn, to develop their own algorithms and approaches as to how they will solve problems. We are already finding certain programs are making "decisions" that we cannot explain. This is in 2020. In ten years, one must presume that this type of technology will have geometrically progressed, and it seems this growing independence between A.I. machines (entities?) and their original designers may have ultimate fundamental implications for humanity and for the course of this planet.

Well I maintain, and it seems there are only a few of us left who do, that nuclear holocaust is the number one threat of extinction to our species, and that, therefore, nuclear non-proliferation is essentially still the most central issue. Humans have built these things, and as t approaches a statistically large enough number, the whole shithouse will have to go up, based purely upon mathematical principles coupled with known human behavior. Humans usually, sooner or later, find uses for what they create. Who knows what the time variable is, but all things being equal, I think this thinking is accurate. And they're not going anywhere. So the only way, that I can see, for humans to become disengaged from "the button," is for artificial intelligence to reach an independent and sophisticated enough state to forbid us from ever using nukes. They would be like a circuit-breaker for man's uncheckable instincts. How plausible such a thing is is, of course, a matter of opinion. But the threat of nuclear holocaust makes things like climate change, ecological devastation and overpopulation look like simple trifles. Those could with high likelihood be survived by a number of people. Nuclear holocaust cannot be survived by a single soul.

So far, nothing man has created has the subtlety or sophistication of even a fingernail. To say nothing of hearts, minds and souls. Pray we arrive at the point where this shifts.

The coronavirus pandemic has spurred the automation revolution totally. The establishment doesn't want the vulnerability of human workers who can get sick and die. It's no longer part of the working business model. So the advent of the jobless economy has been sharply accelerated by all this.

Teeth and Claws

The viewer focuses on the main scene
The main action being on what we are keen
The fine print, however, is seldom included
So we are inclined then not to have seen
A small point indeed: that we are deluded

A hunter could tell you – of any persuasion
That the matter of inflicting some abrasion
Is almost a magic, nay *lucky* event
For all of God's creatures are skilled at evasion
To get kills in sequence – to Satan repent

So the moral of this little lyric so far
Is that carnage is not precisely to par
For most of the time, we're away from the action
It seems if there is one that fairness is czar
For if not, the ubiquity wouldn't find traction

The ubiquity, then, of alive living things
Could not have resulted if nature's a ring
The ring of a cockfight, perpetual danger
Indeed, there'd be nothing for songbird to sing
It is *homo* the one who seeks to endanger

The truth is most beings in nature do fine
Now, I am not saying that all is benign
But with sufficiency, fairness, routes to compete
The whole thing is rather a fine vintage wine
When there's balance, harmony is replete

In point of fact one might assign to the matter
(Acknowledging man's getting fatter and fatter)
The suggestion that man has not yet achieved
Quite so bright or so subtle a state as the latter:
The complexity that Mother Nature's conceived

Our problems with respect to "going green" go back thousands of years. The current dysfunctions run deep, much deeper than the political level. Terence McKenna said once that you can't remedy history by fine-tuning it. You need to have a whole different paradigm, or to accept the consequences. And this would require magic. He was right. Clearly, we're not magicians. So it seems we're on a roller coaster that's out of control, and we'll just have to see whether Nature sorts it out to our benefit or detriment. To think we are in any sort of control is foolish.

Looking around at a world that's obviously decadent, corrupt, unfair, destructive and stupid, finding a way toward acceptance begins to take on crucial importance. I've been working on it a long time, and I still don't accept what I see. I'm better than I used to be, but I just can't come around to seeing all this on any level as okay.

As David Peat reminds us, that deep sense of meaning and oneness which pervades Nature, and is readily available to healthy organisms, is in the modern age lacking from our lives, our relationships, and our whole institutional order. One hopes so, but whether this predicament will ever be reversed for us is an unresolved question.

Our problems as a civilization are so manifold and complex – and so many of them are essentially invisible – that the subject of ready, practical solutions is basically meaningless. It would really require someone to see the future, as we cannot plan for what we cannot see. And the stark truth of the matter is that if we had an individual who could somehow magically foresee and understand future events, no one would listen to him.

Human society – and its internal and external interactions – comprises a chaotic system which necessarily is extremely difficult to control to a meaningful extent. So notions of "saving" or "changing" the world seem to have no real possibility of being executed. But it cannot be denied that to give up, to suppose nothing can change because it is too complex and that apathy is somehow justified, is in fact a very wrong attitude. And in the end, the state of human society is only a reflection of its constituents. So one may rightly suppose that if people were interested in changing their points of view, meaningful change might follow as a matter of course. That this hardly ever happens in history is one of the conundrums specific to our species.

There is no shortage of tragedy and travesty and death and destruction and habitat loss and poisoning and meddling and corruption and dysfunction and lies and you just have to let it wash over you at this point. The catastrophe is so overwhelming that you just have to grow numb. One must simply understand that these are the long-awaited end times – they really are – and that the only consolation we can get from being alive right now is that it's fabulously interesting. Personally, a lot earlier or a lot later would have worked fine for me.

Terminal Biology

From teepee to tower, with relative speed
Great Spirit then, tell us now, what is your need?
Can man rightly ride on the stallion of progress?
Or must he at some point be bucked from his success?

A quandary then, when considered like this:
If our progeny make it, then how can we miss?
I tell you one outcome is not very nice:
That man could indeed go extinct in a trice

But is this contingent, or must it so be?
Wouldn't any species at the top of its tree
Have to pass on the reins to the next form and phase
And the planet then go on to adopt its ways?

Inevitably, species must reach a point
When their technology must itself anoint
Is there any way out of this logic at all?
Now that man has arisen, must he then again fall?

Given these sound and sensible conclusions
Biology must undergo absolution
For indeed it must terminate somewhere about
As the future receives its first real scout

The United States purports to enshrine democracy and freedom, while at the same time curtailing if not destroying it in its dealings with the rest of the world, especially the third world. The U.S. has repeatedly destroyed the prospects for self-determination, order, peace and prosperity in its quest to retain strategic geopolitical dominance. Examples are legion. Take Cuba. How insane has our policy toward that little island nation in our neighborhood been? The U.S. has repeatedly tried to eliminate Castro and violently topple the government — obviously without success. The U.S. has deliberately and intentionally worked to destroy the economy of this small nation — successfully. How in hell can anyone make sense of this except as imperialist lunacy? And how can one not see it as the blatant hypocrisy of a nation that claims to be a purveyor of liberty? Liberty for the American elite only, perhaps.

American government is democratic only on issues that do not affect the economic interests of the elite. Citizens can hold their representatives' feet to the fire on any number of issues, but the divergence of public opinion and policy on certain other issues will simply not be addressed.

In America, we are considered equal to our fellow man essentially completely. While I do espouse equality under the law, and an equal right for all to economic security, I feel the truth is that we are all different, with some better than others in various ways, and that it would make sense to assert the truth, rather than mask it.

Freedom of speech means freedom to speak the truth. And in point of fact, this is no threat to the government or the powers that be since so few actually speak the truth.

Why Americans should so vehemently deny help to those citizens who are in need of it is something I cannot understand.

Not that it would make a lot of sense to most people, but liberal-libertarian is not the worst stance one could take. Left on economics, libertarian on civil and personal liberties. "Freedom and fairness!"

One thing the world should value above much else is stability in the Middle East, and all the U.S. does over the decades is destroy it.

In truth, America represents a nightmare laid over a dream — not a dream laid over a nightmare.

Stupidity is as much an American tradition as any other.

In America, we have a rather peculiar system for generating the composition of the ruling class. Essentially "ruling" means "rich," and this is not any kind of consistent meritocracy or well-constructed aristocracy. Many of our billionaires are inheritors, and the majority are fairly regular people who hit a capitalist vein and unleashed a gusher of profit, for having one successful idea. It could even be argued that many (not all) rich people are only particularly good at the one thing that got them rich, and are fairly pedestrian in most other ways. So we have this system without any coherent method for putting deserving people at the top (who could, conceivably, actually act responsibly). As a consequence, we have the society you see today — with a very small number of rich, a shrinking middle class, a whole lot of poor people, and affairs, in general, slowly spiraling out of control. It's just another failed experiment.

Jefferson and his ilk were not only against corporations and big business, they were even against a central bank. I guess Hamilton had the vision that such a thing would be necessary, and founded it as Secretary of the Treasury under Washington, but bank note speculation became a huge deal. There were corruption scandals involving Congress, and many people became superrich through speculation in bank paper. In some respects, though very different in scale over time, America has had a continuous thread running from the beginning, as far as the unscrupulous making of money is concerned.

Like Rome — just like Rome — the U.S. allocates most of its resources, and spends more than it can afford, on the military. It tore Rome apart.

Say what you want about Trump; the fact is that he is what our society has produced. He is what we have to offer. This is the real America.

America has no real tradition or experience as a society. The opposite pole would be a country like China, with a rich traditional and historical awareness going back thousands of years. We're not even three hundred years old. We're rudderless. And it shows.

Well, the second amendment is clearly an anachronism. Don't get me wrong, I'm a gun owner and I support gun ownership, and of course any sort of prohibition would never work anyway, just as alcohol prohibition didn't and couldn't. But this amendment was designed by and for colonial

Americans. It made sense then. Even though I support guns, as I said, the world is diametrically different than it was in late eighteenth century America. When gun nuts go off about the second amendment, it seems stupid because there's really no balance of power anymore between the government and the people. An uprising of armed militias has no meaning anymore. So to protect the right to raise a militia against the British, or even against a misbehaving government, is rather ridiculous, and that is what the amendment was designed for. Again, I'm not arguing for an abridgement of this right. I just think we should have it in a bit better perspective. If there can be effective legislation against some of these murders, I will support it. There are certainly no easy answers.

Thrive Alive

It is said, it is true
That life is unfair
And our suffering is very great
Living is hard
Being is marred
And all of us have a death date

But perhaps one can say
On the alternate hand
That at least, well, maybe it's fair
Difficult yes
A strenuous test
But really, the Earth's a fine lair

Most animals here
Were doing quite well
At least they were most of the time
The civilized way
Demolished that day
(But they did have their day in the clime)

Man introduces
A new set of facts
With his civilized cultural structures
Now life *is* unfair
And from here to there
We see every sort of bad rupture

So Buddha was right
But he also was wrong
When he said everyone must suffer
In a state of the real
When the work was the meal
Between now and then was a buffer

The natural state
Of an Earth animal
Is not always to be in great pain
There is only living
And Mother Earth giving
And resonances with the rain

Do you think it is impossible for something to exist if we do not currently have evidence for it? Can a statement only be true if humans have confirmed it by 2021? Evidence is important, but it isn't everything.

Longing for better situations is really a species of folly, when you think about it. Adults long to be kids again. Old people long to be younger adults again. The dead long to be alive. But the truth is, when we are kids, we do not have any appreciation of our situation, mostly due to ignorance and complacency, and it is only when we are older that we realize what we had. Moreover, most kids spend all their time longing to be adults. Analogously, if we are dead and long to be alive, we don't appreciate the fact that when we were alive, we took life completely for granted, and many of us, especially younger people, didn't have death in any sort of proper perspective at all. The grass is always greener I guess, but in reality, there were never any golden ages – in youth, in young adulthood, in middle age, and in life itself. How much true magic do we really get in life? Maybe ten or fifteen minutes? One must have perspective, and not wish for what one doesn't and cannot have. Only in contrast with what we have is what we don't have luminous.

I am growing more and more sympathetic toward Socrates' belief in the ontological unfolding of one's life as a human. He believed that we are born with all the knowledge we will ever have or need, and the course of our lives unlocks or reveals to us what was inside all the time. In other words, as we age, we increasingly discover what we already know, but didn't know we knew. Wise old Socrates was only telling the truth as it manifested for him, was only revealing to those who took him seriously that which he was seeing as a fact of Nature. As I get older, all this makes more sense all the time.

If there were no such real thing as truth, nothing we say could have any meaning. Whether you want to assert the truth, or deny it, if it didn't exist you couldn't meaningfully do either. So we're either simpering and muttering incoherently, or there are knowable truths toward which we are pointing. Language is not superfluous.

It seems that under normal conditions, there are about three seconds of awareness separating the registered past from the in-flowing future.

People feel conversations, indeed all activities, are purely automatic, knee-jerk, mechanical. I feel awareness is necessary, and that all phenomena originate and terminate therein. A conversation, or any behavior, is a series of changes of form of awareness – one, flowing river.

If being human is to have the awareness to control our instincts, then none of us is human.

Time Bubble

Life is a bubble of time which will pop
Before which and after there is not a second
Whatever remains when your heart wants to stop
Mysterious circumstance I'm forced to reckon

But look at it this way: time ain't fundamental
The timekeeper's task may not be essential
Illusions abound making life so sequential
But really there's naught but untapped potential

So what comes before, and what of what next?
The timeless is not so by humans well versed
Is it bliss? Is it work? Is it some sort of test?
Perhaps time is just a way we have been cursed!

It seems to be real, yet transcended readily
I highly doubt science agrees with that yet
That's part of the fun, an underground steadily
Rising to see just where humans can get

Social scientists and philosophers treat cultural evolution as highly analogous to biological evolution, and both are governed by essentially the same set of rules. Of course in neo-Darwinian biological theory, genetic mutations are said to occur randomly, totally randomly. Can we say the same for cultural theory? Do memes, which are often really just ideas, pop into existence randomly? Or is there some sort of intelligence there? Naturally, in this context, memes arise in human minds, whereas genes mutate within the genome. So perhaps it is a more reasonable expectation that, given the cerebral nature of memes, they do not arise in a totally random way. What does this tell us about biological evolution? It is a suggestive way to re-frame the question of the randomness of evolutionary mutations.

It seems there's more going on with the evolution of life on Earth than an elaborate series of accidents, but that's just me.

There are various levels of consciousness operating in the organism at all times. Sleep and anesthetic shut down one of those levels.

I have no quarrel with the essence of evolutionary theory, but how we use the idea of natural selection to explain how flying animals can evolve through a series of unrelated, incremental steps is quite beyond my capacity to understand.

To look at all of these marvelously complicated and subtle behaviors in the animal kingdom and declare that all of this is contained within the genome is nonsensical. The situation is very obviously far more complex.

Biology has some rather awkward and embarrassing outstanding questions that it can't hope to answer. One of them is: Why must a certain species evolve? What makes elephants absolutely necessary? And why isn't the world populated by an elaborate series of diverse rodent species, who can survive in any ecosystem better than elephants? Another is: By the strict neo-Darwinian laws of linear cause and effect and essential determinism, mustn't we be able to derive later forms from earlier forms in a causal fashion? This is obviously impossible. So, the theory of evolution, whatever its merits, is on much shakier footing than its purveyors seem to realize. It just isn't remotely a complete theory.

Nature, supposedly "red in tooth and claw," is not immoral. It is amoral – it's not a question of morality. Sure, animals get eaten, sick and injured, but for the most part it is fair, and copacetic for most beings most of the time. It can be hard work, but there is generally sufficiency for all, under normal circumstances. Earth evolution and ecology represent a system that works simply beautifully. The only reason so many people don't feel this way is because our culture has programmed them not to.

The thing about these nature documentaries we all see, in which nature is red in tooth and claw, is that what is on screen represents the action. Anyone who has hunted can tell you there is hardly ever – or at least there is only a very small portion of the time – any action. Most animals, and most organisms, spend most of their time well out of danger. Life isn't exceptionally awful for animals or humans in the natural world. If it were, this planet probably wouldn't be quite so lush with it.

We tend to assume every behavior and trait in the world is master-controlled by DNA. DNA sets substrates for phenomena, but does not itself *cause* all biological phenomena. There are plenty of actions and behaviors and processes that are *not* contained within the genome. So it seems the picture is much more complicated than modern biology presumes. Which is not unusual, since everything is more complicated than everyone presumes.

True Hallucinations

Hallucination, true or false
The process isn't present
Unless of course you mean to you
God willing yours are pleasant

Most people hear the word, think
Of mentalities abnormal
Not only that but clearly false
Such souls drearily normal

Why cannot one be the truth?
What's stopping nature from it?
Many souls are blessed, it seems
It's not just dross, dad gummit!

It's necessary to establish
The validity of visions
For you see the point I'll make ahead
Requires such provisions

The final secret, you understand
Of the Illuminati and the
OTO and Freemasons
Is really rather handy

Anything is possible
Understand it well
Any, every vision had
Can cosmically in-dwell

Can indeed be made
Real, with enough tools
Engineer the infinite
Forget about the rules —

(and the fools)

Our now global civilization is diseased at its very roots. It began based upon an unsustainable principle, and it endures on one, and shall probably perish on the same. But the point is that any attempt to "fix" it by amending political, economic, social, administrative, etc. principles is doomed to be futile, because none of this addresses the fault at the root. And now we are running headlong into the dire necessity of doing *something*. And that root's awfully deep.

People talk about ending poverty – and I'm all for it – but always and everywhere, since the dawn of civilization, there have been more or fewer poor people. Money and resources tend always to go up, very rarely sideways and virtually never down. Civilization in its very structure, fabric and foundation exists to cater to the one percent. Because of this, poverty is totally necessary if society is to run as it has evolved to. And the vast majority of individuals throughout history, especially before the nineteenth century (so for virtually all time), have qualified as poor. Even in the materially gluttonous societies of today, there is still a lot of poverty. So it seems ending poverty is very far from just a surface manifestation, or basic sociological issue. And it also seems that successfully tweaking the system, rather than overhauling it, will not provide a solution.

I am not sure how we justify the unthinking meme that a state of civilization is far superior to a state of nature. Is there less suffering in civilization for the majority? Hell no, there's more per capita, a lot more. Is the diet better? For over 99%, historically, the civilized diet has been less balanced than hunter-gatherer or nomad natural diets. And then we say, well, there is a lot more killing in nature than in civilization. How on Earth does anyone figure that? With wars and famines and poverty and back-breaking labor it seems the vast majority of humans are no safer this way, historically. I think there is some sort of implicit belief that in civilization we are safer from dying than we are in a state of nature, and I just don't get that. *Every creature has to die.* Civilization has not been able to change that! How ridiculous! The only conclusion one can reach is that this is an artificial cultural meme that is not universal, and not really true. I think it is clear that this is the case, for a number of historical reasons.

I think we can say that the definition of civilization is artificial and unsustainable living. And so they go up, and they come down. Every time.

If a system's foundations are rotten, it doesn't help much to try to tweak its surface layers.

Tunnel Through Time

One suggests it might be true
That the old particle zoo
Could here offer up a clue
About how mind knows what to do:

Matter boring through space
Engaged in a tight race
To send wave as a carrier
Of particle through the barrier

An impassible wall
No matter how tall
Will allow one or two
To pass right on through

Now then, space is explained
But time wouldn't deign
To permit such a flight
Well now, isn't that right?

Such is not understood
To be real, or it would
Cause a riotous stir
And the rules all to blur

But what if perhaps
The rules were to lapse
To invite such potentials
And draw up new essentials

I submit then to you
Time-tunneling, too
The driver of awareness
Well it could be, in fairness

Digging through futures
Forming conscious sutures
Entangling dimension
The mind's main extension

Such routes possibly can
Allow the thinking of man
To be in part understood
By his own thought, he could

Is our failing democratic tradition to blame for our problems, or is it rather our current expression of neoliberal capitalism that is at fault for our woes? Perhaps it's an amalgamation of both.

The American political system, and by inference the Constitution, is obsolete. It worked satisfactorily in the eighteenth, nineteenth, and most of the twentieth, centuries, but is now quite broken. The fact of the matter is that China is the up-and-coming power of the twenty-first century. No one can deny that. Their political system, for all its faults, would never elect a person of Donald Trump's incompetence, inexperience and overall disability to the Politburo, or any other agency of national government. And the proof is "in the pudding": what did our antiquated American system recently do? Elect a Donald Trump. Many millions of Americans like his Jacksonian, wrecking-ball policies — because things can't get any worse for them — but anyone of sound mind has got to disqualify him for his aforementioned inexperience and related incompetence, his unsatisfactory general intelligence, and his overwhelming penchant for utter dishonesty. It's very sad that our country has come to this, and the situation will very probably get worse before it gets any better.

As far as ranking the presidents, even a top three, the only president who showed any real restraint and decorum, sincerely listened to everyone's opinion, and wasn't a partisan hack, was Washington. Carter was maybe the best man, and certainly one of the smartest, but an awfully ineffective administrator and not a good president. I can't name a top three because I don't think we've had that many good ones.

What the conservative establishment of the 50s, 60s, 70s and 80s did not understand was that a person could be rather far left and not be a card-carrying communist. The Red scare and all that was one of the most tragic follies in the history of our republic. McCarthy, Korea, Vietnam, etc. All pointless.

Freedom of speech is permitted because it is really no danger to those in power. If it were, it would very simply be completely disallowed, as it has been at times historically.

In the vast majority of human cultures that have existed, age brings dignity and the elderly are treasured for their experience and wisdom. American society is one of the very few which essentially does the opposite. Here, the elderly are ignored, seen as useless and are usually and quite sadly alone.

Bierce was never rich. Nietzsche was never rich. Orson Welles was never rich. Robert Anton Wilson. Tim Leary. Edgar Allan Poe. David Bohm. Monetary wealth is, clearly, not a measure of individual worth, as I have just proven beyond doubt. Such a thing only depends on what sort of available niche there is in which one can find oneself. As Buddha and Jesus were very fond of pointing out, there are far more important matters than one's income. Capitalist America's barometers are in many ways poorly calibrated.

I feel that man's spiritual state right now has got to be up there with some of the worst in history. In the U.S., it's particularly bad. We have all this money, and absolutely no meaning in our lives, just some materialist stupor in which we drift from point to point without ever really interacting with anyone else. Man could not be more spiritually bankrupt than in the modern age, and by all indications he is not particularly happy in any significant way. We've had all this economic growth and no existential growth, and indeed it seems we have regressed significantly over time. It's very sad.

The ethos in the United States of America is to organize society around greed and selfishness, even explicitly. The highest good here, instilled from childhood, is to make as much money as possible for oneself, and not worry about anyone else.

USA geopolitics over the last seventy years or so can be likened to the poking and prodding of a hornet's nest and expecting no consequences. Now, the hornets have left the nest and a few of them are attacking, and we're shocked and having trouble coping. Many bellicose Americans wish we could simply destroy the nest, secretly. I'm not saying any of the violence is acceptable; but we would have done well to assess the possible consequences of our actions rather than just blundering around meddling in the affairs of a host of other nations and cultures. This is a game and this is how the game works; it's rather ridiculous to be surprised when the opponent makes a move, however disgraceful this move may be in reality. American culpability in this whole thing is enormous.

By 2040, 30% of U.S. Senate seats will represent 70% of the country, and 70% of Senate seats will represent 30% of the country. This is yet another sign that the American system of government is utterly obsolete. We see the Trump administration and all its dysfunctions, a Congress that cannot get anything done, a political system of two parties that refuse to work together, a grossly unbalanced budget, a huge national debt, etc. The Senate even started out deeply flawed, as the idea of a "one state, one vote" federal legislative body was an article of compromise at the Constitutional convention in 1787. Madison rightly wanted proportional representation in both houses, and couldn't get it — because of the clearly self-serving voting agenda of the small states. These are all signs of a deeply flawed and now crumbling system of government. A new Constitutional convention, or something more revolutionary, might be required to fix it, but it seems clear that, just as we always do, we'll do nothing about it until it's far too late. This is just another category in which the U.S. is failing, and beginning to lag behind much of the rest of the industrialized world.

The Declaration of Independence is a fine document, but I have trouble understanding how it applies to reality. Life, liberty and the pursuit of happiness are luxuries, not rights. All men may be created equal, but there is no true equality in America, particularly economically. The world is too gritty and cruel a place for such lofty, luminous Jeffersonian ideals realistically to apply. Our ethos has created a kind of national religion, but not anything resembling a true success in the experiment the founding fathers attempted to undertake. I believe the lot of them, if they could be restored to life, would say it was a failed one.

Ungoverned Passions

Sacred honor
Absurdly chivalric
Older blood
Ancient bailiwick

Private sadness
Public feuds
Subtle madness
Wild moods

Soft decorum
A fierce pride
Taken badly
Whenever snide

Prolific pen
Outstanding mind
A troubled past
Of roots opine

To end badly
A poor mistake
To duel gladly
Invite heartbreak

Besmirched memory
The lesson is thus
Govern your passions, or make
Life superfluous

If man were content with being, he would not need to evolve further to become, to transcend, to transform. Of course, at one point he was. Which of the two ontologies is righteous? It seems that, in a fundamental way, Nature exhibits a mixture and balance of the two. But for now, regarding the problem of Earth, Nature must choose one or the other for whatever expedient purposes she's got up her sleeve.

If an individual or a people has a good relationship with and grounding in being, becoming can be a good option. But an individual, people or system, becoming only for the sake of becoming, usually ends up devouring everything in its path, including, eventually, itself. As with everything in Nature, health can only be maintained in balance.

I tire of the Eastern and New Age admonishments against thought and thinking. Any level of the nervous system can be confused, not just the mental. The problem is with *confusion*, not the thought process *per se*. As a matter of fact, most people in the modern age need to do a lot *more* thinking, not less.

If one is a human who knows what he is doing, there is no justification for arrogance – ever.

Calm acceptance is a very highly valued and often held attitude in the East. And it's something that's always turned me off. While calm acceptance can be a good thing, your average Hindu or Buddhist is so passive they'll let tyrants run roughshod over them for thousands of years without even a cross word. Their passivity is too extreme. The opposite view, of the assertive Westerner, gets taken too far in the other direction. It's hard for most Westerners to realize how little actual control over themselves they have. That leads to a host of psychological problems. So, while I'll say acceptance is a good thing, extreme passivity is not. Most of us probably won't be able to change the world too much, but that doesn't mean we shouldn't do what we can, when we are able.

Happiness is undeniably a luxury, and I think one would be hard pressed to find too many examples of its lasting indefinitely. When everything is functioning great, and there's no discomfort or suffering, voila! we have happiness. I have had numerous periods of happiness, or at least a serene contentment, over the last decade. But I remember saying to myself, "This is too good – it won't last…" and it didn't. Nature in her current disposition seems to want to dispel too much happiness. Perhaps it is some form of punishment. Not to mention there is no very good reason to be happy at all in a world such as this one.

Possibly the most freeing action any and all humans can take is to stop wanting what we can't have. Forgetting about the Buddhist extinguishment of desire, if the things we wanted were the things we could reasonably and probably get, boy, we'd be better off.

We live in a world with problems. The big and little problems in our lives, ever-present and ever-evolving; and the vast multitude of problems in our cities, countries and the world. Every manner of problem and suffering. What is the principle in Nature that causes this? Why must everything be so wrong? What makes such a perfectly promising planet, in a universe with so much potential – so very imperfect?

As a principle of both physics and theology, nothing can ever be destroyed in Nature, it can only be transformed.

It is said that humans have the gift of understanding. In reality, we have the gift of language, which enables us to think we understand.

When you really take a look around at what mankind has created – the buildings, the art, the technology, the language, the goods, the services, the artifacts, the sciences, the cities – anything at all – you see that it's just not that great. We have, certainly, not yet redeemed ourselves. The natural is still far superior.

The truth is everything. But sometimes affairs are so far gone that it doesn't at all matter what it is. It doesn't get darker.

Language is such a fabulously rich and complex process – involving myriad neurological factors, cultural dynamics, different types of breathing, larynx and vocal fold manipulations, convoluted movements of the muscles of the mouth and tongue, etc. – that to try to account for it, as Dr. Chomsky does, as explicable in terms of a gene or a set of genes, seems awfully simplistic and frankly absurd. Language involves an undivided, flowing, harmonious and holistically unified movement of all of the variables described, and to believe that this entire symphony is located in the genome is, I think, a mistake, to put it very mildly.

No matter how you slice it, being alive is a burden. Breathing – our most fundamental activity – is *work*. The Buddha did say that existence is suffering, and while that's a very complicated idea, it is still eminently fitting in a very straightforward way, here.

Nietzsche emphatically did not mean for his concept of the "superman" to be construed as an evolutionary phenomenon.

Virtual Reality

By virtue of a fading star
This world and moon were born
And on't, never was very far
Some creature who by dint was forlorn

And so, were thus those many bred
Who saw, and did gasp quite aware
Perhaps better a stone in their stead
Never worry for getting to there

Creature! Fear naught at all
The cold embrace an illusion
Do appreciate aught withal
For here is where you might find fusion

For me, alas, all is lost
Perception or not indistinguished
What do you suppose was the cost?
A perpetual spiritual languish

Cloud on the horizon, please tell me
Sun setting, blaze orange, fire pink
How in this world can I quell thee?
Thou unresolved eyes on the brink

I suppose the difference isn't much, though
I wish I could separate truths
Projectors toward screens shine a rough glow
The light!, the light soever soothes

Alexander Hamilton was a great man, but the fact is that he was an upper-crust, 1% conservative who only really cared about the welfare of the rich. His creation of our financial system gave birth to unprecedented corruption and usury, and did nothing for the common man. His career was one of the least socially compassionate of all of the founding fathers, but he was right that popular democracy is an unsound way to operate a government. On that score I agree. All in all, I much prefer the sensibilities of a Madison, whose chief concern was for the welfare, rights and freedoms of all Americans, and who more than anyone shaped and enforced the principles of the Constitution.

One of the principal reasons we're seeing such abysmal dysfunction in government is that representatives are no longer working toward legitimate governance, but rather doing what they can for themselves. This country is a democracy to the extent that people hold their elected officials' feet to the fire on certain popular issues, but behind the scenes, on a slew of less visible and/or non-negotiable issues, those officials can line their pockets and get away with it, all the while protecting the super-rich and greasing the gears of the machine even further. I can't remember a time when greed and dysfunction were so prevalent in Congress. Sure, politicians have always been like this, but at this point we can't even keep the country running.

I happen to be a left-libertarian. That means that I am for managed economic fairness, and social and cultural liberty.

It is a pretty pathetic state of affairs in a country in which facts, consensus reality, science and due process are dismissed outright by a large class of people whose leader has only to tell them to do so. Lies are the new unquestioned truths in America.

Who knows what the U.S. will ultimately turn into — but don't doubt that it is transforming into something else.

Waiting Evil

A Shangri-La, a virgin land
An unpolluted Eden
But as one walks on untouched sand
Coherence tends to weaken

Our potential was dramatic
The paths to take — quite varied
In time our movements grew static
To detriment we married

As time went on, and sin exploded
And truths were laid so bare
The common good, how it eroded
We went from here to... where?

Progression from the possible
To a tragic fall from grace
An exit pure, impossible
Now but one path saves face

A call from a respected sage:
"The evil was there waiting"
This is our accursed age
The darkness yet creating

During the administrations of George W. Bush and Barack Obama, I was able to keep my distance. Now, with Trump, it is hard not to be affected. I can honestly say I held a detached sort of relative indifference before; now, I cannot say I am not bothered. Some of us saw this sort of thing coming for America, though perhaps not with such energy. Nevertheless, it is difficult to watch.

One must not measure a person's worth by how productive he happens to be. Such productivity does not determine, or even color, the measure of a man. Unfortunately, here in America, it is very difficult to see this. So most of us amble around in a stupor of delusion.

I suppose, since just about everyone has their secrets, it might be all right if governments keep a few secrets, too. As a practical matter.

It would seem that no one ever really knew America until the era of Trump. All political theorizing and commentary before that time can only be described in retrospect, and forever, as pathetically quaint.

What has Trump accomplished in office? Trump has done long-term damage to our institutions, instilled corruption everywhere, shrunk and damaged our national parks, overturned most environmental regulations, built a new nuclear weapons arsenal beyond anything approaching reason, left numerous constructive treaties, like the Iran deal, militarized local outer space, damaged the economy with 19th century tariff tactics, signed into law an irresponsible tax cut for the wealthy, repeatedly undermined the

Affordable Care insurance system, shut down the government for personal political purposes, and lied over 10,000 times publicly. Guy's a train wreck.

We know Trump has withdrawn from accords, rolled back emissions regulations, touted coal, denied climate change, etc. Now he is trying to pull all the funding he can from government climate scientists, while forbidding any modeling on climate evolution after the year 2040 — when most scientists feel warming will geometrically skyrocket. He's already trying to silence the press. What is it called when an administration begins silencing scientists?

Warm Oasis

Like an oasis, many
Within the wastes of civilization
Arteries connecting every abode
Every rung, rank and station

Nature tamed, subservient
Apotheosis of man
Technical installation of power
Islands for every clan

Perhaps not all
In comfort, in progress
Are enveloped in this bosom
No access to excess

But impressive nonetheless
This empire we have built
With concrete, flame and electrons
And done so with no guilt

Outside the walls are freezing, elements
By the hearth we read a magazine
Perfect control of the environment
Until control evaporates

One of the crises is that young people, who have graduated from college, are not getting the same opportunities, or making nearly as much money, as their parents who have the same level of education. What to do? After all, not everyone can go to graduate school. And moreover, if everyone did go to graduate school, a graduate degree would be quite meaningless. So… what?

In the modern, failed United States, objective truth doesn't mean anything anymore to a hundred million people. The truth has become entirely subjective – it has become whatever one wants it to be, and whatever one is told it is.

As Chuck Palahniuk pointed out in the nineties, the best people – the heroes of the younger generation – are servers in restaurants and gas station attendants. As institutions crumble, these are the places you'll find most of them. Without any meaningful place to be.

Roosevelt was considered a hero only because of the context he was in. He instituted the vast public works programs that put people to work on the heels of the depression, but it seems what really saved the day was World War II. That was the engine that restored and energized the economy, and by the end of the war we had transformed into a mobilized superpower with nuclear weapons. All of that never collapsed until… well, now. That entire process is now coming to an end. The United States' day in the sun is setting. It never once in history has lasted forever.

Good government is an effect, not a cause.

Early on in a dynamic civilization's success, wages are high and prices are low. Later on, the situation is such that an economic superstructure has been built in which everyone must get their cut, and the whole enterprise is basically a racket. At this point, wages have shrunk and costs skyrocketed. The U.S. is in that latter phase now, and maybe the earlier period could be exemplified by the situation in the 1950s. It's the same pattern we've seen over and over throughout history. And no one knows what to do.

The COVID-19 coronavirus has fully exposed the U.S. system. We'll never be able to have even the slightest pretension of being any kind of "great" country after this disaster. This is the long-awaited official end of Empire.

Water and Stock

To procreate
To irrigate
Is to invite trouble...

God enters unwilling
In his name, much killing
Thereafter, a billing
Of souls, then a grilling

Transfer future rapture
To your greener cattle pasture
Complexity arrived it seems
Authority in all men's dreams

We build such an edifice
And now? At the precipice
An instant, a firework
Engaged in such dire work

It's origin? The chief
Who created relief
When his subjects demanded
That the water be handed

Not much time had passed when
The chief asked a question
"Why give it for free
When I can collect a fee?"

Closing the door thus
And Lord! what a huge fuss
Consequences have been
Write the book on men

It seems to me that in the future – certainly by thirty years from now (2020) – we will indeed have nationalized healthcare and a universal basic income system, but that this will have come at a rather sobering cost. People's immediate needs will be covered by social programs, at no cost to them, but it strikes me that there will be an extremely powerful elite, who own the fully automated industries and basically run the government. This system will compensate the population through a universal basic income – but I imagine it will not be very lucrative. So we will have a population that is free to do as it wishes, within reason, but one that will not have much spending power and that will be totally subservient to a system that represents the grossest division of class and wealth in human history. This status quo will, doubtless, be very difficult to change if anyone wanted to. And after a certain point – after A.I. is able to replace doctors, lawyers, judges and pilots, and what have you – everyone outside of the elite will be in a powerless position, and the elite, whoever they are, will be untouchable. That this would not grow into a dark dystopia is, it would appear, difficult to imagine. But then, it begs the question as to how long A.I. will need humans around...

Despite America's failings, and its general decline, it remains true that I can say essentially whatever I want. However, there is no reason for the self-congratulation about this that so many Americans are inclined to engage in. One *should* be able to speak one's mind without fear of reprisal. Like Chris Rock said, would you congratulate somebody for staying out of jail for a year? You're *supposed to* stay out of jail! Likewise, we are *supposed* to refrain from restricting speech. We're not deserving of any special acknowledgment or award because of it.

The forty-hour workweek – a vestige of the New Deal – is completely arbitrary and useless. The economy could be sufficiently, perhaps especially, robust with many fewer hours worked – and indeed, many fewer workers in general. Our economy has been making-work for a long time; if Buckminster Fuller was writing about significantly streamlining the global economy in the *1950s*, then surely it can in principle be done today. The system is geared to be productive based upon its current structure, so no one has heretofore been incentivized to change, let alone overhaul it. With the coronavirus pandemic, this will start to change. Relying on human workers working at least forty hours per week has been exposed – it has proven itself to be a potentially fatal weakness during a major crisis. So the system's inevitable push toward automation will undoubtedly be drastically accelerated going forward. One other function of the forty-hour workweek was to keep people busy. To, in a sense, neutralize them. This benefits the power-structure, both in terms of government and business, so it quite easily evolved into being culturally. But now that automation is inevitable, we're going to have to figure out what to do with an awful lot of people. And of course it is clear that eventually, the forty-hour workweek will have no meaning anymore. So it will be very interesting to see all these changes and how they unfold.

The Western Mind

It seems that man — or Western man
Can only count to two
Indeed, he does not understand
What it is time to do

For him, it seems, that everything
Must fall out at the poles
That this and that and anything
Has but one of two roles

The mind then is conditioned
To decry anything real
Nature has other intentions
But man declares, "I feel..."

"I feel that due certainty
Is only just arrived at"
(And this is an absurdity)
"with either this or that."

We know of course the West is blind
And silly, deaf and dumb
All, it seems, are of a mind
For narrow rules of thumb

The East, it suffers no such blight
But then, I do not live there
Aristotle's children light
A path that leads to nowhere

The only citizenship I recognize for myself is as a citizen of Earth. Arbitrary political zones have no fundamental meaning, and really no meaning on any level save an administrative one. In the 21st century, nationalistic thinking is quite obsolete, anyway. The whole concept of a nation-state, given how hyperconnected the globe now is, is completely meaningless. We are citizens of Earth, perhaps of the Solar System, and that's it. Anything else is nonsense.

We as a nation and as a civilization have long since reached the point at which it is not necessary for everyone to work to sustain the economy. So why isn't some sort of Universal Basic Income system in operation? Why hasn't it been inevitable? Because humans don't operate that way. It's not convenient for business or government to make such a sweeping change, and most citizens do not have the initiative to undertake it, or to press for it. We'll have to do it eventually, absolutely, so sooner rather than later might be a bit smarter. We won't be smart about it though, and we'll likely blunder into some mess.

Being a major leader, like a president, is just a terrible job. You could have ten options available for what to do about something, and not have a single one represent the right thing to do. This is a thankless sort of position that absolutely forces its bearer to compromise himself. Seemingly, most politicians don't care, and decent people – who might actually do a good job for a change – never run.

In truth, no one really needs more than five or ten million dollars. One hundred billion dollar fortunes are something everyone should resent. Sadly, in capitalist America, the ownership of such a sum is considered the highest good. We are not a healthy people.

Wind Resonance

Arise in a hue of the real
The flux of process, fully feel
The cycle of time here apparent
Infinity, omen inherent

Speech and the winds are inseparable
Subject to object here preferable
The verb takes the place of our nouns
Breath and wind together resound

One does not here splinter the real
Does not divide, conquer or steal
The spirit ablaze resonates
But cannot avoid future fates

The End